COURSE BOOK

LEVEL 2 BEGINNER

Author

Rachel Harding has a background in English-language teaching and is now a full-time author of English-language learning materials. She has written for major English-language publishers including Oxford University Press.

Course consultant

Tim Bowen has taught English and trained teachers in more than 30 countries worldwide. He is the co-author of works on pronunciation teaching and language-teaching methodology, and author of numerous books for English-language teachers. He is currently a freelance materials writer, editor, and translator. He is a member of the Chartered Institute of Linguists.

Language consultant

Professor Susan Barduhn is an experienced English-language teacher, teacher trainer, and author, who has contributed to numerous publications. In addition to directing English-language courses in at least four different continents, she has been President of the International Association of Teachers of English as a Foreign Language, and an adviser to the British Council and the US State Department. She is currently a Professor at the School for International Training in Vermont, USA.

ENGLISH
FOR EVERYONE

COURSE BOOK
LEVEL 2 BEGINNER

SECOND EDITION
Senior Editor Ankita Awasthi Tröger
Editor Elizabeth Blakemore
Art Editor Amy Child
Managing Editor Carine Tracanelli
Managing Art Editor Anna Hall
Production Editor Gillian Reid
Senior Production Controller Meskerem Berhane
Jacket Designer Surabhi Wadhwa-Gandhi
Jacket Design Development Manager Sophia MTT
Publisher Andrew Macintyre
Managing Director, DK Learning Hilary Fine

DK INDIA
Senior Jackets Coordinator Priyanka Sharma Saddi
DTP Designer Rakesh Kumar

FIRST EDITION
US Editors Allison Singer, Jenny Siklos
Editors Gareth Clark, Lisa Gillespie, Andrew Kerr-Jarrett
Art Editors Chrissy Barnard, Ray Bryant
Senior Art Editor Sharon Spencer
Editorial Assistants Jessica Cawthra, Sarah Edwards
Illustrators Edwood Burn, Denise Joos, Michael Parkin, Jemma Westing
Audio Producer Liz Hammond
Managing Editor Daniel Mills
Managing Art Editor Anna Hall
Project Manager Christine Stroyan
Producer, Pre-Production Luca Frassinetti
Producer Mary Slater
Jacket Designer Natalie Godwin
Jacket Editor Claire Gell
Jacket Design Development Manager Sophia MTT
Publisher Andrew Macintyre
Art Director Karen Self
Publishing Director Jonathan Metcalf

DK INDIA
Jacket Designer Surabhi Wadhwa
Managing Jackets Editor Saloni Singh
Senior DTP Designer Harish Aggarwal

This American Box Set Edition, 2024
First American Edition, 2016
Published in the United States by DK Publishing,
a division of Penguin Random House LLC
1745 Broadway, 20th Floor, New York, NY 10019

Copyright © 2016, 2018, 2024 Dorling Kindersley Limited
25 26 27 28 10 9 8 7 6 5 4 3
003–342958–Sep/2024

All rights reserved.
Without limiting the rights under the copyright reserved above, no part of this publication may be reproduced, stored in or introduced into a retrieval system, or transmitted, in any form, or by any means (electronic, mechanical, photocopying, recording, or otherwise), without the prior written permission of the copyright owner.
Published in Great Britain by Dorling Kindersley Limited

A catalog record for this book is available from the Library of Congress.
Box Set ISBN 978-0-5938-4961-3
ISBN 978-0-5938-4228-7

DK books are available at special discounts when purchased in bulk for sales promotions, premiums, fund-raising, or educational use. For details, contact:
DK Publishing Special Markets, 1745 Broadway, 20th Floor, New York, NY 10019
SpecialSales@dk.com

Printed and bound in China

www.dk.com

This book was made with Forest Stewardship Council™ certified paper – one small step in DK's commitment to a sustainable future.
Learn more at
www.dk.com/uk/information/sustainability

Contents

How the course works

English for Everyone is designed for people who want to teach themselves the English language. Like all language courses, it covers the core skills: grammar, vocabulary, pronunciation, listening, speaking, reading, and writing. Unlike in other courses, the skills are taught and practiced as visually as possible, using images and graphics to help you understand and remember. The best way to learn is to work through the book in order, making full use of the audio available on the website and app. Turn to the practice book at the end of each unit to reinforce your learning with additional exercises.

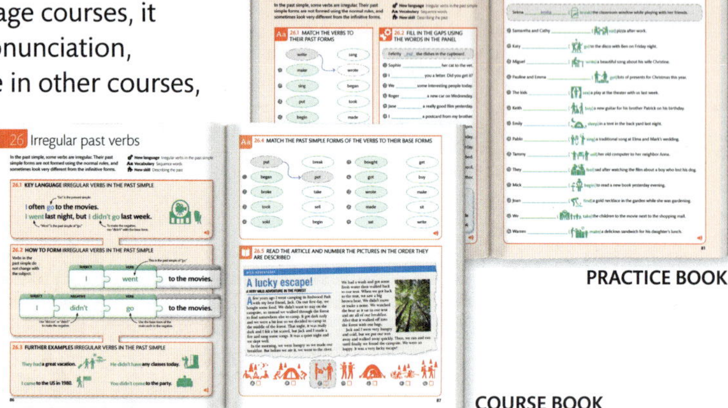

Unit number The book is divided into units. The unit number helps you keep track of your progress.

Learning points Every unit begins with a summary of the key learning points.

Modules Each unit is broken down into modules, which should be done in order. You can take a break from learning after completing any module.

Language learning Modules with colored backgrounds teach new vocabulary and grammar. Study these carefully before moving on to the exercises.

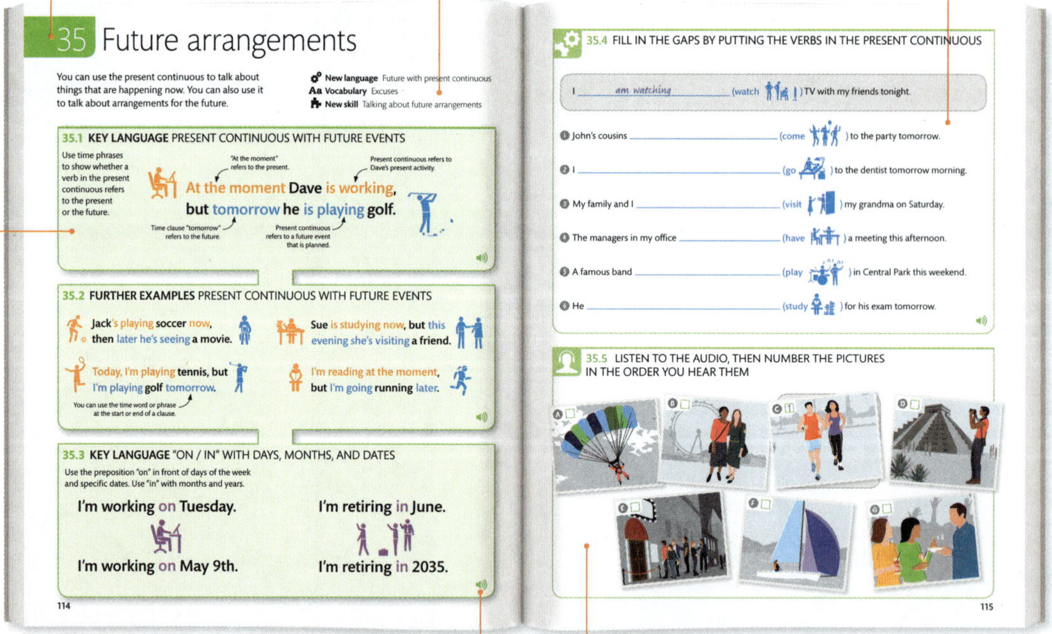

35 Future arrangements

You can use the present continuous to talk about things that are happening now. You can also use it to talk about arrangements for the future.

New language Future with present continuous
Aa Vocabulary Excuses
New skill Talking about future arrangements

35.1 KEY LANGUAGE PRESENT CONTINUOUS WITH FUTURE EVENTS

Use time phrases to show whether a verb in the present continuous refers to the present or the future.

At the moment Dave is working, but tomorrow he is playing golf.

"At the moment" refers to the present. Present continuous refers to Dave's present activity. Time clause "tomorrow" refers to the future. Present continuous refers to a future event that is planned.

35.2 FURTHER EXAMPLES PRESENT CONTINUOUS WITH FUTURE EVENTS

Jack's playing soccer now, then later he's seeing a movie.

Sue is studying now, but this evening she's visiting a friend.

Today, I'm playing tennis, but I'm playing golf tomorrow.

I'm reading at the moment, but I'm going running later.

You can use the time word or phrase at the start or end of a clause.

35.3 KEY LANGUAGE "ON / IN" WITH DAYS, MONTHS, AND DATES

Use the preposition "on" in front of days of the week and specific dates. Use "in" with months and years.

I'm working on Tuesday. I'm retiring in June.

I'm working on May 9th. I'm retiring in 2035.

114

35.4 FILL IN THE GAPS BY PUTTING THE VERBS IN THE PRESENT CONTINUOUS

I am watching (watch) TV with my friends tonight.

1 John's cousins ______ (come) to the party tomorrow.
2 I ______ (go) to the dentist tomorrow morning.
3 My family and I ______ (visit) my grandma on Saturday.
4 The managers in my office ______ (have) a meeting this afternoon.
5 A famous band ______ (play) in Central Park this weekend.
6 He ______ (study) for his exam tomorrow.

35.5 LISTEN TO THE AUDIO, THEN NUMBER THE PICTURES IN THE ORDER YOU HEAR THEM

A B C D E F G

115

Audio support Most modules have supporting audio recordings of native English speakers to help you improve your speaking and listening skills.

Exercises Modules with white backgrounds contain exercises that help you practice your new skills to reinforce learning.

FREE AUDIO
website and app
www.dkefe.com

Language modules

New language points are taught in carefully graded stages, starting with a simple explanation of when they are used, then offering further examples of common usage, and a detailed breakdown of how key constructions are formed.

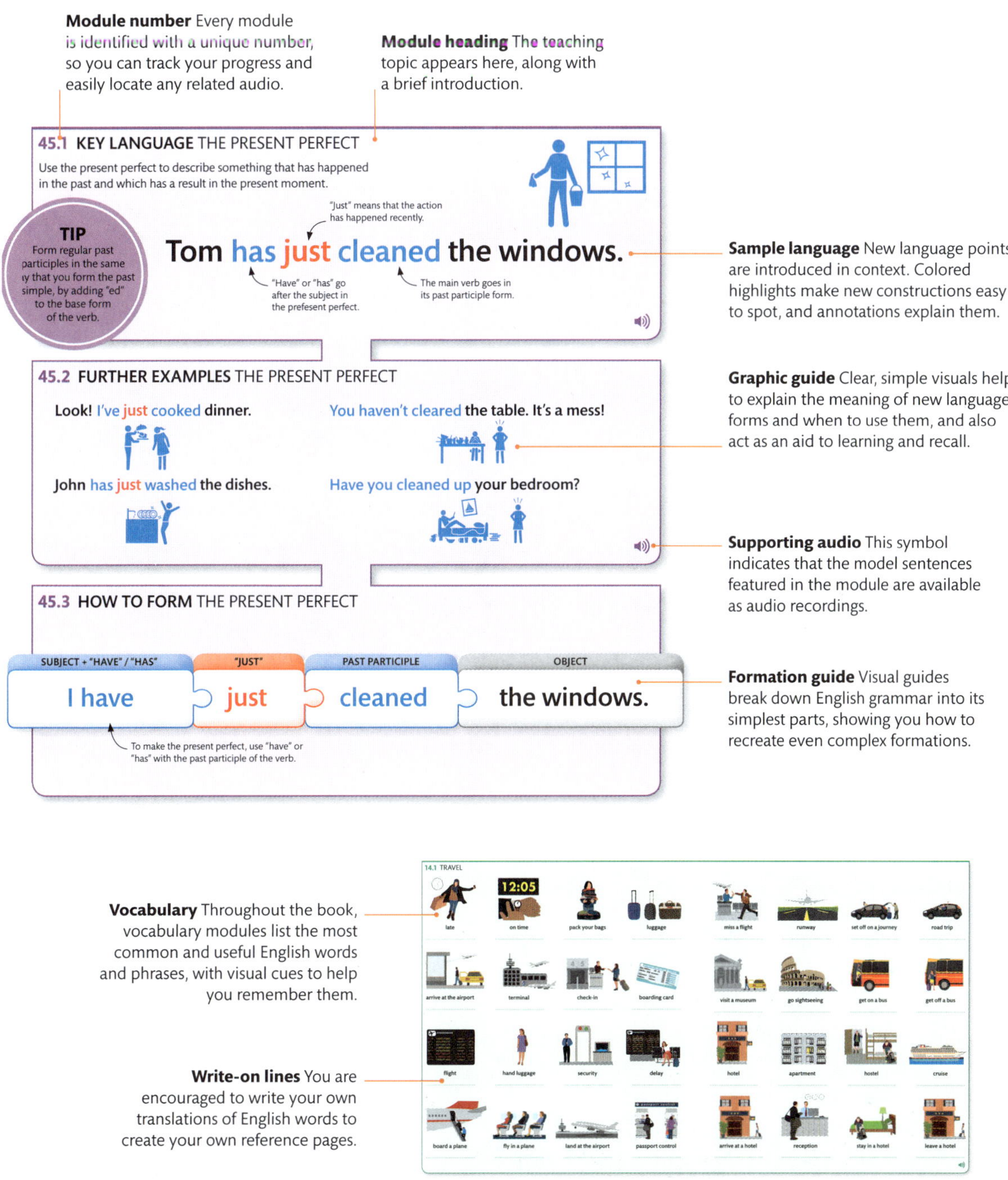

Module number Every module is identified with a unique number, so you can track your progress and easily locate any related audio.

Module heading The teaching topic appears here, along with a brief introduction.

Sample language New language points are introduced in context. Colored highlights make new constructions easy to spot, and annotations explain them.

Graphic guide Clear, simple visuals help to explain the meaning of new language forms and when to use them, and also act as an aid to learning and recall.

Supporting audio This symbol indicates that the model sentences featured in the module are available as audio recordings.

Formation guide Visual guides break down English grammar into its simplest parts, showing you how to recreate even complex formations.

Vocabulary Throughout the book, vocabulary modules list the most common and useful English words and phrases, with visual cues to help you remember them.

Write-on lines You are encouraged to write your own translations of English words to create your own reference pages.

Practice modules

Each exercise is carefully graded to drill and test the language taught in the corresponding course book units. Working through the exercises alongside the course book will help you remember what you have learned and become more fluent. Every exercise is introduced with a symbol to indicate which skill is being practiced.

GRAMMAR
Apply new language rules in different contexts.

READING
Examine target language in real-life English contexts.

LISTENING
Test your understanding of spoken English.

VOCABULARY
Cement your understanding of key vocabulary.

SPEAKING
Compare your spoken English to model audio recordings.

Module number Every module is identified with a unique number, so you can easily locate answers and related audio.

Exercise instruction Every exercise is introduced with a brief instruction, telling you what you need to do.

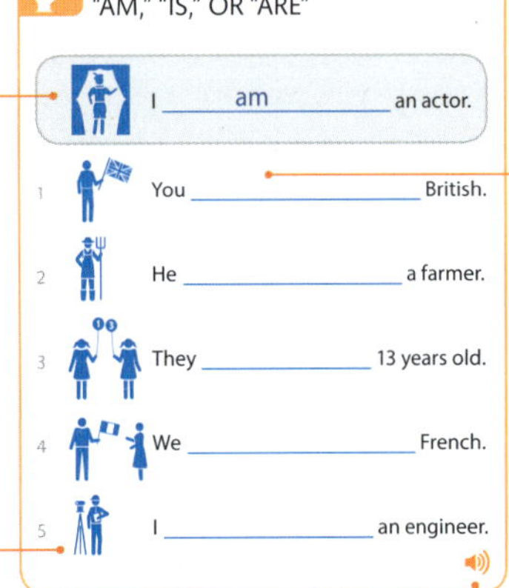

Sample answer The first question of each exercise is answered for you, to help make the task easy to understand.

Space for writing You are encouraged to write your answers in the book for future reference.

Supporting graphics Visual cues are given to help you understand the exercises.

Supporting audio This symbol shows that the answers to the exercise are available as audio tracks. Listen to them after completing the exercise.

Speaking exercise This symbol indicates that you should say your answers out loud, then compare them to model recordings included in your audio files.

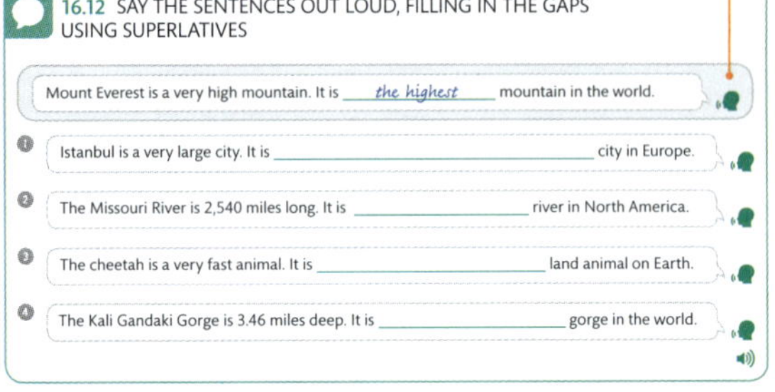

Listening exercise This symbol indicates that you should listen to an audio track in order to answer the questions in the exercise.

Audio

English for Everyone features extensive supporting audio materials. You are encouraged to use them as much as you can, to improve your understanding of spoken English, and to make your own accent and pronunciation more natural. Each file can be played, paused, and repeated as often as you like, until you are confident you understand what has been said.

LISTENING EXERCISES
This symbol indicates that you should listen to an audio track in order to answer the questions in the exercise.

SUPPORTING AUDIO
This symbol indicates that extra audio material is available for you to listen to after completing the module.

Track your progress

The course is designed to make it easy to monitor your progress, with regular summary and review modules. Answers are provided for every exercise, so you can see how well you have understood each teaching point.

Checklists Every unit ends with a checklist, where you can check off the new skills you have learned.

13 CHECKLIST

Weather descriptions ☐ Aa Temperature words ☐ Talking about the weather ☐

Review modules At the end of a group of units, you will find a more detailed review module, summarizing the language you have learned.

Check boxes Use these boxes to mark the skills you feel comfortable with. Go back and review anything you feel you need to practice further.

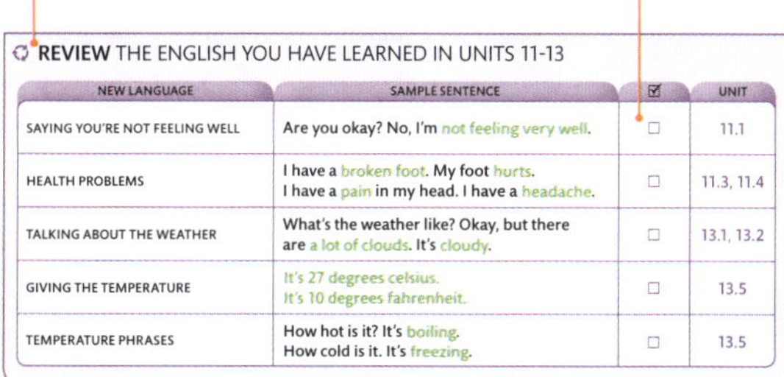

REVIEW THE ENGLISH YOU HAVE LEARNED IN UNITS 11-13

NEW LANGUAGE	SAMPLE SENTENCE	☑	UNIT
SAYING YOU'RE NOT FEELING WELL	Are you okay? No, I'm not feeling very well.	☐	11.1
HEALTH PROBLEMS	I have a broken foot. My foot hurts. I have a pain in my head. I have a headache.	☐	11.3, 11.4
TALKING ABOUT THE WEATHER	What's the weather like? Okay, but there are a lot of clouds. It's cloudy.	☐	13.1, 13.2
GIVING THE TEMPERATURE	It's 27 degrees celsius. It's 10 degrees fahrenheit.	☐	13.5
TEMPERATURE PHRASES	How hot is it? It's boiling. How cold is it. It's freezing.	☐	13.5

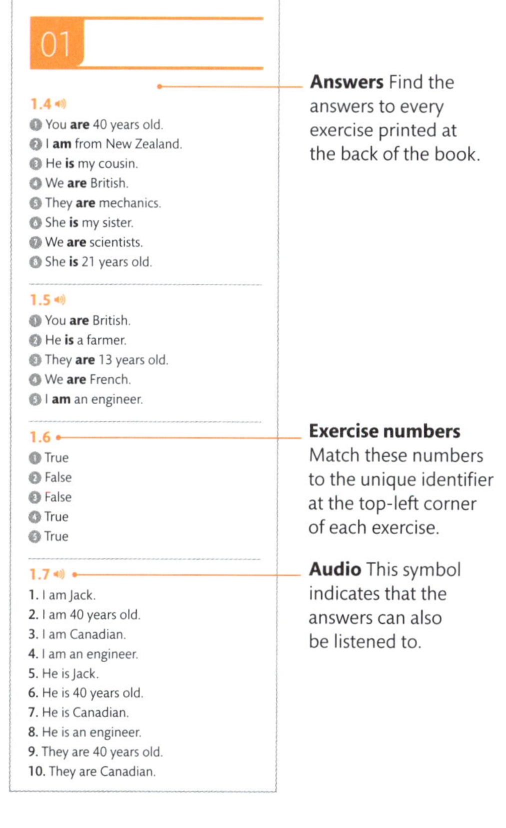

01

1.4
1. You **are** 40 years old.
2. I **am** from New Zealand.
3. He **is** my cousin.
4. We **are** British.
5. They **are** mechanics.
6. She **is** my sister.
7. We **are** scientists.
8. She **is** 21 years old.

1.5
1. You **are** British.
2. He **is** a farmer.
3. They **are** 13 years old.
4. We **are** French.
5. I **am** an engineer.

1.6
1. True
2. False
3. False
4. True
5. True

1.7
1. I am Jack.
2. I am 40 years old.
3. I am Canadian.
4. I am an engineer.
5. He is Jack.
6. He is 40 years old.
7. He is Canadian.
8. He is an engineer.
9. They are 40 years old.
10. They are Canadian.

Answers Find the answers to every exercise printed at the back of the book.

Exercise numbers Match these numbers to the unique identifier at the top-left corner of each exercise.

Audio This symbol indicates that the answers can also be listened to.

01 Talking about yourself

When you want to tell someone about yourself, or about people and things that relate to you, use the present simple form of "to be."

New language Using "to be"
Aa Vocabulary Names, jobs, and family
New skill Talking about yourself

1.1 KEY LANGUAGE "TO BE" STATEMENTS

Use the verb "to be" to talk about your name, age, nationality, and job.

Hi! I am Noah. I'm 25 years old. I'm Australian and I'm a doctor.

In conversational English, speakers often use contractions. These are shortened versions of pairs of words. "I am" can be shortened to "I'm."

1.2 FURTHER EXAMPLES "TO BE" STATEMENTS

Mia is 72 years old.

Aban is a police officer.

Jack's aunt is Canadian.

They are the Jackson family.

1.3 HOW TO FORM "TO BE" STATEMENTS

"You" in English is the same in the singular and plural.

These are pronouns. They are the subjects of these sentences.

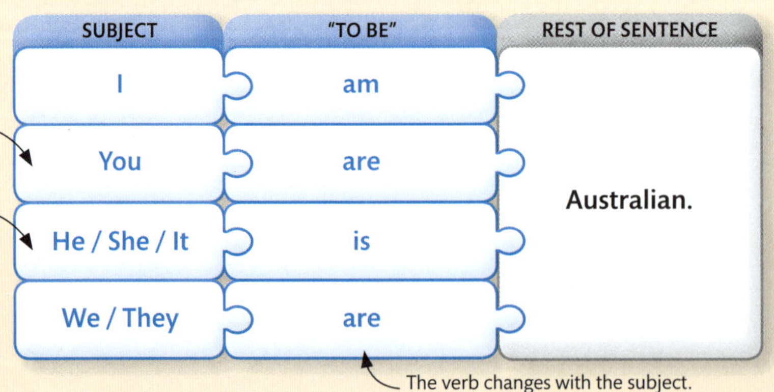

1.4 CROSS OUT THE INCORRECT WORD IN EACH SENTENCE

They are / ~~is~~ builders.

1. You are / is 40 years old.
2. I am / is from New Zealand.
3. He is / are my cousin.
4. We am / are British.
5. They is / are mechanics.
6. She is / are my sister.
7. We is / are scientists.
8. She is / are 21 years old.

1.5 FILL IN THE GAPS WITH "AM," "IS," OR "ARE"

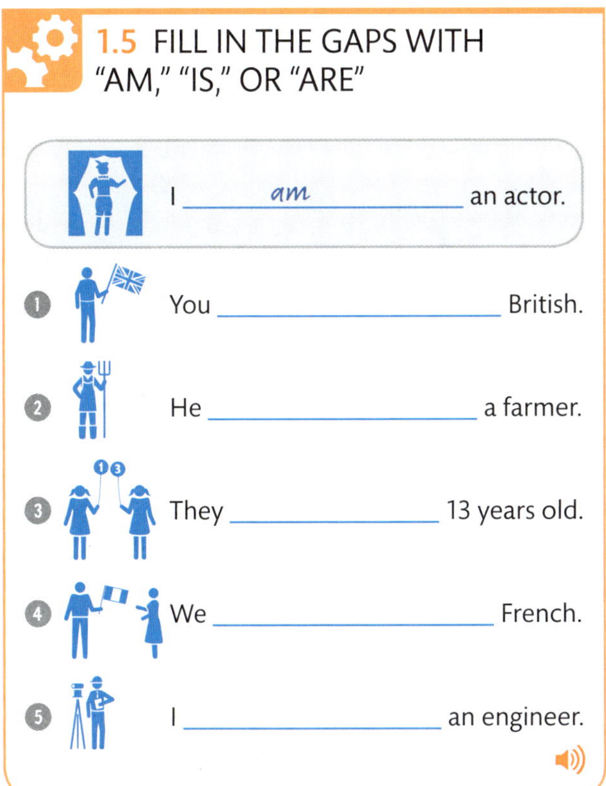

I *am* an actor.

1. You ______ British.
2. He ______ a farmer.
3. They ______ 13 years old.
4. We ______ French.
5. I ______ an engineer.

1.6 LISTEN TO THE AUDIO AND ANSWER THE QUESTIONS

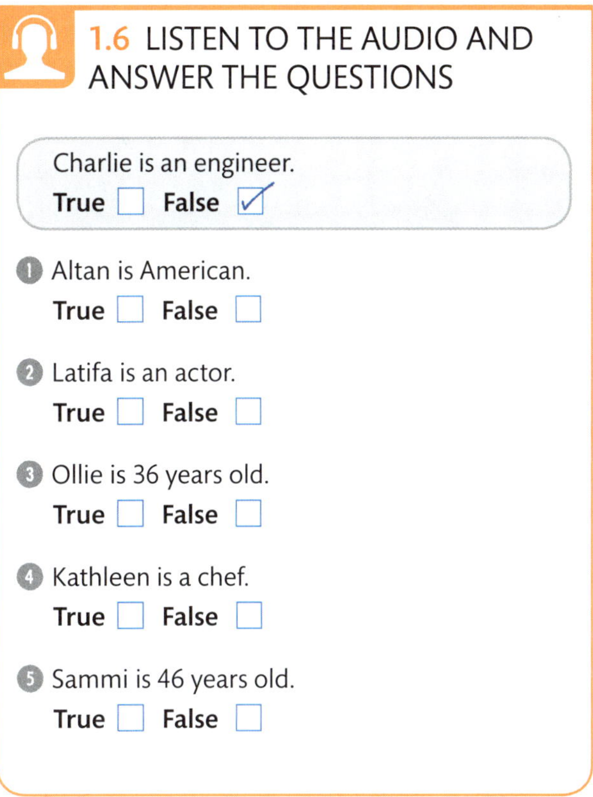

Charlie is an engineer.
True ☐ **False** ☑

1. Altan is American.
True ☐ **False** ☐
2. Latifa is an actor.
True ☐ **False** ☐
3. Ollie is 36 years old.
True ☐ **False** ☐
4. Kathleen is a chef.
True ☐ **False** ☐
5. Sammi is 46 years old.
True ☐ **False** ☐

1.7 USE THE CHART TO CREATE 10 CORRECT SENTENCES, THEN SAY THEM OUT LOUD

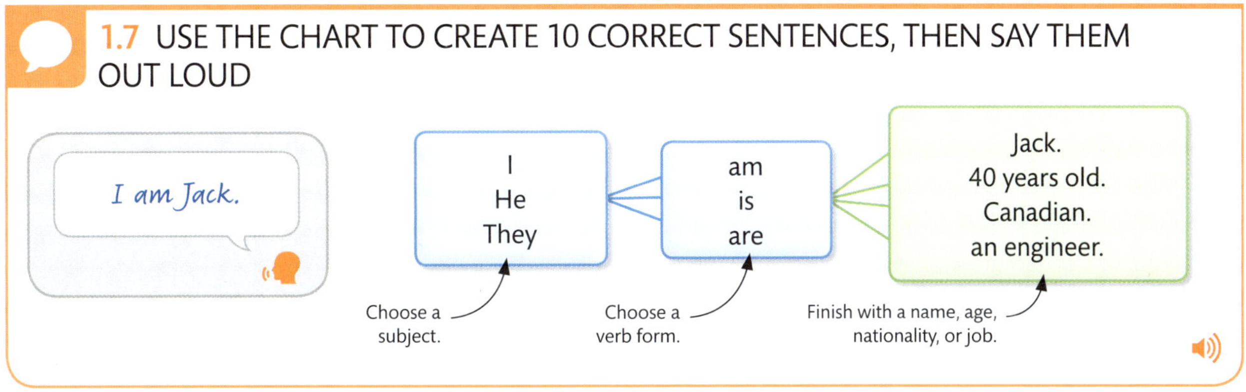

1.8 KEY LANGUAGE NEGATIVE "TO BE" STATEMENTS

To make a negative statement, add "not" after the verb.

I am not a nurse. I am a scientist.

1.9 FURTHER EXAMPLES NEGATIVE "TO BE" STATEMENTS

"Are not" is often contracted to "aren't."

They aren't Canadian.

I'm not happy today.

"Is not" is often contracted to "isn't."

He isn't at work this morning.

Lucy is not my friend.

1.10 FILL IN THE GAPS TO MAKE NEGATIVE SENTENCES

It *is not* 11 o'clock.

1. He ______ playing tennis.
2. She ______ a waitress.
3. He ______ 30 years old.
4. We ______ teachers.
5. I ______ at work.
6. Lyla ______ a cat.

1.11 WRITE EACH SENTENCE IN ITS NEGATIVE FORM

I **am** an engineer.
I am not an engineer.

1. Kaleh **is** their mother.
______
2. There **is** a bank on this street.
______
3. That **is** his laptop.
______
4. They **are** her grandparents.
______
5. Alyssa and Logan **are** your friends.
______

1.12 KEY LANGUAGE "TO BE" QUESTIONS

To ask a "to be" question, put the verb before the subject.

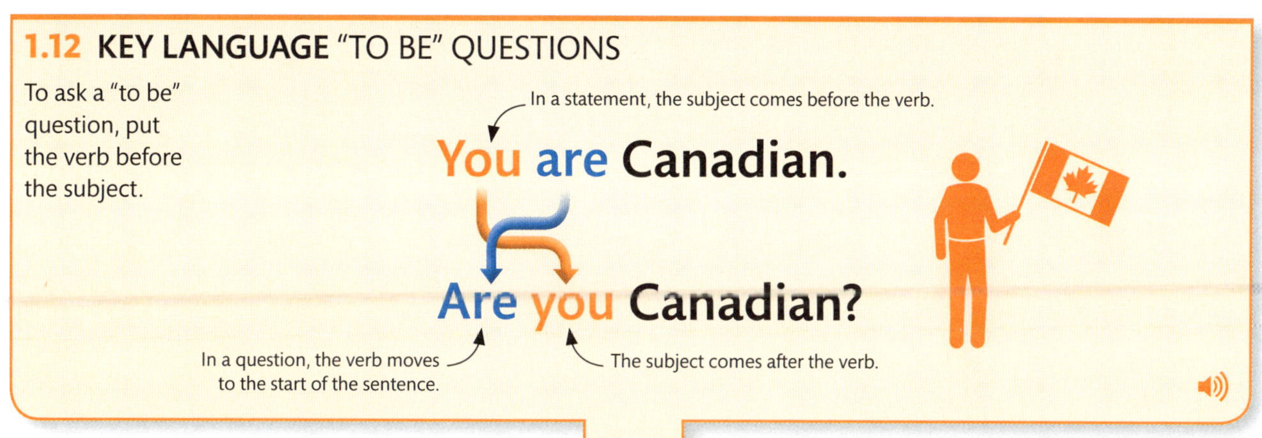

1.13 FURTHER EXAMPLES "TO BE" QUESTIONS

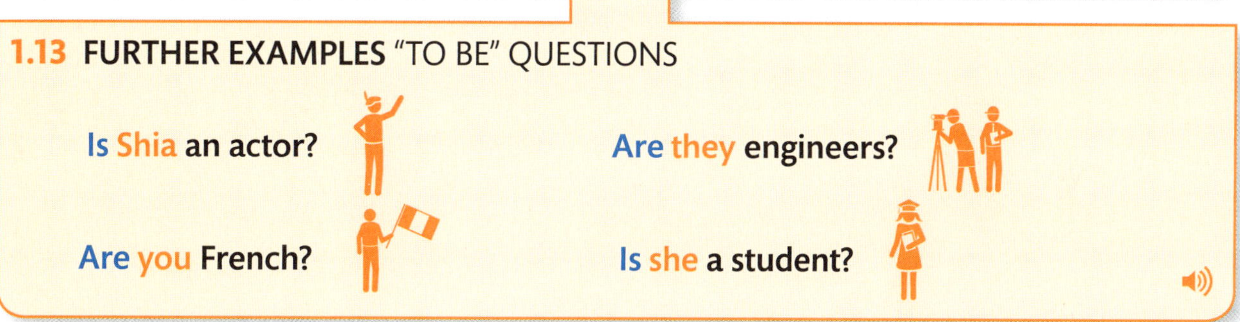

1.14 REWRITE THE SENTENCES AS QUESTIONS

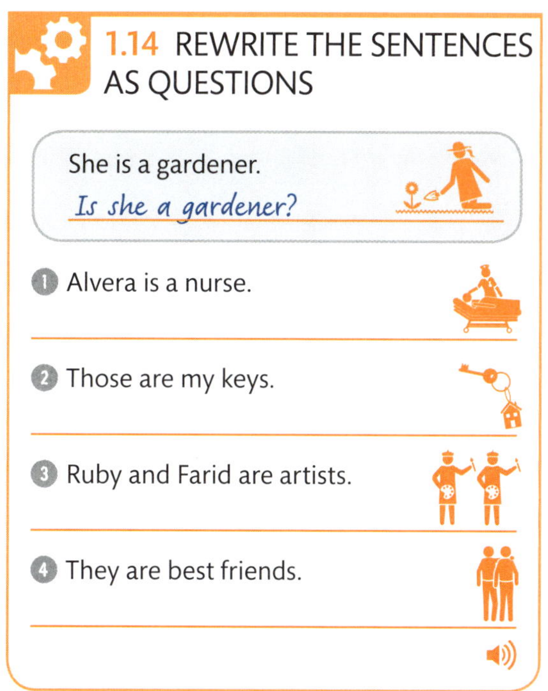

1.15 SAY THESE QUESTIONS OUT LOUD, FILLING IN THE GAPS

01 CHECKLIST

Using "to be" ☐ Aa Names, jobs, and family ☐ Talking about yourself ☐

02 Talking about routines

You can use present simple statements to describe your daily routines, pastimes, and possessions. Use "do" to form negatives and ask questions.

New language The present simple
Aa Vocabulary Routines and pastimes
New skill Talking about routines

2.1 KEY LANGUAGE THE PRESENT SIMPLE

2.2 FURTHER EXAMPLES THE PRESENT SIMPLE

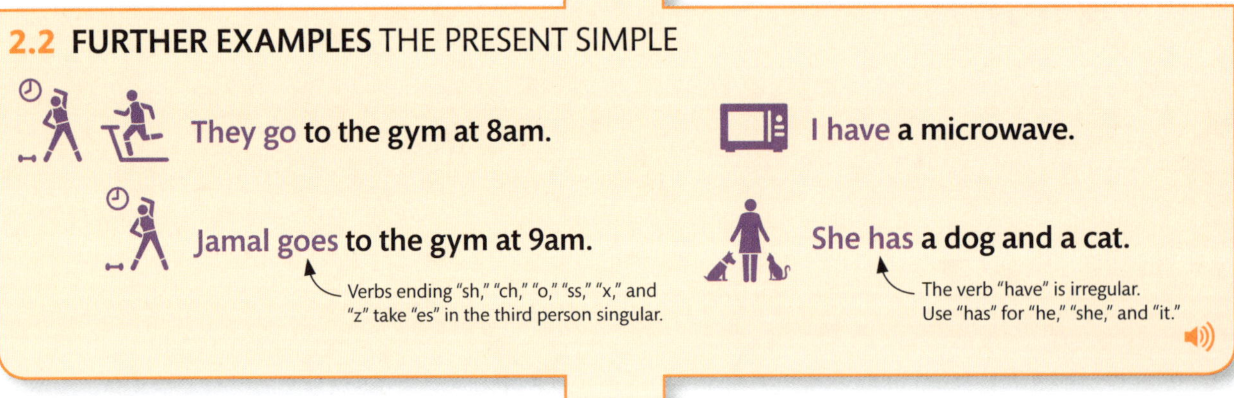

2.3 HOW TO FORM THE PRESENT SIMPLE

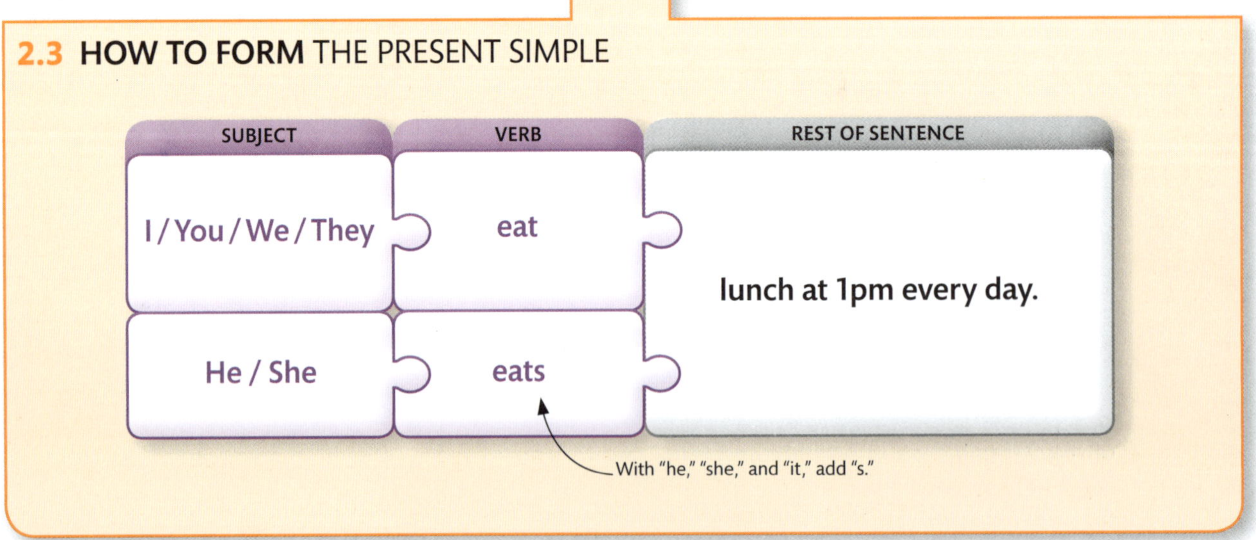

2.4 CROSS OUT THE INCORRECT WORD IN EACH SENTENCE

She ~~eat~~ / eats dinner in the evening.

1. He wake up / wakes up at 7 o'clock.
2. I start / starts work at 10am.
3. They leave / leaves home at 8:45am.
4. We finish / finishes work at 4pm.
5. My friend has / have dinner at 6:30pm.
6. I cook / cooks dinner every night.
7. My parents eat / eats lunch at 2pm.
8. Mia get / gets up at 5 o'clock.
9. My cousin work / works with animals.

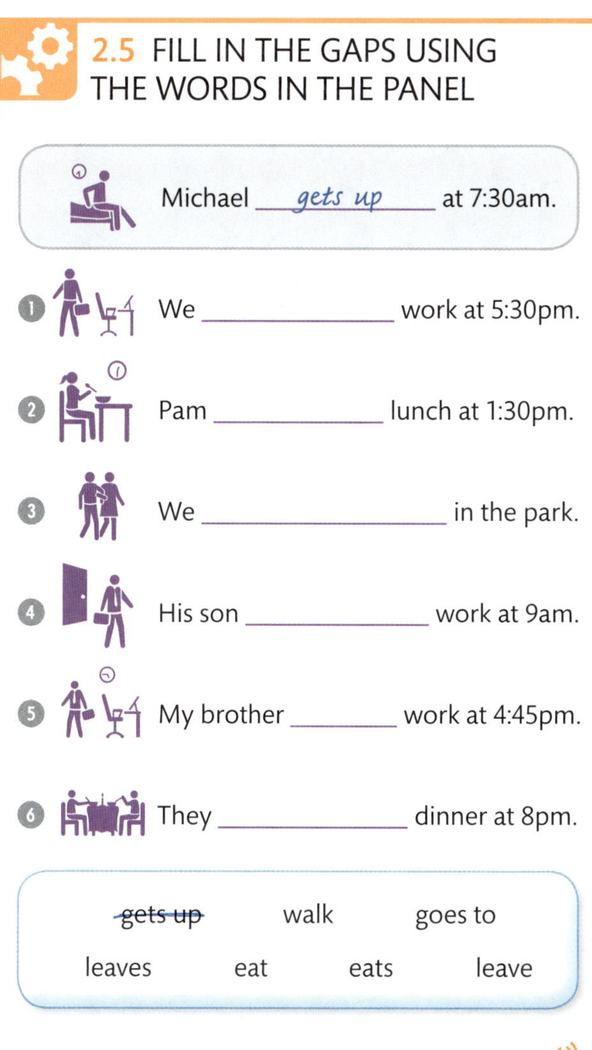

2.5 FILL IN THE GAPS USING THE WORDS IN THE PANEL

Michael *gets up* at 7:30am.

1. We __________ work at 5:30pm.
2. Pam __________ lunch at 1:30pm.
3. We __________ in the park.
4. His son __________ work at 9am.
5. My brother __________ work at 4:45pm.
6. They __________ dinner at 8pm.

~~gets up~~ walk goes to
leaves eat eats leave

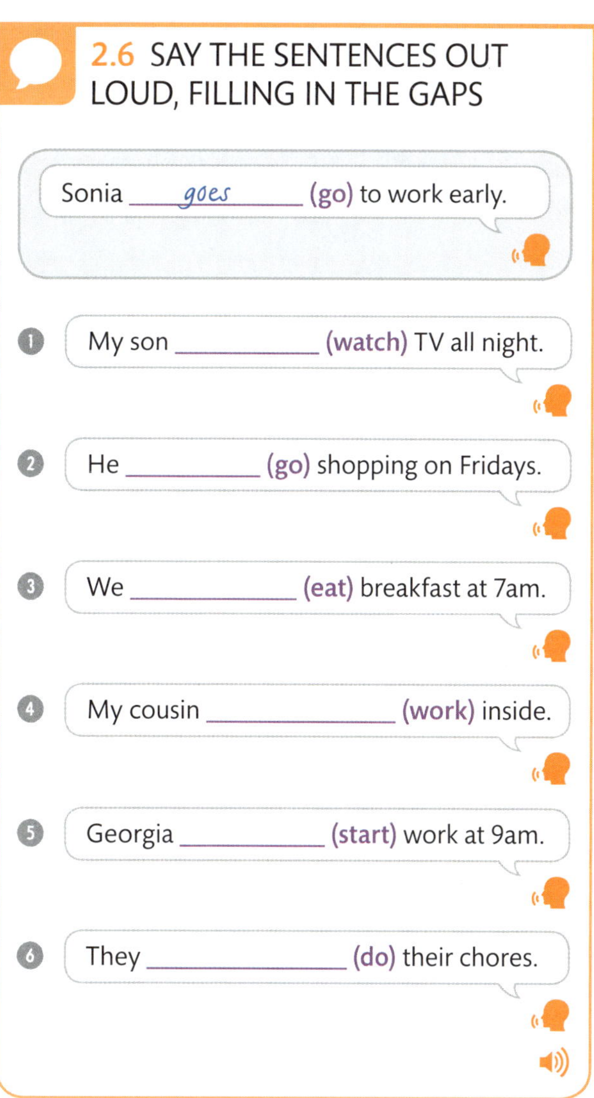

2.6 SAY THE SENTENCES OUT LOUD, FILLING IN THE GAPS

Sonia *goes* (go) to work early.

1. My son __________ (watch) TV all night.
2. He __________ (go) shopping on Fridays.
3. We __________ (eat) breakfast at 7am.
4. My cousin __________ (work) inside.
5. Georgia __________ (start) work at 9am.
6. They __________ (do) their chores.

2.7 **KEY LANGUAGE** THE PRESENT SIMPLE NEGATIVE

Use "do not" before the main verb to make the negative. If the subject is "he," "she," or "it," use "does not."

The main verb does not change.

I do not work outside.
I work inside.

He does not work inside.
He works outside.

2.8 **FURTHER EXAMPLES** THE PRESENT SIMPLE NEGATIVE

He does not live in France.

You can contract "do not" to "don't" and "does not" to "doesn't."

This house doesn't have a yard.

2.9 **HOW TO FORM** THE PRESENT SIMPLE NEGATIVE

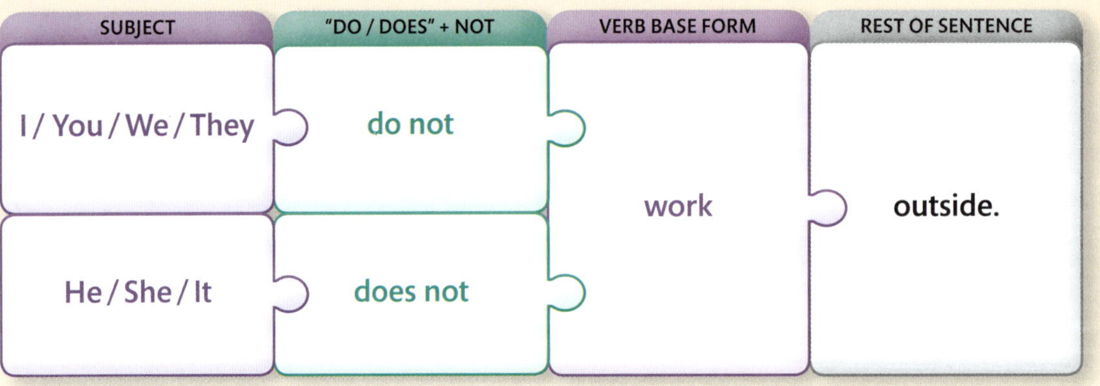

SUBJECT	"DO / DOES" + NOT	VERB BASE FORM	REST OF SENTENCE
I / You / We / They	do not	work	outside.
He / She / It	does not		

2.10 FILL IN THE GAPS TO WRITE EACH SENTENCE THREE DIFFERENT WAYS

	He gets up at 5am.	*He does not get up at 5am.*	*He doesn't get up at 5am.*
1	______	______	I don't go to work every day.
2	______	He does not watch TV in the evening.	______
3	They work in an office.	______	______

2.11 **KEY LANGUAGE** QUESTIONS WITH "DO" AND "DOES"

For most verbs other than "to be," add "do" or "does" to turn a statement into a question.

You work in an office. → **Do you work in an office?**

Use "do" in questions for "I," "you," "we," and "they."

She works in a school. → **Does she work in a school?**

Use "does" in questions for "he," "she," and "it."

The main verb is in its base form.

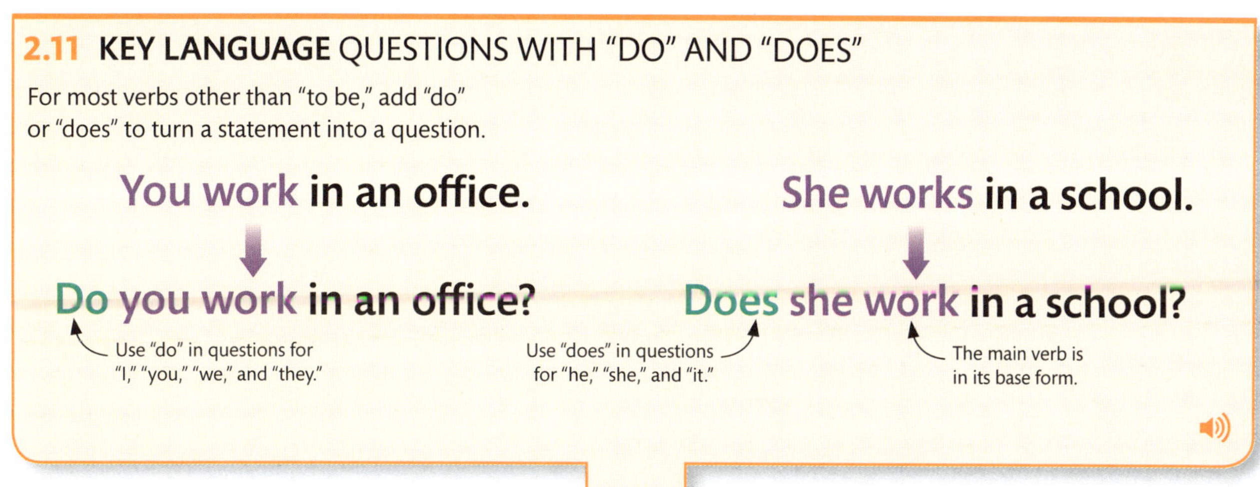

2.12 **FURTHER EXAMPLES** QUESTIONS WITH "DO" AND "DOES"

Do they live in London?

Does Tom get up at 7am?

Do I need a new coat?

Does she go swimming?

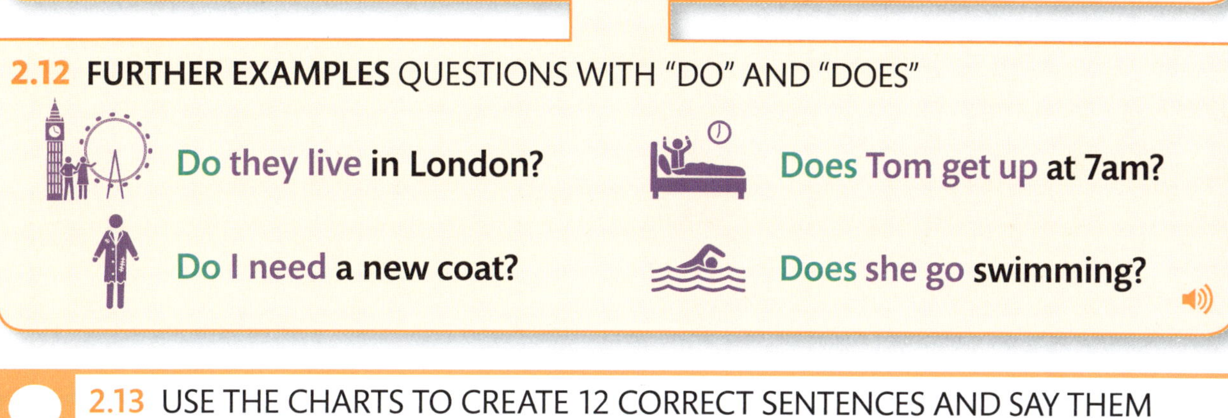

2.13 USE THE CHARTS TO CREATE 12 CORRECT SENTENCES AND SAY THEM OUT LOUD

Do you like basketball?

Do you / Does he → like → basketball? / running? / pizza?

I / My sister / They → don't / doesn't → work → on the weekend. / on Mondays.

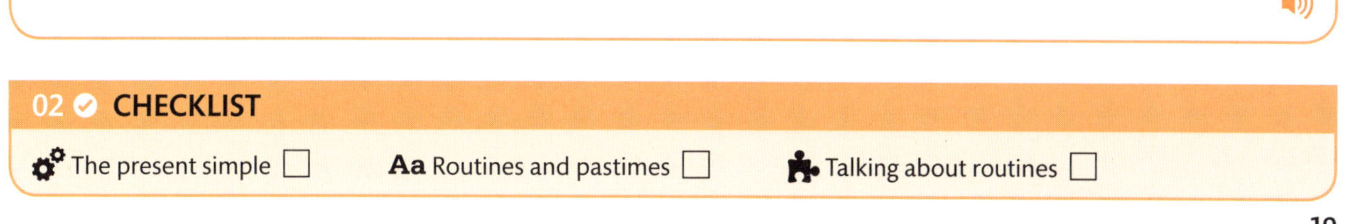

02 CHECKLIST

The present simple ☐ **Aa** Routines and pastimes ☐ Talking about routines ☐

03 Today I'm wearing...

You can use the present continuous to describe something that is happening now. It is often used to describe what people are wearing, using, or doing.

New language The present continuous
Aa Vocabulary Clothes and activities
New skill Talking about what's happening now

3.1 KEY LANGUAGE THE PRESENT CONTINUOUS

Use the present continuous form to describe what is happening right now.

This is the present simple. It describes a regular action.

Julie doesn't usually wear dresses, but today she is wearing a bright red dress.

This is the present continuous. It describes what is happening right now.

3.2 HOW TO FORM THE PRESENT CONTINUOUS

Use "to be" plus the present participle (this is the "-ing" form of the verb) to form the present continuous.

SUBJECT	"TO BE"	VERB + "-ING"	REST OF SENTENCE
She	is	wearing	a red dress.

This is the present participle. These follow the same spelling rules as gerunds.

3.3 FURTHER EXAMPLES THE PRESENT CONTINUOUS

She is walking the dog.

He is washing the dishes.

We are using our phones.

For verbs ending in "e" (such as "use"), take off the "e" and add "ing."

Remember, you can use contractions.

They're fighting with each other.

She is relaxing at the moment.

I am cutting some apples.

For single-syllable words ending consonant-vowel-consonant, double the final letter before adding "ing."

3.4 CROSS OUT THE INCORRECT WORDS IN THE SENTENCES

They ~~is~~ / are wearing hats.

1. Sharon is / are reading a book.
2. I am / is carrying my laptop.
3. My cat is / are climbing a tree.
4. We is / are working at the moment.
5. They is / are having their dinner.
6. He is / are talking to his dad.
7. I am / are driving to work right now.
8. They am / are watching the movie.

3.5 FILL IN THE GAPS TO COMPLETE THE SENTENCES

She *is sleeping* (sleep) in her bed.

1. They ________________ (come) home now.
2. We ________________ (play) a board game.
3. Jane ________________ (cook) dinner.
4. He ________________ (drink) some water.
5. We ________________ (listen) to music.
6. I ________________ (wash) my hair.
7. You ________________ (win) the game.
8. We ________________ (visit) New Zealand.

3.6 LISTEN TO THE AUDIO AND MATCH THE PORTRAITS TO THE NAMES

1 2 3 4

Emma — Emma's dad — Julie — Max — Emma's cousin

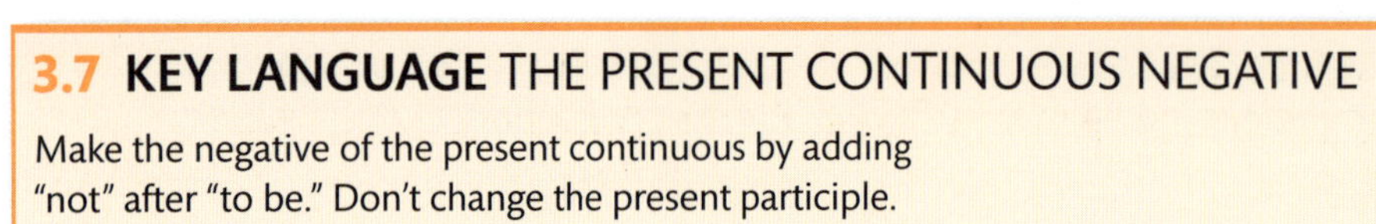

3.7 KEY LANGUAGE THE PRESENT CONTINUOUS NEGATIVE

Make the negative of the present continuous by adding "not" after "to be." Don't change the present participle.

He is wearing a tie, but he { is not / isn't } wearing a hat.

Add "not" after "to be" to make the negative. You can use contractions, too.

You still use the present participle when you make the negative.

3.8 HOW TO FORM THE PRESENT CONTINUOUS NEGATIVE

3.9 FURTHER EXAMPLES THE PRESENT CONTINUOUS NEGATIVE

She isn't walking **the dog.**

We aren't taking **the bus today.**

They aren't singing **well today.**

You aren't doing **your job!**

3.10 CROSS OUT THE INCORRECT WORDS IN THE SENTENCES

They ~~isn't~~ / aren't wearing coats.

1. We isn't / aren't playing with them.
2. The baby isn't / aren't sleeping.
3. He isn't / aren't watching the game.
4. You isn't / aren't wearing boots.
5. She isn't / aren't cooking lunch.
6. We isn't / aren't meeting right now.
7. I am not / aren't eating with them.

3.11 FILL IN THE GAPS WITH THE PRESENT CONTINUOUS NEGATIVE

Sheila _isn't walking_ (walk) the dog.

1. They ______________ (go) to the park.
2. I ______________ (eat) this meal.
3. You ______________ (wear) this coat again.
4. Frank's dog ______________ (sit) by the fire.
5. My dad ______________ (carry) the heavy box.

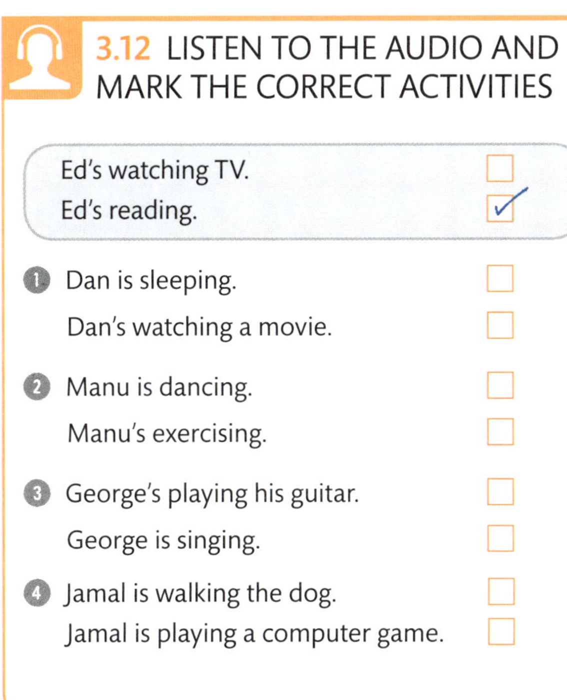

3.12 LISTEN TO THE AUDIO AND MARK THE CORRECT ACTIVITIES

Ed's watching TV. ☐
Ed's reading. ☑

1. Dan is sleeping. ☐
   Dan's watching a movie. ☐
2. Manu is dancing. ☐
   Manu's exercising. ☐
3. George's playing his guitar. ☐
   George is singing. ☐
4. Jamal is walking the dog. ☐
   Jamal is playing a computer game. ☐

3.13 SAY POSITIVE AND NEGATIVE SENTENCES BASED ON THE IMAGES

They are running.
They aren't running.

1.

2.

3.

03 CHECKLIST

The present continuous ☐ Aa Clothes and activities ☐ Talking about what's happening now ☐

04 What's happening?

You can use the present continuous to ask about things that are happening now, at the time of speaking.

New language Present continuous questions
Aa Vocabulary Activities and gadgets
New skill Asking about the present

4.1 KEY LANGUAGE PRESENT CONTINUOUS QUESTIONS

Use present continuous questions to ask about what is happening now.

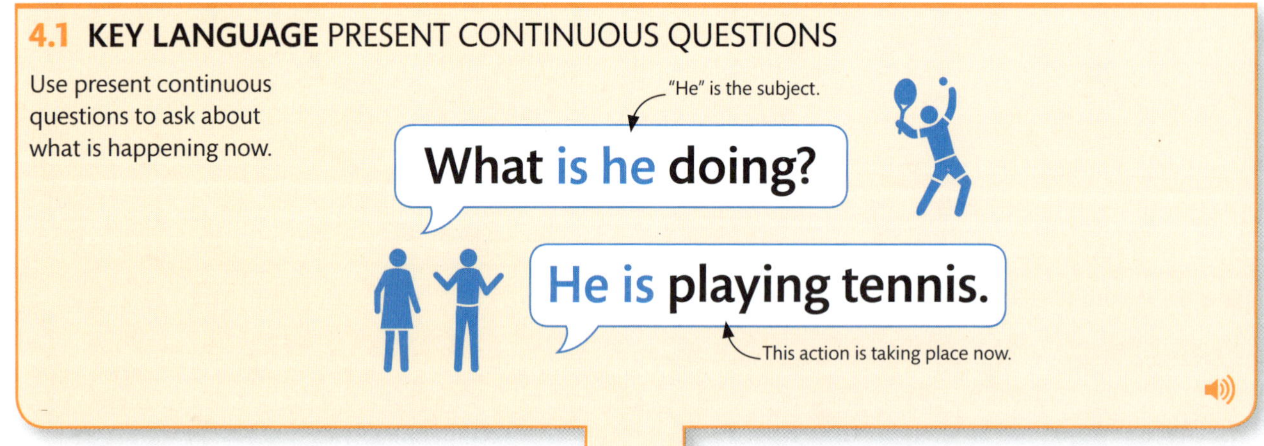

4.2 HOW TO FORM PRESENT CONTINUOUS QUESTIONS

To make a question in the present continuous, swap the subject and "to be." You can also add question words.

4.3 FURTHER EXAMPLES PRESENT CONTINUOUS QUESTIONS

4.4 VOCABULARY COMMON PRESENT CONTINUOUS VERBS

4.5 LISTEN TO THE AUDIO AND WRITE WHO'S DOING EACH ACTIVITY

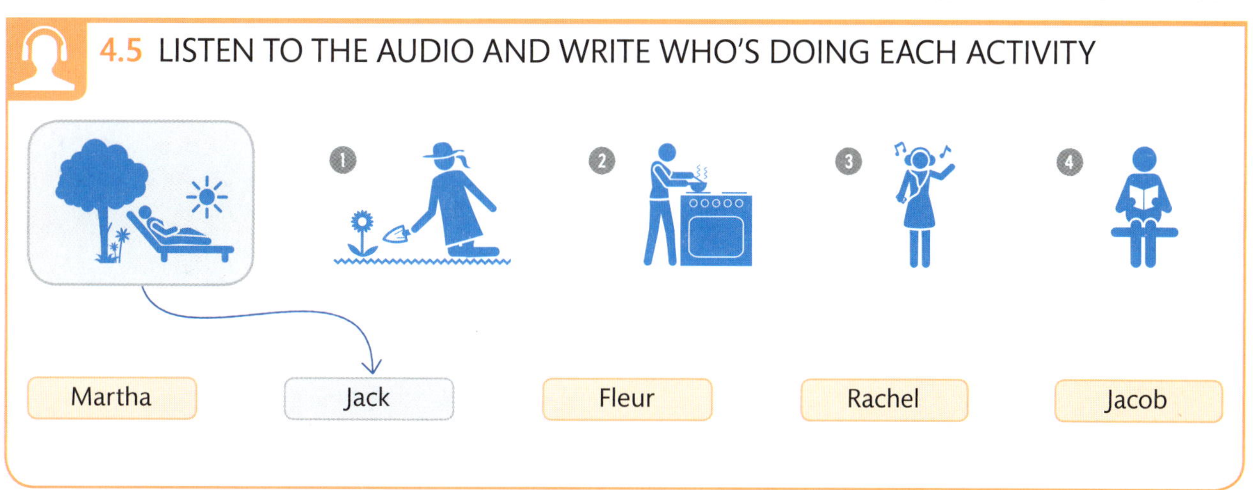

4.6 MATCH THE QUESTIONS TO THE ANSWERS

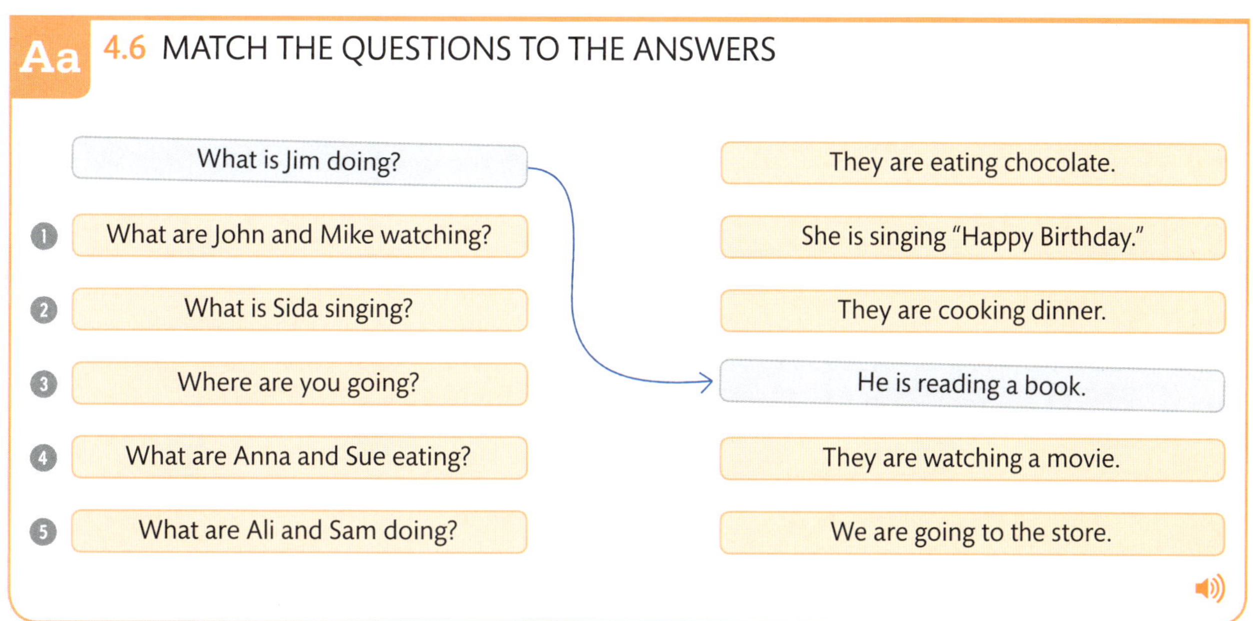

4.7 VOCABULARY DIGITAL GADGETS

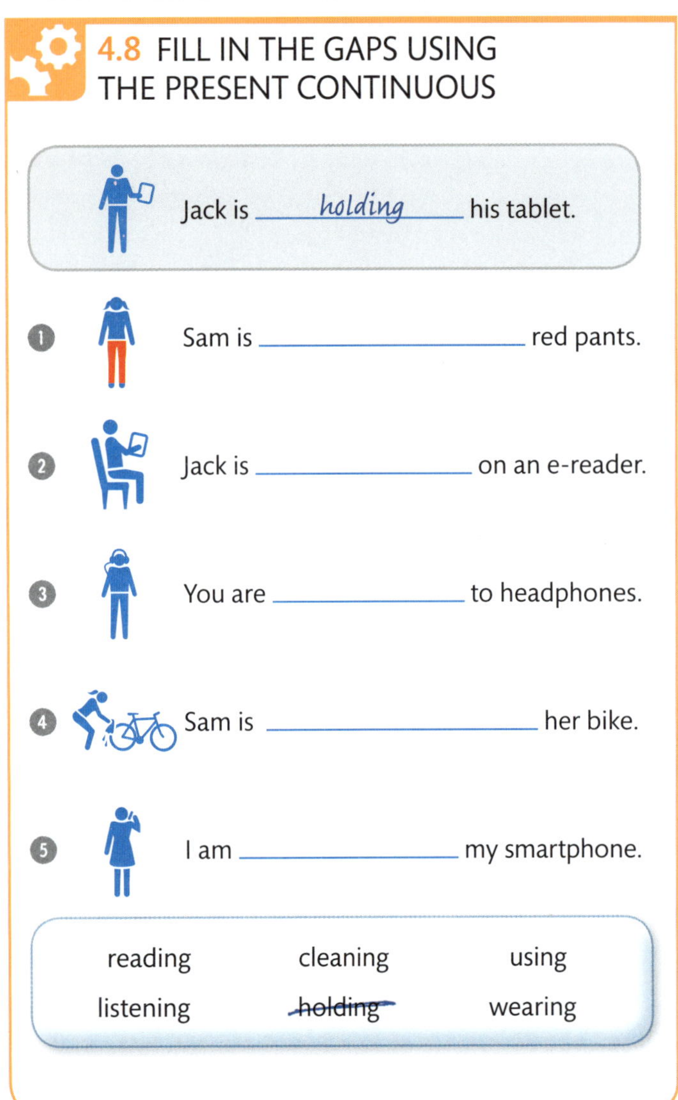

4.8 FILL IN THE GAPS USING THE PRESENT CONTINUOUS

Jack is *holding* his tablet.

1. Sam is ______________ red pants.
2. Jack is ______________ on an e-reader.
3. You are ______________ to headphones.
4. Sam is ______________ her bike.
5. I am ______________ my smartphone.

reading	cleaning	using
listening	~~holding~~	wearing

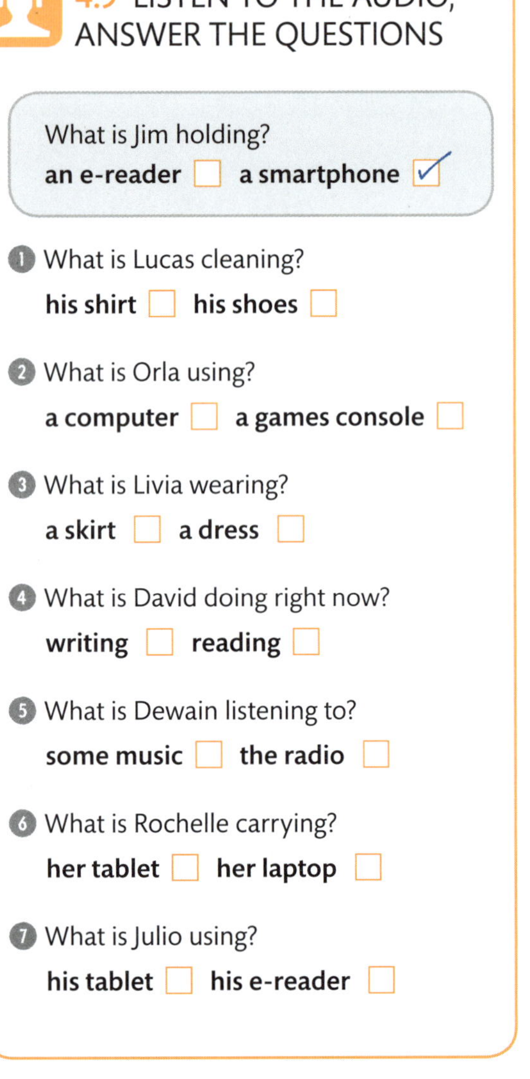

4.9 LISTEN TO THE AUDIO, ANSWER THE QUESTIONS

What is Jim holding?
an e-reader ☐ **a smartphone** ☑

1. What is Lucas cleaning?
   his shirt ☐ **his shoes** ☐
2. What is Orla using?
   a computer ☐ **a games console** ☐
3. What is Livia wearing?
   a skirt ☐ **a dress** ☐
4. What is David doing right now?
   writing ☐ **reading** ☐
5. What is Dewain listening to?
   some music ☐ **the radio** ☐
6. What is Rochelle carrying?
   her tablet ☐ **her laptop** ☐
7. What is Julio using?
   his tablet ☐ **his e-reader** ☐

4.10 REWRITE THE QUESTIONS, CORRECTING THE ERRORS

Where Lill is going?
Where is Lill going?

1. What cleaning is Kimi?

2. What is doing Jill?

3. Using what is Jack?

4. Max what is holding?

5. Is what carrying Marge?

4.11 LOOK AT THE PICTURES AND ANSWER THE QUESTIONS, SPEAKING OUT LOUD

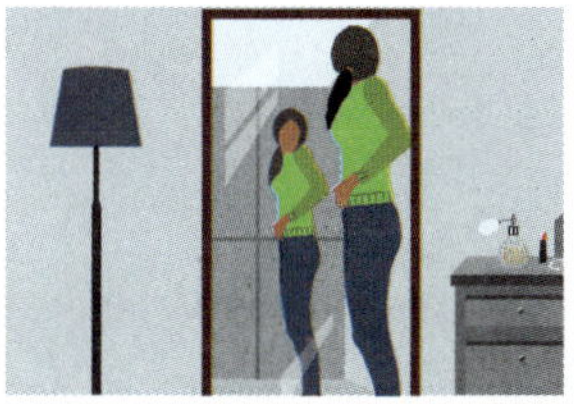

What is Alvita wearing?
Alvita is wearing a green sweater.

1. Where is Emir going?

2. What are they holding?

3. What is she carrying?

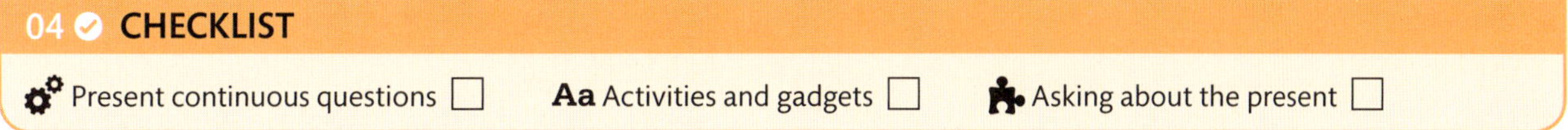

04 CHECKLIST

Present continuous questions ☐ Aa Activities and gadgets ☐ Asking about the present ☐

05 Types of verbs

You can use most verbs in the continuous form to describe ongoing actions. Some verbs cannot be used in this way. These are called "state" verbs.

New language Action and state verbs
Aa Vocabulary Activities
New skill Using state verbs

5.1 KEY LANGUAGE ACTION AND STATE VERBS

Action verbs usually describe what people or things do. State verbs usually say how things are or how someone feels.

ACTION VERB

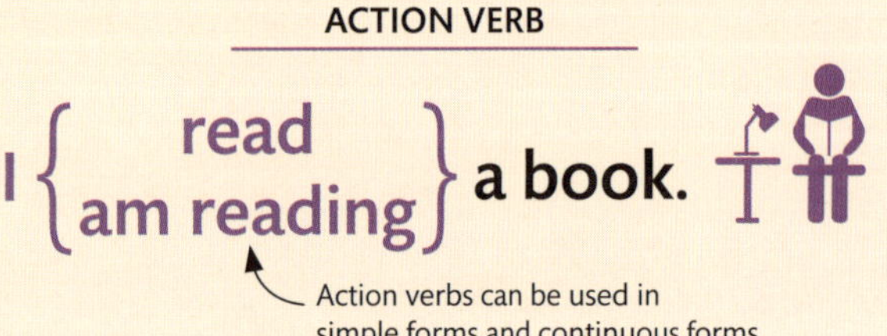

Action verbs can be used in simple forms and continuous forms.

STATE VERB

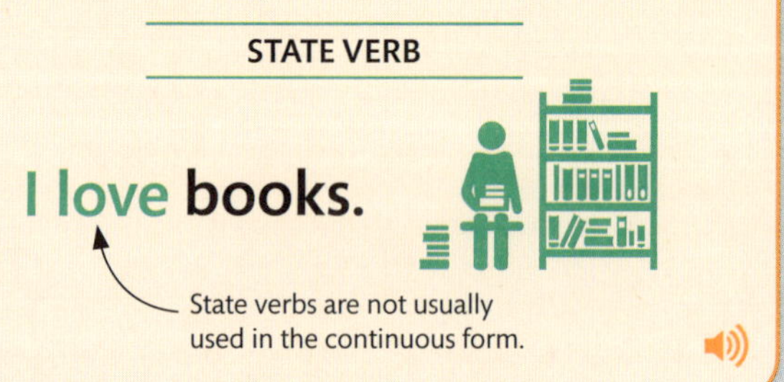

State verbs are not usually used in the continuous form.

5.2 FURTHER EXAMPLES ACTION AND STATE VERBS

Dominic is eating ice cream.

I want to go on vacation.

Gayle is lying on the couch.

She has two cats and a dog.

Aa 5.3 FIND EIGHT VERBS IN THE GRID AND WRITE THEM UNDER THE CORRECT HEADING

L O V E B I R A C S A H
T P Q A Y H E N V T Q A
R E M E M B E R D H M T
W A N T L E R E A D T E
L T B C O W D K S V X C
E E D E V T W E E E A I
L E A R N L A O E R G O

ACTION VERBS:	STATE VERBS:
1 ______	1 want
2 ______	2 ______
3 ______	3 ______
4 ______	4 ______

5.4 ⚠ COMMON MISTAKES STATE VERBS

It is incorrect to use state verbs in the continuous form.

I want a new laptop. ✓
You can usually only use state verbs in the simple form.

I am wanting a new laptop. ✗
You can't usually use state verbs in the continuous form.

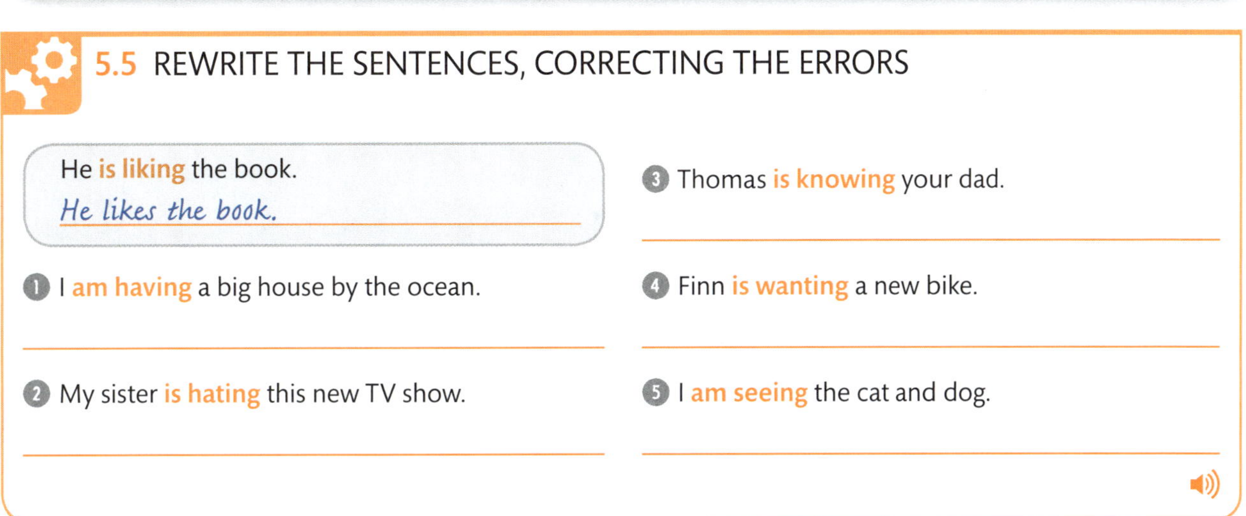

5.5 REWRITE THE SENTENCES, CORRECTING THE ERRORS

He is liking the book.
He likes the book.

1. I am having a big house by the ocean.
2. My sister is hating this new TV show.
3. Thomas is knowing your dad.
4. Finn is wanting a new bike.
5. I am seeing the cat and dog.

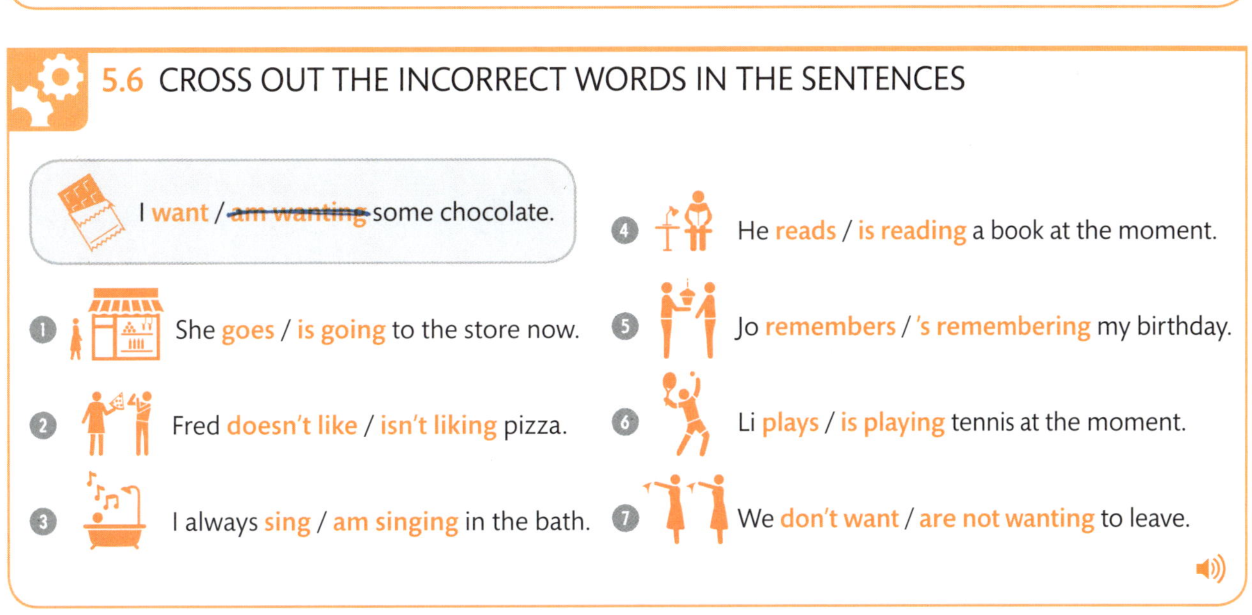

5.6 CROSS OUT THE INCORRECT WORDS IN THE SENTENCES

I want / ~~am wanting~~ some chocolate.

1. She goes / is going to the store now.
2. Fred doesn't like / isn't liking pizza.
3. I always sing / am singing in the bath.
4. He reads / is reading a book at the moment.
5. Jo remembers / 's remembering my birthday.
6. Li plays / is playing tennis at the moment.
7. We don't want / are not wanting to leave.

05 ✓ CHECKLIST

Action and state verbs ☐ Aa Activities ☐ Using state verbs ☐

06 Vocabulary

6.1 FEELINGS AND MOODS

calm

relaxed

happy

confident

proud

excited

surprised

pleased

cheerful

amused

irritated

angry

annoyed

furious

sad

unhappy

worried

lonely

scared

terrified

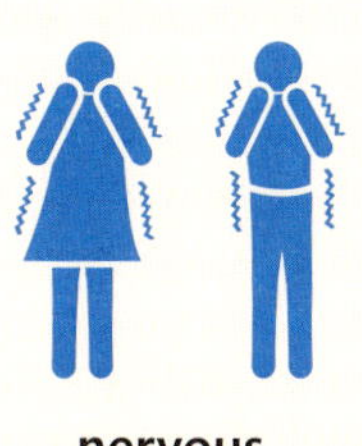
nervous

anxious

distracted

confused

disappointed

miserable

stressed

jealous

tired

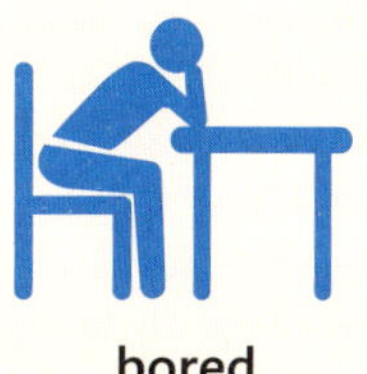
bored

curious

grateful

07 How are you feeling?

Talking about your feelings is an important part of everyday conversation. Use the present continuous to talk about how you're feeling.

New language "Feeling" and emotions
Vocabulary Adjectives of emotions
New skill Talking about your feelings

TIP
"Feel" is a state verb that can be used in continuous forms.

7.1 KEY LANGUAGE TALKING ABOUT YOUR FEELINGS

You can use the verb "to be" plus "feeling" to talk about your feelings.

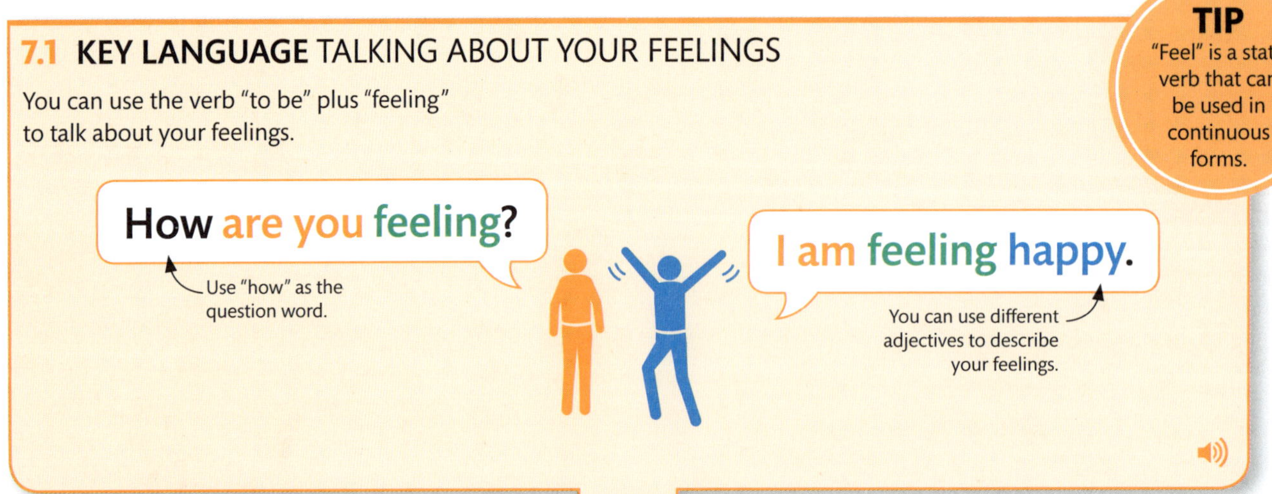

7.2 HOW TO FORM TALKING ABOUT YOUR FEELINGS

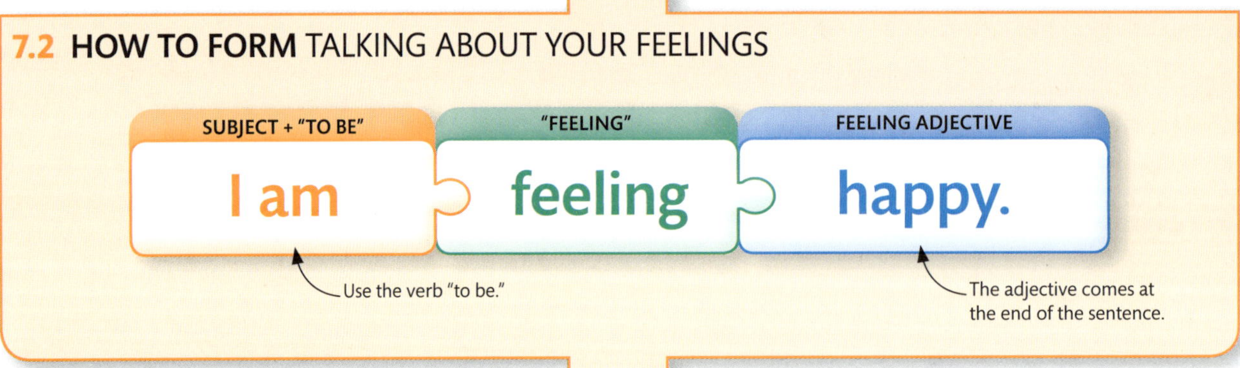

7.3 FURTHER EXAMPLES TALKING ABOUT YOUR FEELINGS

7.4 MATCH THE FEELINGS TO THEIR OPPOSITES

7.5 FILL IN THE GAPS TO COMPLETE THE SENTENCES

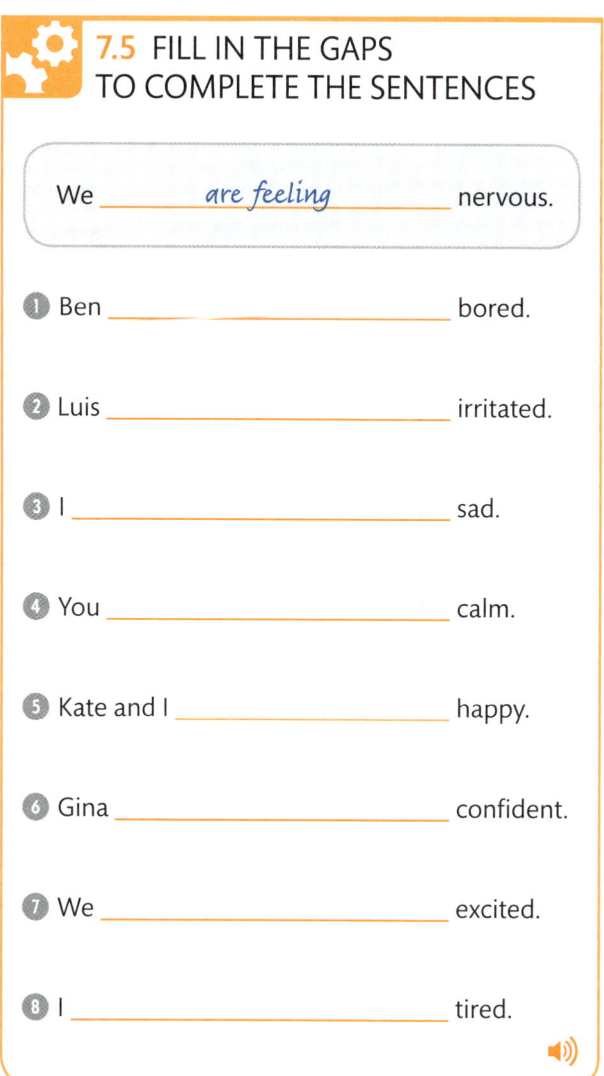

7.6 LISTEN TO THE AUDIO AND ANSWER THE QUESTIONS

Jack is feeling confident.
True ☐ **False** ☑

1. Jill is feeling happy.
True ☐ **False** ☐

2. Sami is feeling nervous.
True ☐ **False** ☐

3. Ian is feeling bored.
True ☐ **False** ☐

4. Lindi is feeling annoyed.
True ☐ **False** ☐

5. Jenny is feeling happy.
True ☐ **False** ☐

6. Jimmi is feeling excited.
True ☐ **False** ☐

7. Minna is feeling scared.
True ☐ **False** ☐

8. Aziz is feeling tired.
True ☐ **False** ☐

7.7 ANOTHER WAY TO SAY IT TALKING ABOUT YOUR FEELINGS

You can also ask how someone is, without using "feeling."

7.8 HOW TO FORM TALKING ABOUT YOUR FEELINGS

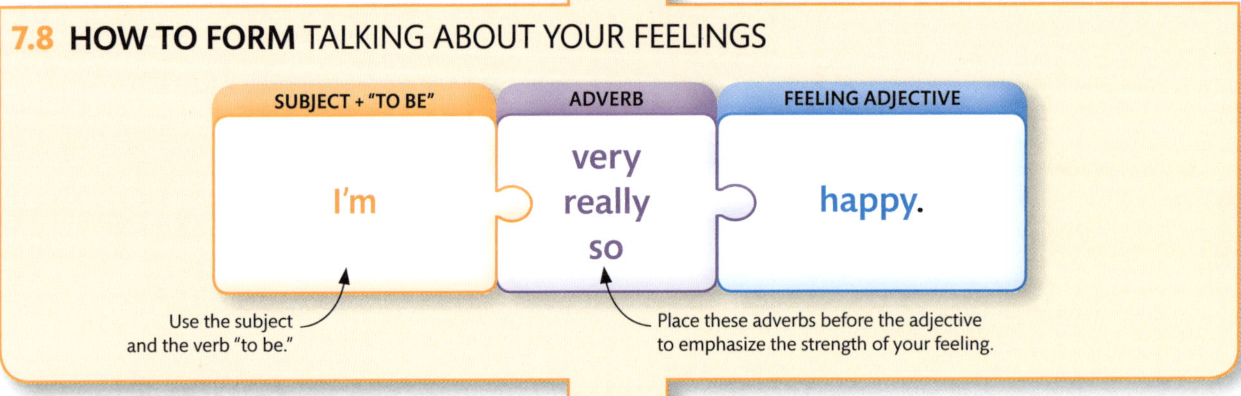

7.9 FURTHER EXAMPLES TALKING ABOUT YOUR FEELINGS

7.10 REWRITE THE SENTENCES, ADDING ADVERBS

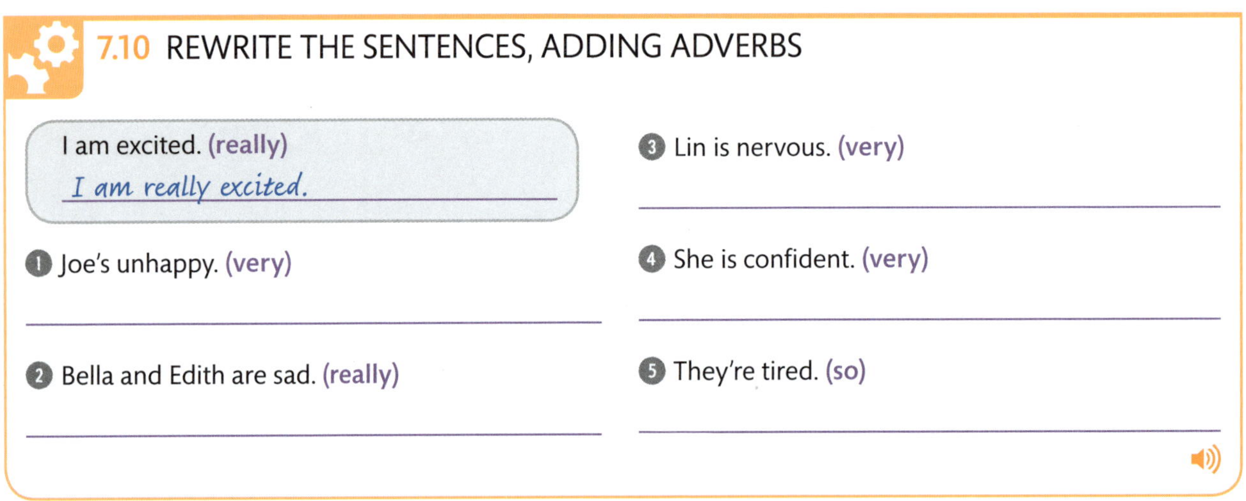

I am excited. (really)
I am really excited.

1. Joe's unhappy. (very)

2. Bella and Edith are sad. (really)

3. Lin is nervous. (very)

4. She is confident. (very)

5. They're tired. (so)

Aa 7.11 FILL IN THE GAPS USING THE WORDS IN THE PANEL

I'm having a great day at the beach. All my friends are here and we're playing volleyball. I'm really happy.

1. I'm at the airport. I'm waiting for the flight. I don't have a book. There's nothing to do. I'm really ______ .

2. I'm watching a movie on TV. It's a love story. The man and his wife are in different countries. They're very ______ .

3. We're at the concert. We're waiting for my favorite band in the world to come on stage. We're at the front. I'm so ______ .

4. I'm at the supermarket. There's no milk, no butter, no flour, and no sugar. All the things that I need for the cake. I'm so ______ .

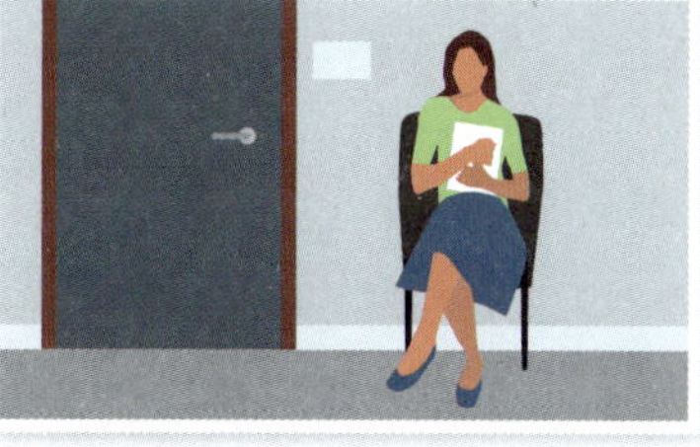

5. I'm waiting to meet my new boss. She's talking to everyone in the office. I don't know what to say to her. I'm very ______ .

sad ~~happy~~ bored angry excited nervous

07 CHECKLIST

"Feeling" and emotions ☐ Aa Adjectives of emotions ☐ Talking about your feelings ☐

08 Vocabulary

8.1 TRANSPORTATION

car

taxi

bus

coach

plane

train

tram

motorcycle (US)
motorbike (UK)

bicycle

boat

yacht

ship

helicopter

bus stop

train station

taxi rank

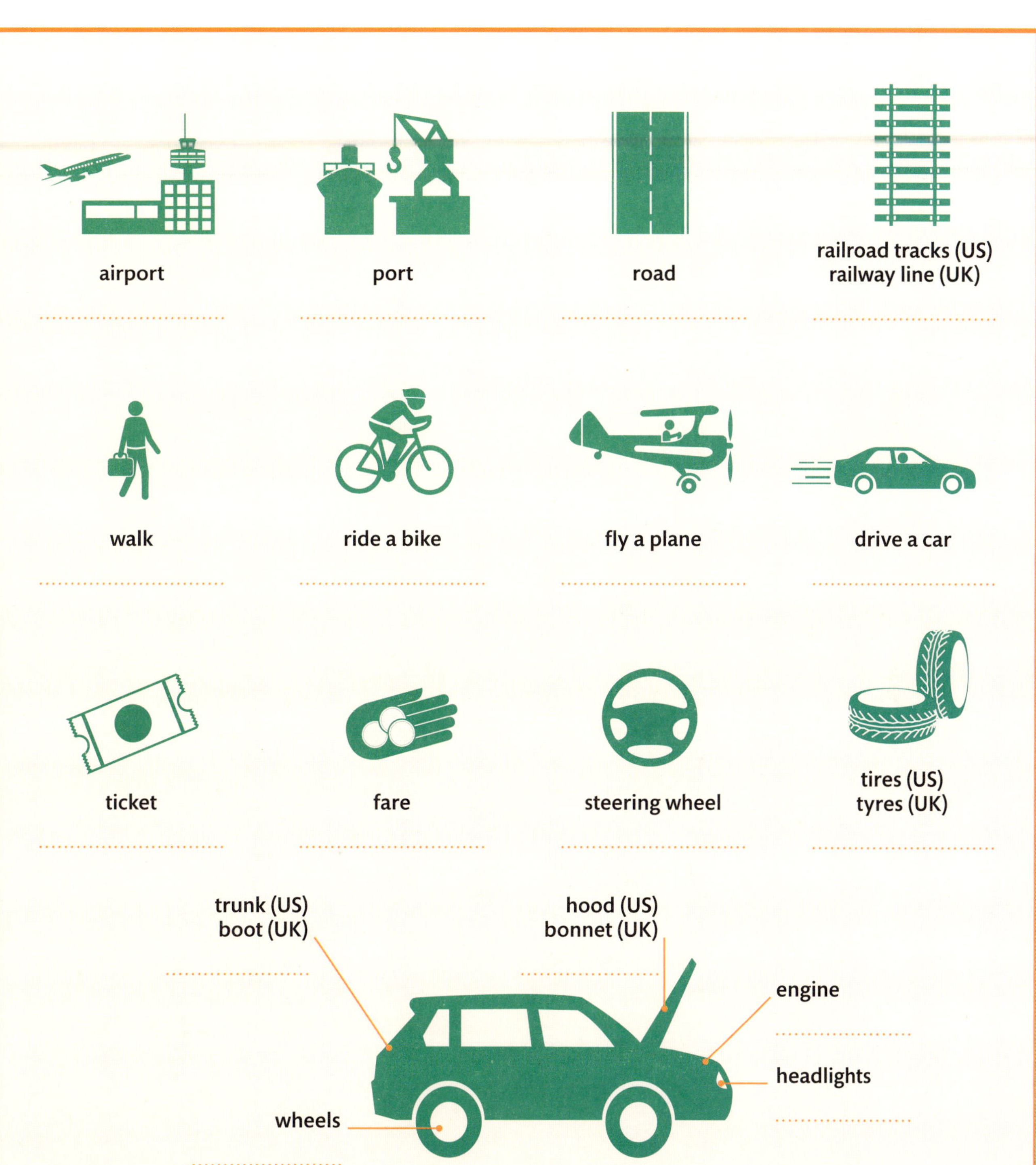

airport
port
road
railroad tracks (US)
railway line (UK)
walk
ride a bike
fly a plane
drive a car
ticket
fare
steering wheel
tires (US)
tyres (UK)
trunk (US)
boot (UK)
hood (US)
bonnet (UK)
engine
headlights
wheels

09 Routines and exceptions

Use the present simple to describe routines, and the present continuous to say what you are doing now. These tenses are often used together.

New language Exceptions
Vocabulary Time markers
New skill Contrasting routines and exceptions

9.1 KEY LANGUAGE CONTRASTING ROUTINES AND EXCEPTIONS

You can contrast a routine action with an exception to that routine by using "but."

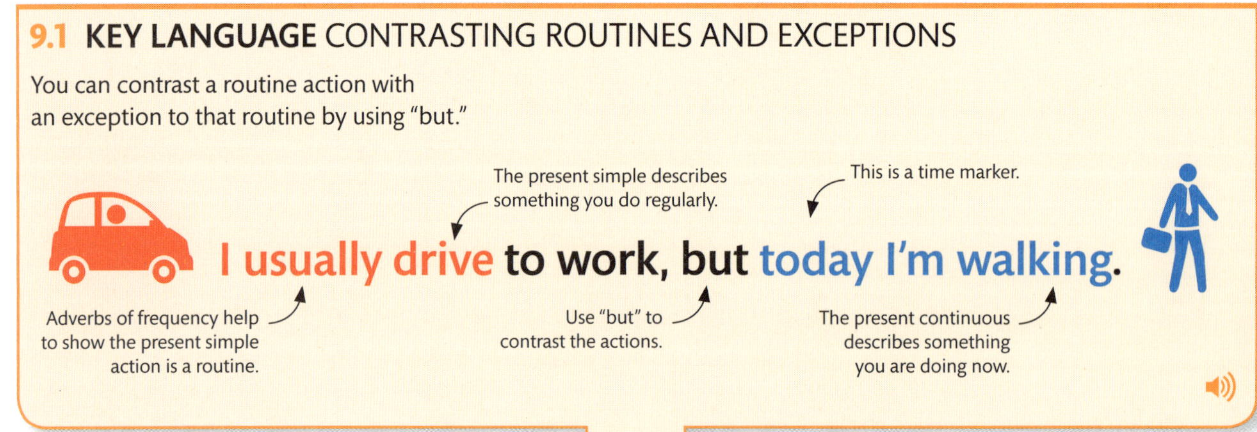

9.2 HOW TO FORM CONTRASTING ROUTINES AND EXCEPTIONS

SUBJECT	ADVERB OF FREQUENCY	VERB	"BUT"	TIME MARKER	PRESENT CONTINUOUS
I	usually mostly often	drive,	but	right now today tonight	I'm walking.

9.3 FURTHER EXAMPLES CONTRASTING ROUTINES AND EXCEPTIONS

I often stay at home on the weekends, but today I'm shopping in town.

They usually go to the gym after work, but tonight they're going to the movies.

Tonight, we're celebrating my birthday, but normally we don't eat out.

You can put the exception first.

9.4 FILL IN THE GAPS BY PUTTING THE VERBS IN THE CORRECT TENSES

Ben usually _sings_ (sing) in the school band, but today he _is playing_ (play) the guitar.

1. Sarah and I normally ______ (play) tennis on Wednesdays, but today we ______ (swim).
2. Today, I ______ (have) soup for lunch, but I usually ______ (have) a sandwich.
3. We often ______ (watch) TV in the evenings, but tonight we ______ (have) a party.
4. Ben and Tom usually ______ (work) until 6pm, but tonight they ______ (work) until 9pm.
5. Melanie ______ (ski) in France this winter, but she normally ______ (go) to Italy.
6. Today, you ______ (drink) water, but you often ______ (have) coffee after lunch.

9.5 VOCABULARY TIME MARKERS

At the moment, I'm knitting.

....

I'm leaving right now.

....

I'm in a meeting this morning.

....

This afternoon, we're shopping.

....

Today, I'm on vacation.

....

They're seeing a play tonight.

....

9.6 READ THE MESSAGES AND FILL THE GAPS USING THE PRESENT CONTINUOUS

Chrissy *is watching a movie* .

1 Denzel ______________________ .

2 Selma ______________________ .

3 Marlow ______________________ .

4 Roxy ______________________ .

4 Rainey ______________________ .

6 Malala ______________________ .

7 Altan ______________________ .

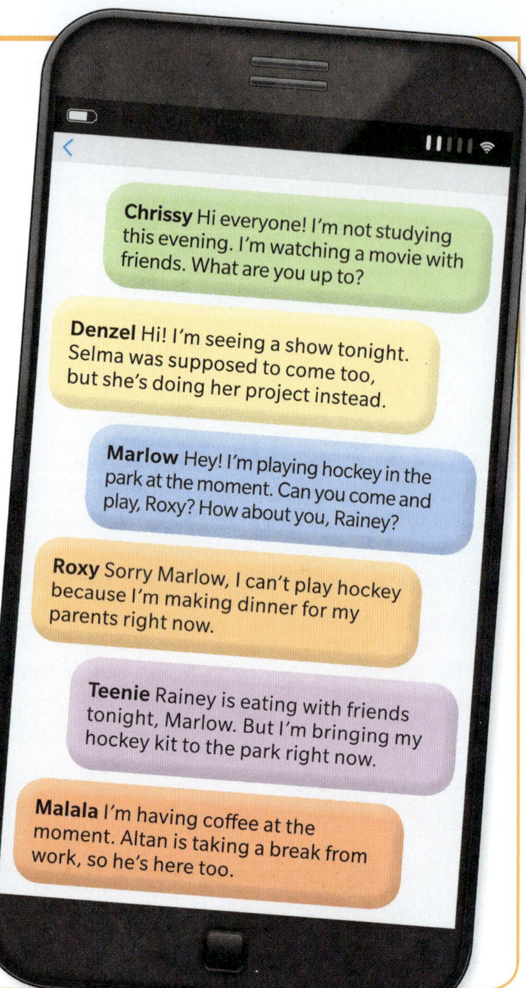

9.7 LISTEN TO THE AUDIO AND MARK WHICH ACTIVITIES ARE EXCEPTIONS

A ☐ B ☐ C ☑

1

A ☐ B ☐ C ☐

2

A ☐ B ☐ C ☐

3

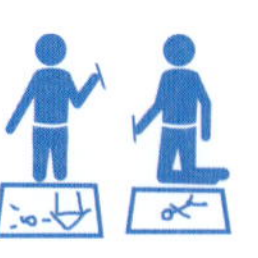

A ☐ B ☐ C ☐

9.8 SAY THE SENTENCES OUT LOUD, PUTTING THE VERBS IN THE CORRECT TENSES

Phil usually *runs* (run), but today *he is cycling* (cycle).

1. Sally usually ______ (swim), but right now ______ (play) soccer.
2. Abe normally ______ (read), but tonight ______ (listen) to music.
3. They often ______ (play) golf, but today ______ (play) hockey.
4. I usually ______ (take) a shower, but today ______ (take) a bath.

09 CHECKLIST

Exceptions ☐ Aa Time markers ☐ Contrasting routines and exceptions ☐

REVIEW THE ENGLISH YOU HAVE LEARNED IN UNITS 01–09

NEW LANGUAGE	SAMPLE SENTENCE	☑	UNIT
TALKING ABOUT YOURSELF AND YOUR DAILY ROUTINE	I am Noah. I'm 25 years old. I eat lunch at 1pm every day.	☐	1.1, 2.1
THE PRESENT CONTINUOUS	She is wearing a red dress.	☐	3.1
PRESENT CONTINUOUS QUESTIONS	What is he doing?	☐	4.1
ACTION AND STATE VERBS	I am reading a book. I love books.	☐	5.1
TALKING ABOUT YOUR FEELINGS	How are you feeling? I am feeling happy.	☐	7.1
ROUTINES AND EXCEPTIONS	I usually drive to work, but today I'm walking.	☐	9.1

10 Vocabulary

10.1 THE BODY

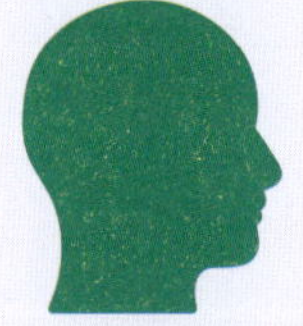
head

hair

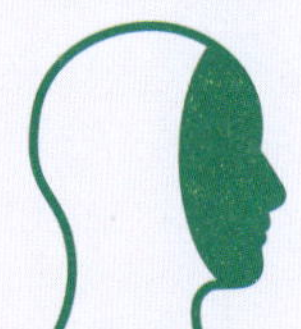
face

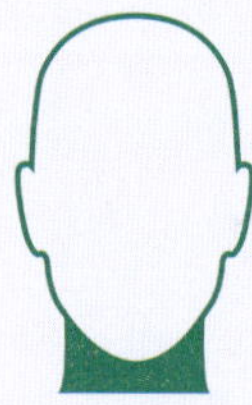
neck

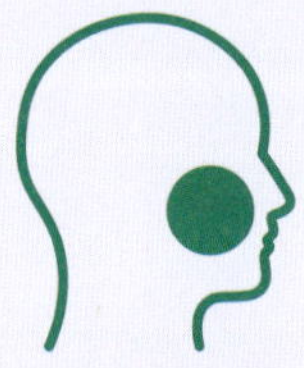
cheek

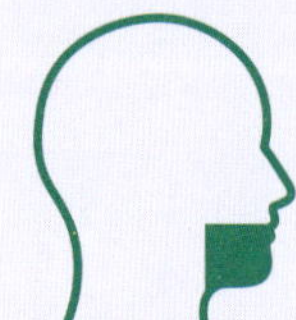
chin

shoulders

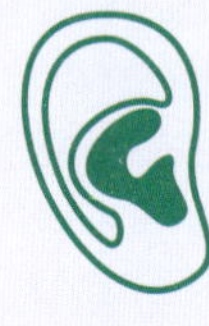
ear

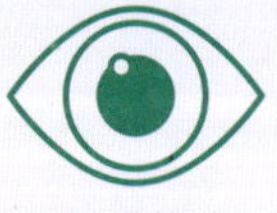
eye

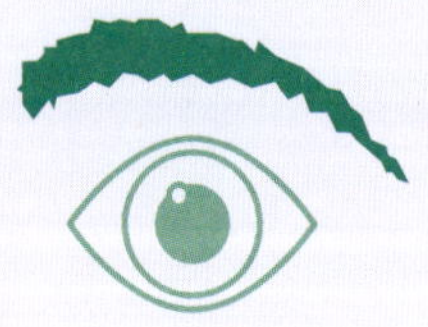
eyebrow

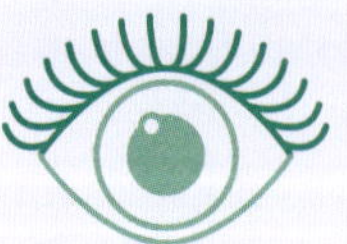
eyelashes

nose

mouth

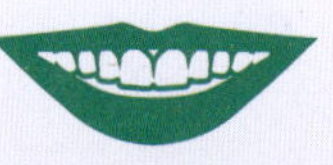
lips

teeth

tooth

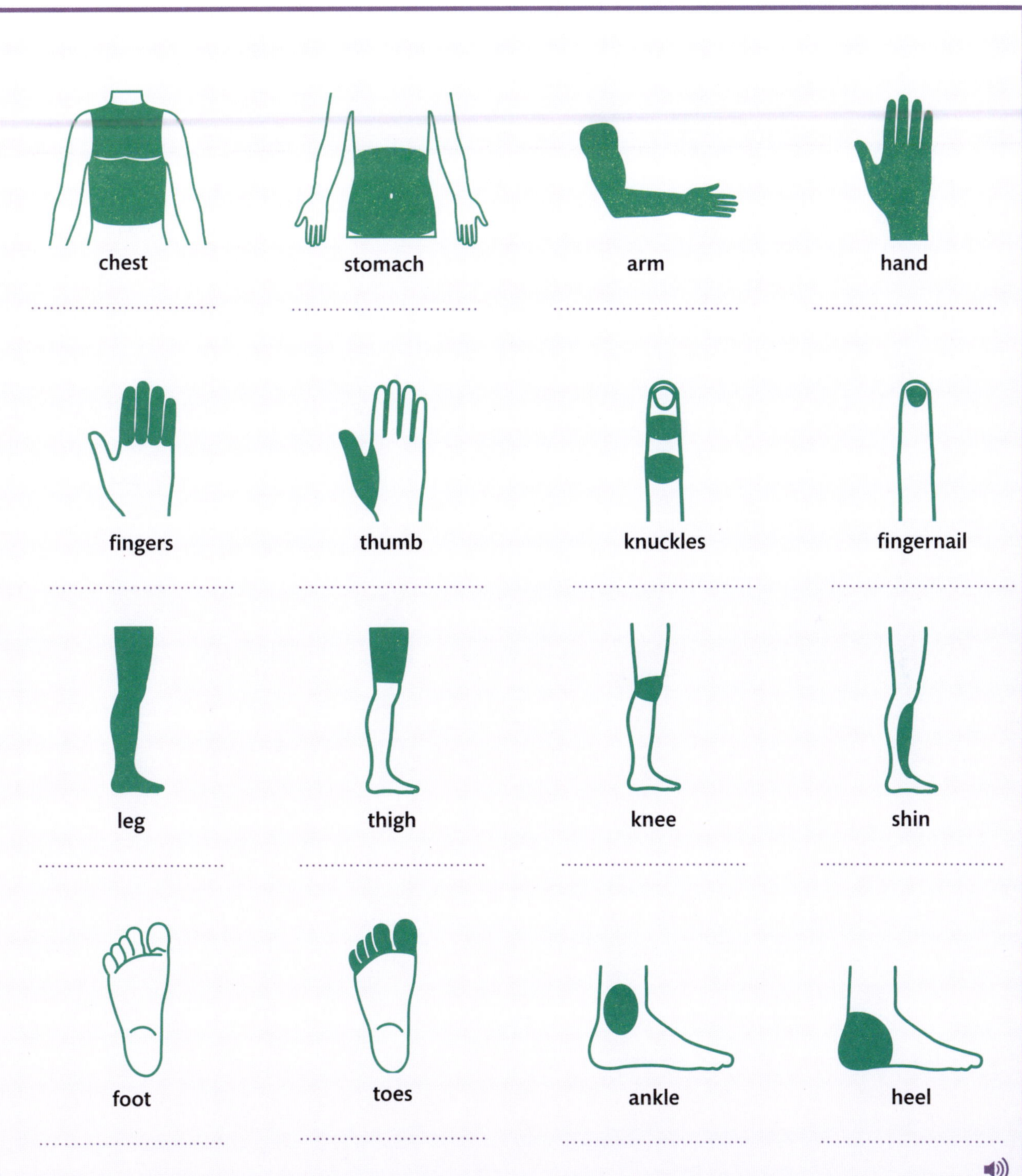
chest
stomach
arm
hand
fingers
thumb
knuckles
fingernail
leg
thigh
knee
shin
foot
toes
ankle
heel

11 What's the matter?

There are many different ways to say you're sick. You often use the negative, "not well," to talk about general illness, and "hurts," "ache," or "pain" for specific problems.

New language Health complaints
Aa Vocabulary Body parts and pain phrases
New skill Saying what's wrong

11.1 KEY LANGUAGE SAYING YOU'RE NOT FEELING WELL

To say what's wrong, use the verb "to be" with "well," "sick," or "ill." You can also use "to be" with "feeling" and an adverb to show the problem continues and to explain how bad it is.

Are you okay?

Negative form.

No, I'm not very well.

Use verb "to be" with present continuous to say the problem is ongoing.

No, I'm not feeling very well.

Use "don't" and "doesn't" with the base form of "to feel."

No, I don't feel very well.

In UK English, "I'm feeling sick" or "I feel sick" mean you might vomit.

No, I'm sick.

No, I feel ill.

"Ill" is more often used in UK English. "Sick" is more common in US English.

No, I'm feeling ill.

11.2 REWRITE THE SENTENCES CORRECTING THE ERRORS

Hilary not feeling well. She's at the doctor.
Hilary's not feeling well. She's at the doctor.

1. My brother isn't **feel** very well this morning.

2. George **are** sick, so he's staying in bed today.

3. I **is** sick, so I'm not going to work.

4. Ayshah **doesn't** feeling well, so she's going home.

5. Luca and Ben **isn't** feeling well today.

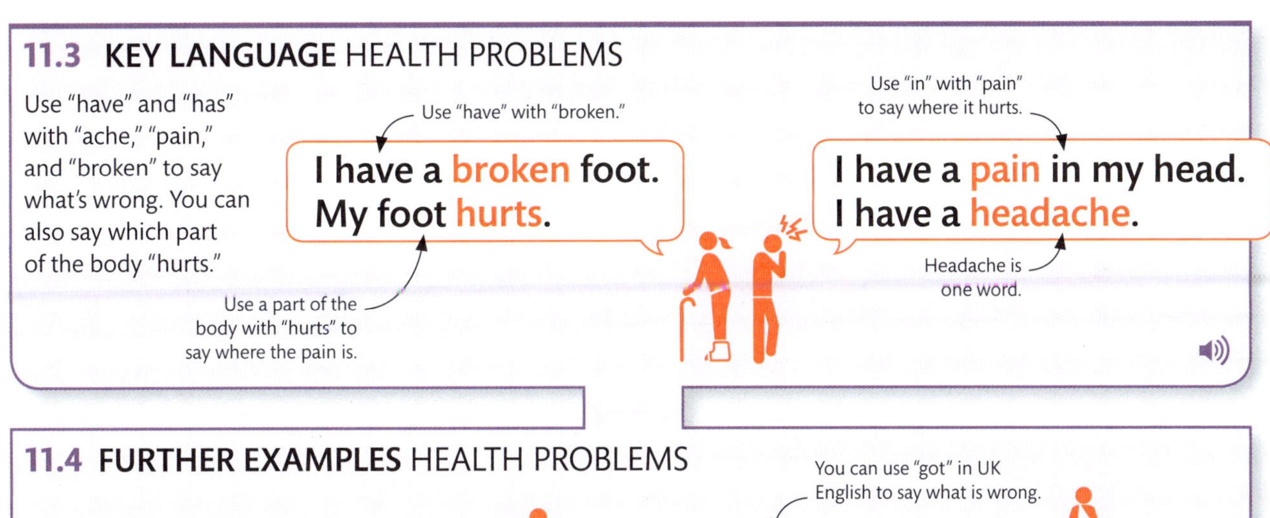

11.3 KEY LANGUAGE HEALTH PROBLEMS

Use "have" and "has" with "ache," "pain," and "broken" to say what's wrong. You can also say which part of the body "hurts."

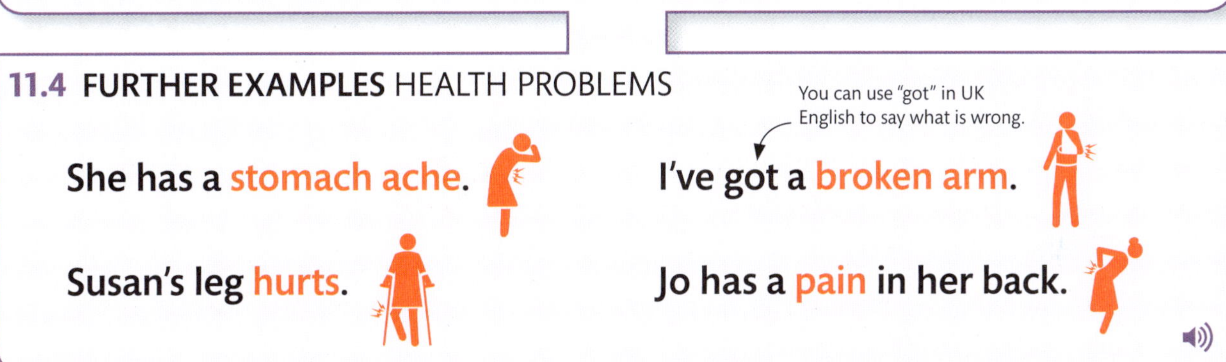

11.4 FURTHER EXAMPLES HEALTH PROBLEMS

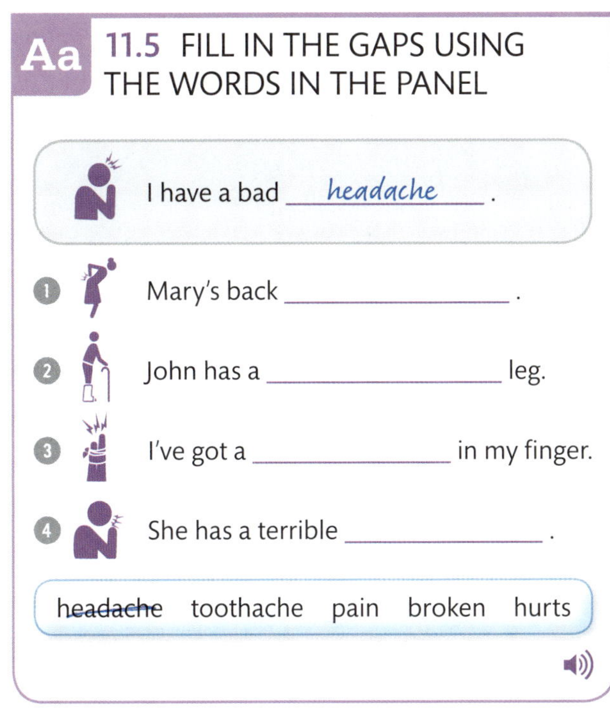

11.5 FILL IN THE GAPS USING THE WORDS IN THE PANEL

I have a bad *headache* .

1. Mary's back ______________ .
2. John has a ______________ leg.
3. I've got a ______________ in my finger.
4. She has a terrible ______________ .

~~headache~~ toothache pain broken hurts

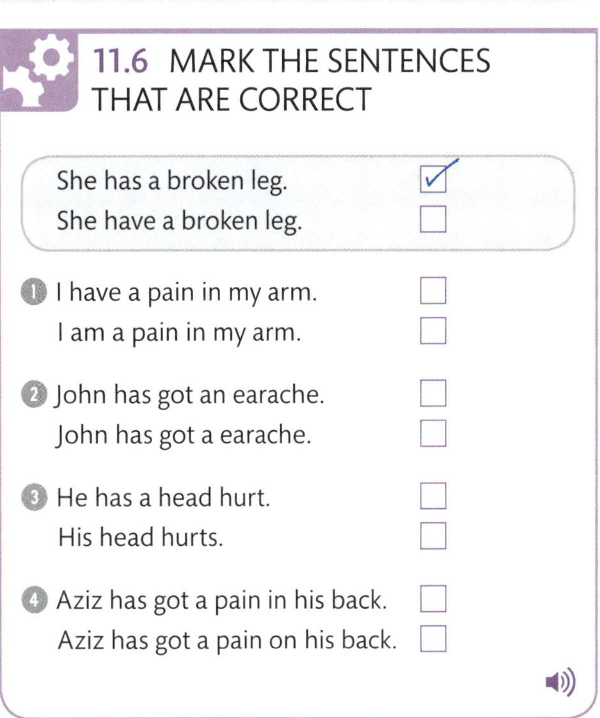

11.6 MARK THE SENTENCES THAT ARE CORRECT

She has a broken leg. ☑
She have a broken leg. ☐

1. I have a pain in my arm. ☐
   I am a pain in my arm. ☐
2. John has got an earache. ☐
   John has got a earache. ☐
3. He has a head hurt. ☐
   His head hurts. ☐
4. Aziz has got a pain in his back. ☐
   Aziz has got a pain on his back. ☐

11 ✓ CHECKLIST

Health complaints ☐ Aa Body parts and pain phrases ☐ Saying what's wrong ☐

12 Vocabulary

12.1 WEATHER

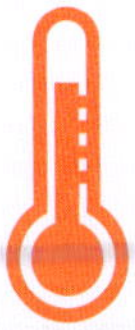

temperature

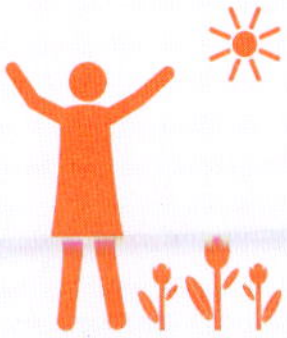

warm

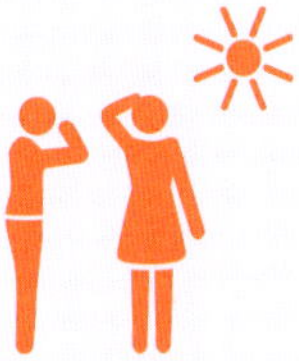

hot

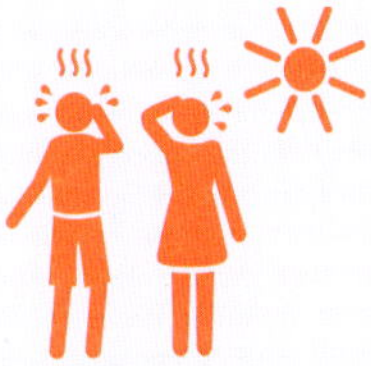

boiling

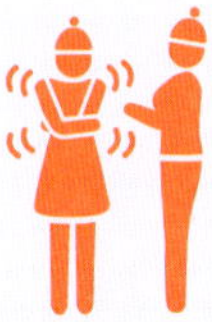

cold

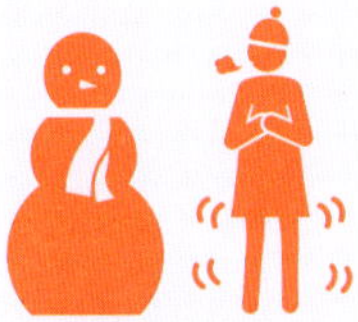

freezing

rainbow

puddle

gray sky (US)
grey sky (UK)

blue sky

12.2 WEATHER ADJECTIVES

sun → sunny

cloud → cloudy

fog → foggy

rain → rainy

snow → snowy

ice → icy

frost → frosty

wind → windy

storm → stormy

thunder → thundery

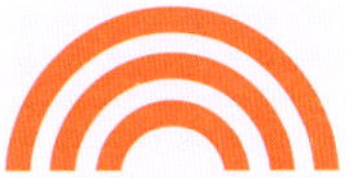

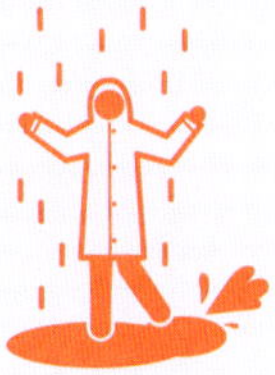

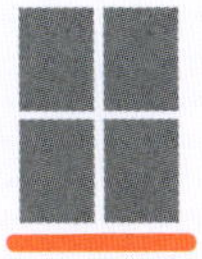

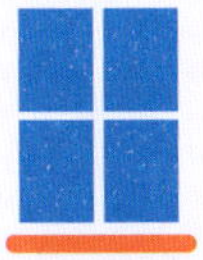

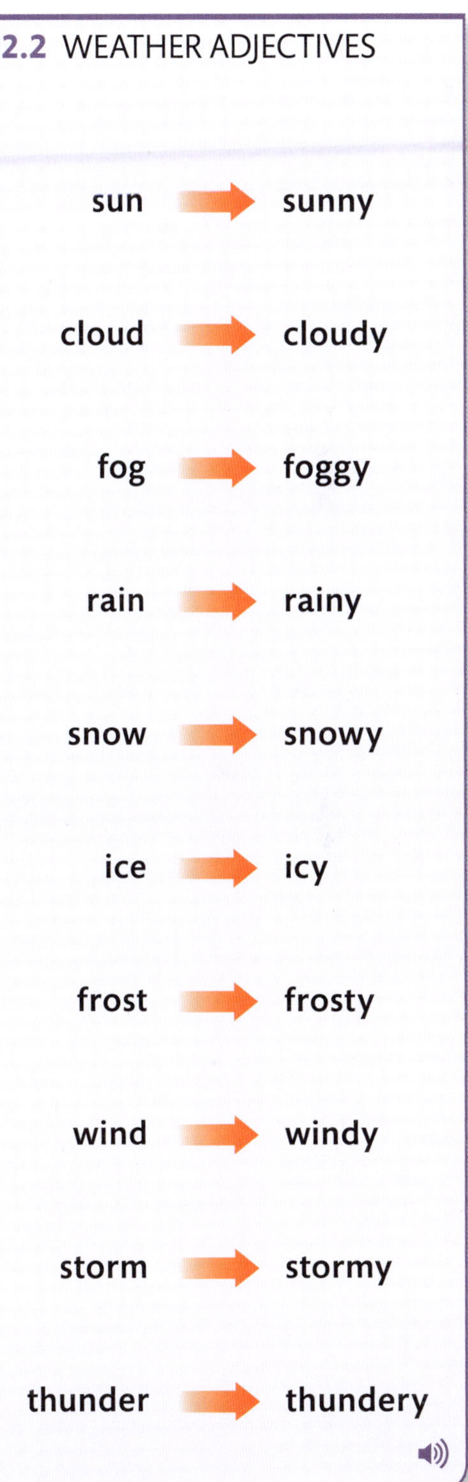

13 What's the weather like?

There are many ways to talk about the weather. Use the verb "to be" with weather words and phrases to describe the temperature and conditions.

New language Weather descriptions
Vocabulary Temperature words
New skill Talking about the weather

13.1 KEY LANGUAGE TALKING ABOUT THE WEATHER

To ask about the weather, say: "What's the weather like?" To answer, use the verb "to be" with the correct weather word or phrase.

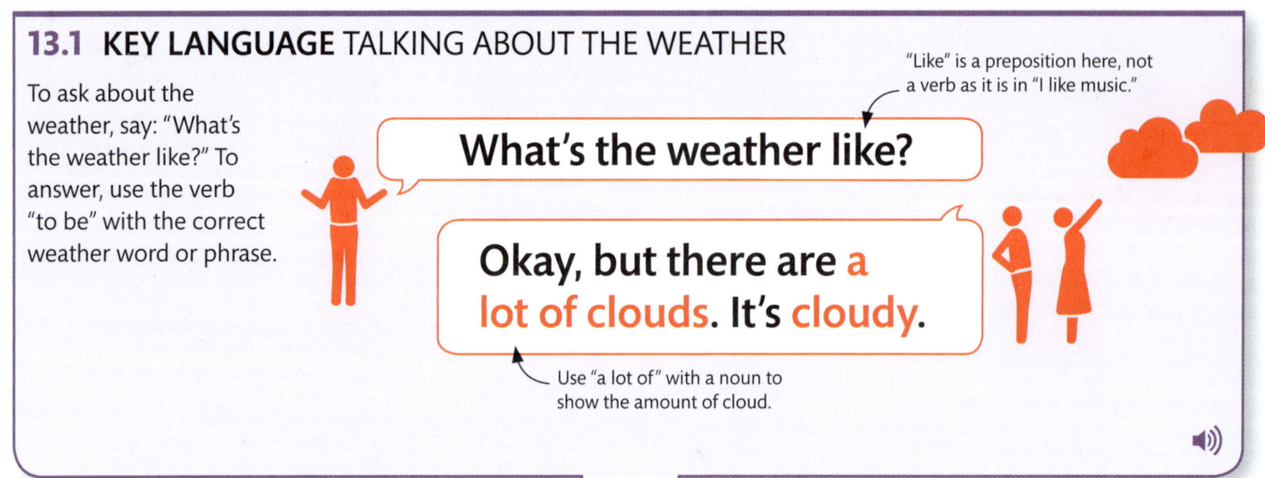

13.2 FURTHER EXAMPLES TALKING ABOUT THE WEATHER

Beautiful! It's really hot and sunny.

Horrible! It's raining. It's wet and cold.

Use the present continuous to say what is happening with the weather now.

Really cold. It's snowing a lot and it's very icy.

There's a storm coming. It's very windy.

Aa 13.3 MATCH THE PICTURES TO THE CORRECT SENTENCES

This is a beautiful place, but I really want it to be sunny. It's dark and cloudy all the time.

The weather's good, and it's windy today, so we're going sailing with Sue and Louis.

The weather is beautiful here. It's hot and sunny, and I'm having a great time.

There's a lot of snow, so the children are having a great time. They want to learn how to ski.

1

2

3

Aa 13.4 FILL IN THE GAPS USING THE WORDS IN THE PANEL

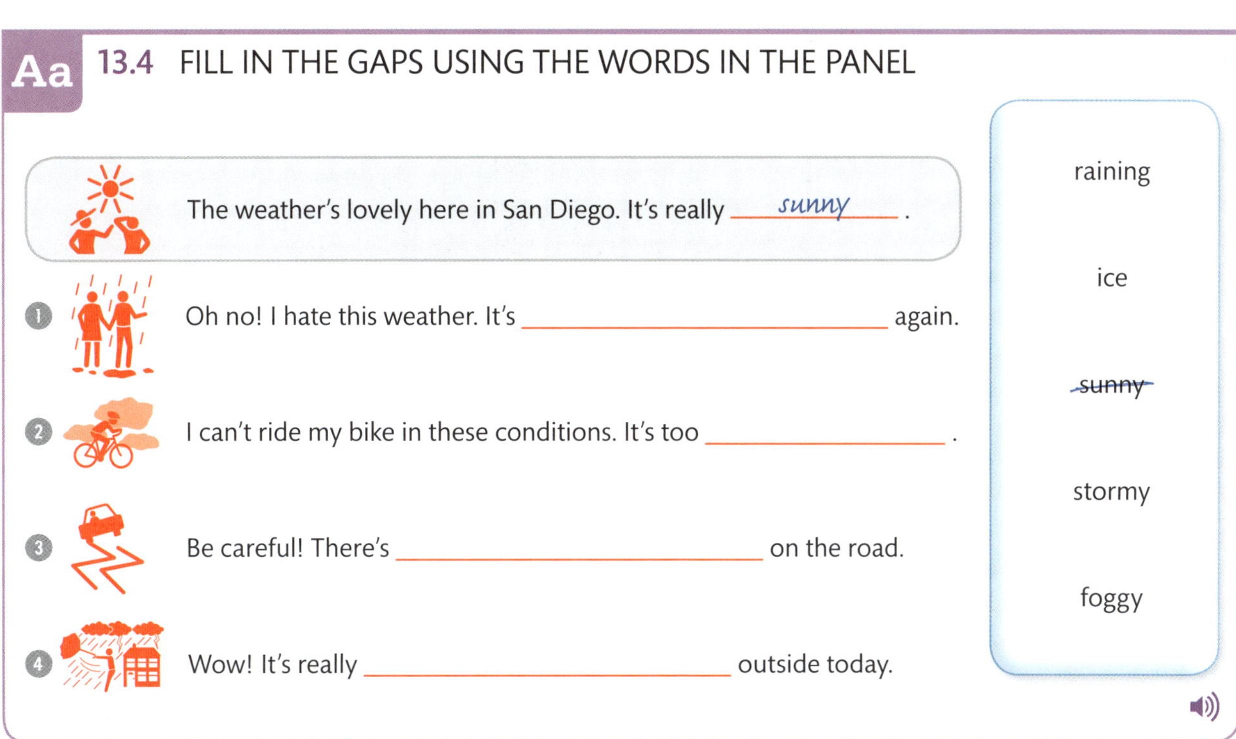

The weather's lovely here in San Diego. It's really *sunny* .

1 Oh no! I hate this weather. It's ____________________ again.

2 I can't ride my bike in these conditions. It's too ____________________ .

3 Be careful! There's ____________________ on the road.

4 Wow! It's really ____________________ outside today.

raining

ice

~~sunny~~

stormy

foggy

13.5 KEY LANGUAGE THE TEMPERATURE

Temperature can be given in "Fahrenheit (°F)" or "Celsius (°C)." In spoken English, use the verb "to be" with a temperature phrase to talk about how hot or cold it is.

How **hot** is it?

How **cold** is it?

TIP
You mostly hear "Fahrenheit (°F)" in US English, and "Celsius (°C)" in UK English.

In spoken English, "boiling" means "very hot."

It's **boiling**.

It's 27 degrees Celsius. I'm **hot**.

It's **warm**.

It's **cold**.

It's 10 degrees Fahrenheit. I'm **freezing**.

In spoken English, "freezing" means "very cold."

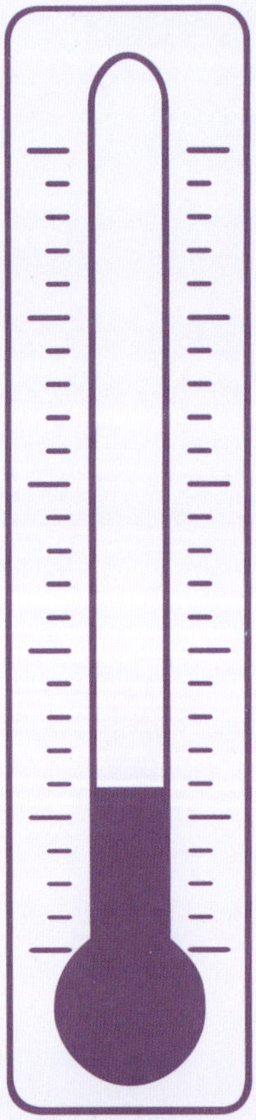

13.6 READ THE CLUES AND WRITE THE ANSWERS IN THE CORRECT PLACES ON THE GRID

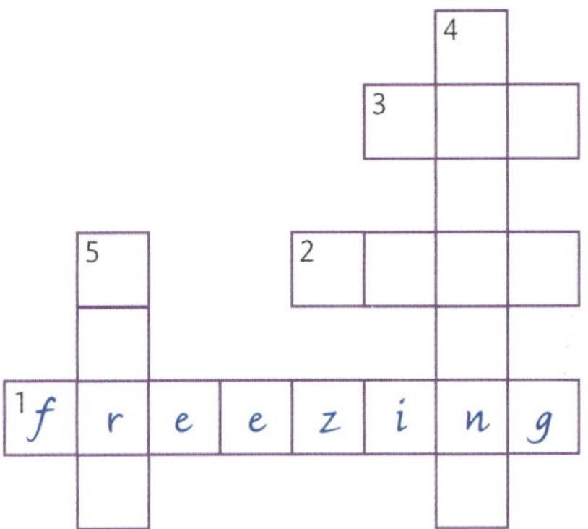

ACROSS

1. It's very cold outside. The temperature is 5°F at the moment, and I'm *freezing* .

2. I'm really ______________ . Can we have the heating on tonight?

3. Sandra says it's ______________ in France today. It's more than 85°F.

DOWN

4. The sun is out and it's 115°F in Turkey today. It's ______________ .

5. It's ______________ outside today. Everyone's wearing T-shirts.

~~freezing~~ hot warm boiling cold

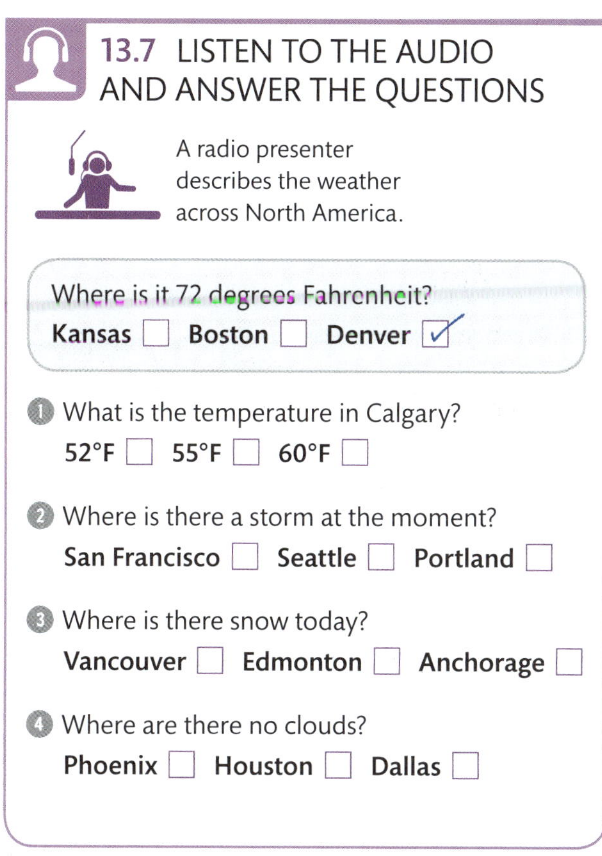

13.7 LISTEN TO THE AUDIO AND ANSWER THE QUESTIONS

A radio presenter describes the weather across North America.

Where is it 72 degrees Fahrenheit?
Kansas ☐ Boston ☐ Denver ☑

1. What is the temperature in Calgary?
52°F ☐ 55°F ☐ 60°F ☐

2. Where is there a storm at the moment?
San Francisco ☐ Seattle ☐ Portland ☐

3. Where is there snow today?
Vancouver ☐ Edmonton ☐ Anchorage ☐

4. Where are there no clouds?
Phoenix ☐ Houston ☐ Dallas ☐

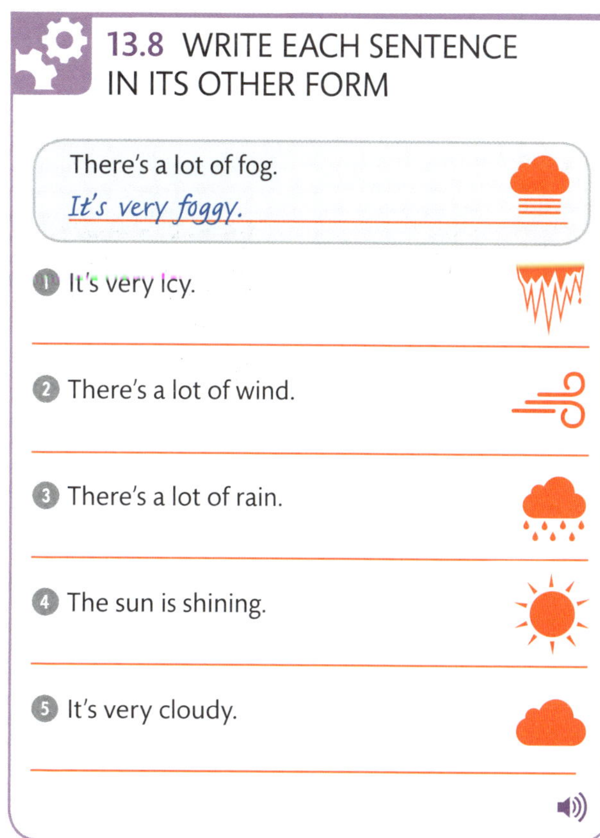

13.8 WRITE EACH SENTENCE IN ITS OTHER FORM

There's a lot of fog.
It's very foggy.

1. It's very icy.
______

2. There's a lot of wind.
______

3. There's a lot of rain.
______

4. The sun is shining.
______

5. It's very cloudy.
______

13 CHECKLIST

Weather descriptions ☐ **Aa** Temperature words ☐ Talking about the weather ☐

REVIEW THE ENGLISH YOU HAVE LEARNED IN UNITS 11-13

NEW LANGUAGE	SAMPLE SENTENCE	☑	UNIT
SAYING YOU'RE NOT FEELING WELL	Are you okay? No, I'm not feeling very well.	☐	11.1
HEALTH PROBLEMS	I have a broken foot. My foot hurts. I have a pain in my head. I have a headache.	☐	11.3, 11.4
TALKING ABOUT THE WEATHER	What's the weather like? Okay, but there are a lot of clouds. It's cloudy.	☐	13.1, 13.2
GIVING THE TEMPERATURE	It's 27 degrees Celsius. It's 10 degrees Fahrenheit.	☐	13.5
TEMPERATURE PHRASES	How hot is it? It's boiling. How cold is it? It's freezing.	☐	13.5

14 Vocabulary

14.1 TRAVEL

late

on time

pack your bags

luggage

arrive at the airport

terminal

check-in

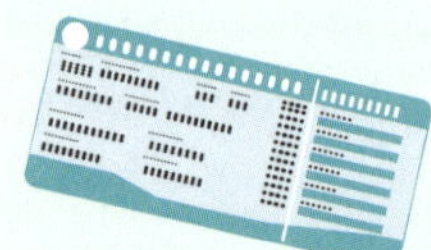
boarding card

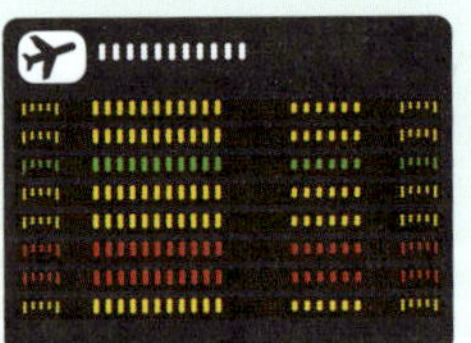
flight

hand luggage

security

delay

board a plane

fly in a plane

land at the airport

passport control

miss a flight

runway

set off on a journey

road trip

visit a museum

go sightseeing

get on a bus

get off a bus

hotel

apartment

hostel

cruise

arrive at a hotel

reception

stay in a hotel

leave a hotel

15 Making comparisons

A comparative adjective is used to describe the difference between two nouns. Use it before the word "than" to compare people, places, or things.

New language Comparative adjectives
Aa Vocabulary Travel and countries
New skill Comparing things

15.1 KEY LANGUAGE COMPARATIVE ADJECTIVES

For most adjectives with one or two syllables, add "er" to make the comparative.

Greece is warm.

Greece is warmer than France.

Add "er" to make the comparative.

Use "than" after the comparative adjective.

15.2 FURTHER EXAMPLES COMPARATIVE ADJECTIVES

Ahmed is taller than Jonathan.

A plane is faster than a train.

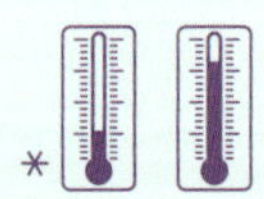

5°F is colder than 85°F.

Sanjay is younger than Tina.

15.3 KEY LANGUAGE FORMING COMPARATIVES

There are special rules for adjectives ending in "e," "y," and with a single consonant.

fast → faster

Add "er" to most adjectives of one or two syllables.

close → closer

If the adjective ends in "e," just add "r."

early → earlier

For some adjectives ending in "y," take off the "y" and add "ier."

big → bigger

For single-syllable adjectives ending consonant-vowel-consonant, double the final letter and add "er."

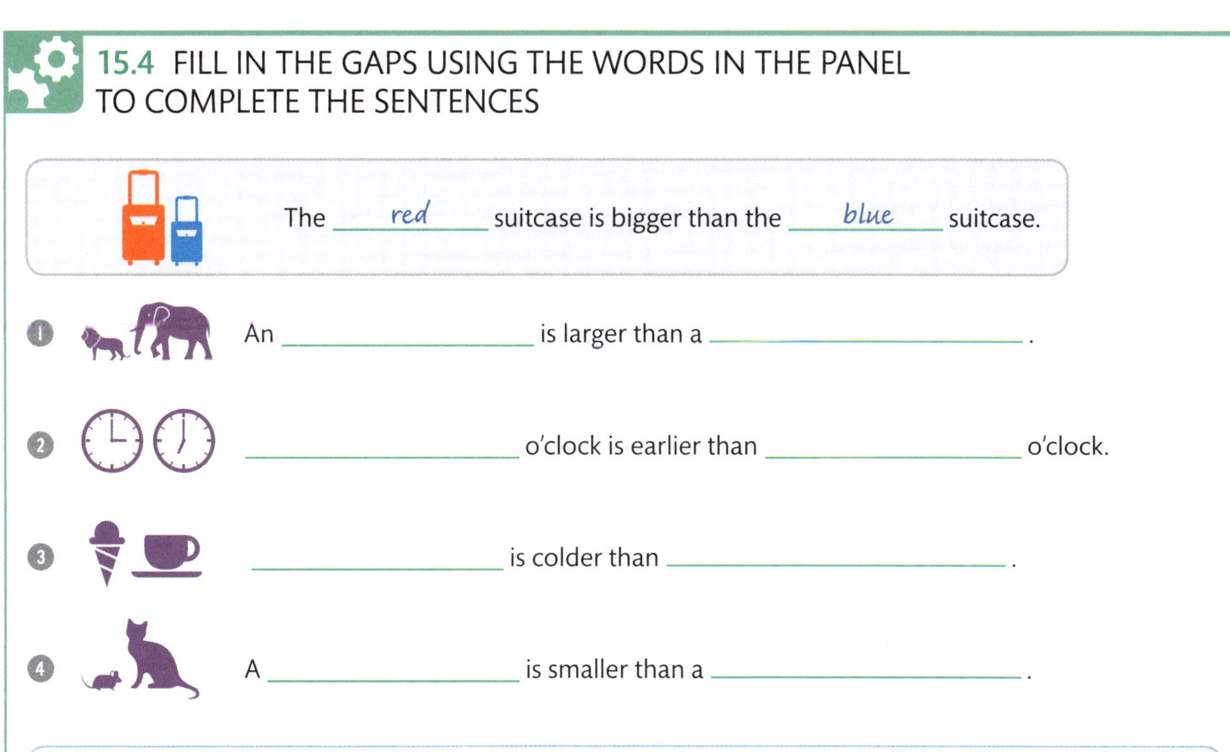

15.4 FILL IN THE GAPS USING THE WORDS IN THE PANEL TO COMPLETE THE SENTENCES

The ___red___ suitcase is bigger than the ___blue___ suitcase.

1. An ______________ is larger than a ______________ .
2. ______________ o'clock is earlier than ______________ o'clock.
3. ______________ is colder than ______________ .
4. A ______________ is smaller than a ______________ .

~~red~~ seven coffee mouse ~~blue~~ three cat elephant ice cream lion

15.5 FIND NINE COMPARATIVES IN THE GRID AND WRITE THEM NEXT TO THE CORRECT ADJECTIVE

E	R	P	W	T	I	E	V	E	H	C	L
H	V	K	K	R	K	N	I	A	I	F	O
O	H	M	E	A	S	I	E	R	G	V	W
T	L	A	T	E	R	C	Y	L	H	F	E
T	Y	T	X	E	L	I	C	I	E	Q	R
E	F	L	A	R	G	E	R	E	R	L	T
R	K	T	H	I	N	N	E	R	E	V	K
J	A	K	I	O	H	M	R	N	P	L	Q
G	D	H	B	C	L	O	S	E	R	E	D

thin = ___thinner___

1. low = ______________
2. high = ______________
3. large = ______________
4. late = ______________
5. easy = ______________
6. early = ______________
7. hot = ______________
8. close = ______________

15.6 KEY LANGUAGE COMPARATIVES WITH LONG ADJECTIVES

For some two-syllable adjectives and those of three syllables or more, use "more" and "than" to make the comparative.

This beach is beautiful.

The adjective "beautiful" has three syllables, so you say "more beautiful than."

This beach is more beautiful than that one.

Use "more" before the adjective.

Use "than" after the adjective.

15.7 HOW TO FORM COMPARATIVES WITH LONG ADJECTIVES

SUBJECT + VERB	"MORE"	ADJECTIVE	"THAN"	REST OF SENTENCE
This beach is	more	beautiful	than	that one.

15.8 FURTHER EXAMPLES COMPARATIVES WITH LONG ADJECTIVES

Surfing is more exciting than going to the gym.

Flying is more expensive than traveling by car.

This book is more interesting than that one.

For me, science is more difficult than history.

15.9 FILL IN THE GAPS USING THE CORRECT COMPARATIVES

This movie is really exciting. It's *more exciting than* the book.

1. The Hotel Supreme is very expensive. It's ______________ the Motel Excelsior.
2. The physics exam is really difficult. It's ______________ the biology exam.
3. Your dress is very beautiful. It's ______________ my dress.
4. This TV program is really interesting. It's ______________ the other ones.

15.10 FILL IN THE GAPS BY PUTTING THE ADJECTIVES INTO THEIR COMPARATIVE FORMS

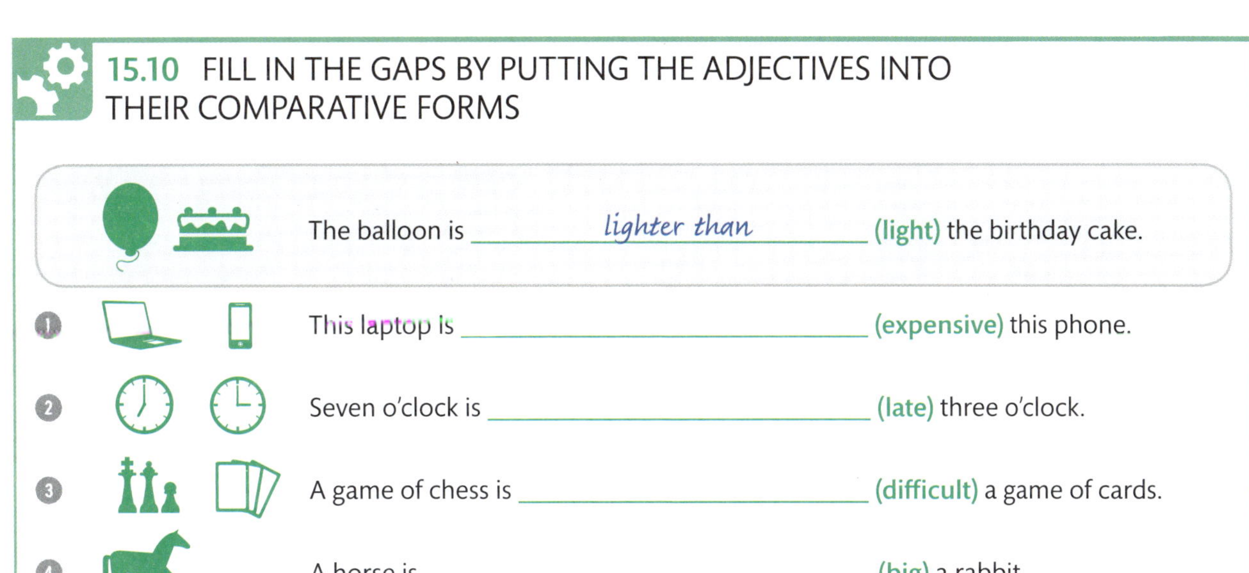

The balloon is *lighter than* (light) the birthday cake.

1. This laptop is ______________ (expensive) this phone.
2. Seven o'clock is ______________ (late) three o'clock.
3. A game of chess is ______________ (difficult) a game of cards.
4. A horse is ______________ (big) a rabbit.

15.11 LISTEN TO THE AUDIO AND ANSWER THE QUESTIONS

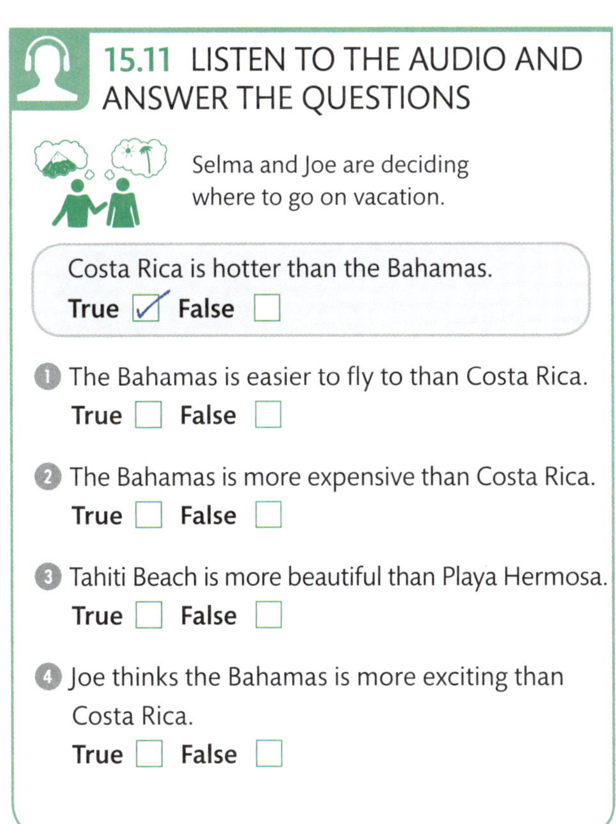

Selma and Joe are deciding where to go on vacation.

Costa Rica is hotter than the Bahamas.
True ☑ **False** ☐

1. The Bahamas is easier to fly to than Costa Rica.
   True ☐ **False** ☐
2. The Bahamas is more expensive than Costa Rica.
   True ☐ **False** ☐
3. Tahiti Beach is more beautiful than Playa Hermosa.
   True ☐ **False** ☐
4. Joe thinks the Bahamas is more exciting than Costa Rica.
   True ☐ **False** ☐

15.12 CROSS OUT THE INCORRECT WORDS IN EACH SENTENCE

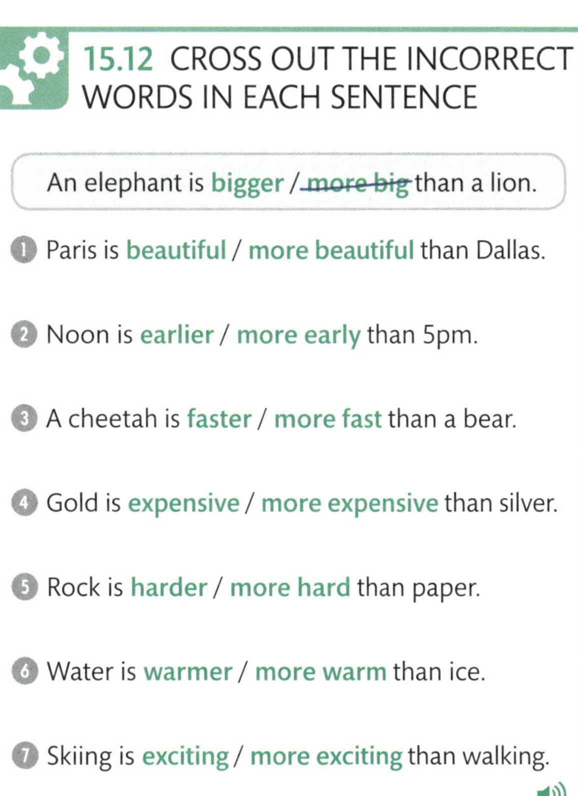

An elephant is bigger / ~~more big~~ than a lion.

1. Paris is beautiful / more beautiful than Dallas.
2. Noon is earlier / more early than 5pm.
3. A cheetah is faster / more fast than a bear.
4. Gold is expensive / more expensive than silver.
5. Rock is harder / more hard than paper.
6. Water is warmer / more warm than ice.
7. Skiing is exciting / more exciting than walking.

15 CHECKLIST

Comparative adjectives ☐ **Aa** Travel and countries ☐ Comparing things ☐

16 Talking about extremes

Use superlative adjectives to talk about extremes, such as "the biggest" or "the smallest." For long adjectives, use "the most" to make the superlative.

New language Superlative adjectives
Aa Vocabulary Animals, facts, and places
New skill Talking about extremes

16.1 KEY LANGUAGE SUPERLATIVE ADJECTIVES

For most adjectives with one or two syllables, add "est" to make the superlative.

The comparative describes the difference between two things.

K2 is higher than Annapurna, but Everest is the highest mountain in the world.

Always use the definite article ("the") before the superlative.

The superlative describes which thing is the most extreme.

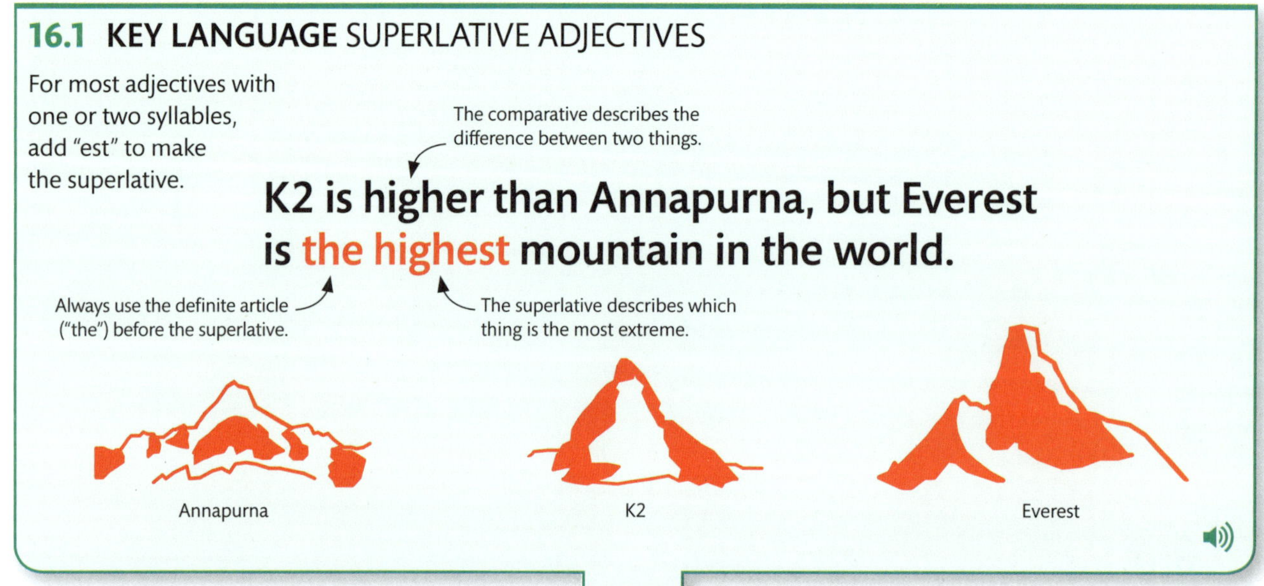

16.2 FURTHER EXAMPLES SUPERLATIVE ADJECTIVES

Rhinos are bigger than cows, but elephants are the biggest land animals.

Great white sharks are larger than dolphins, but blue whales are the largest animals in the world.

16.3 HOW TO FORM SENTENCES WITH SUPERLATIVES

SUBJECT + VERB	"THE" + SUPERLATIVE	REST OF SENTENCE
Everest is	the highest	mountain in the world.

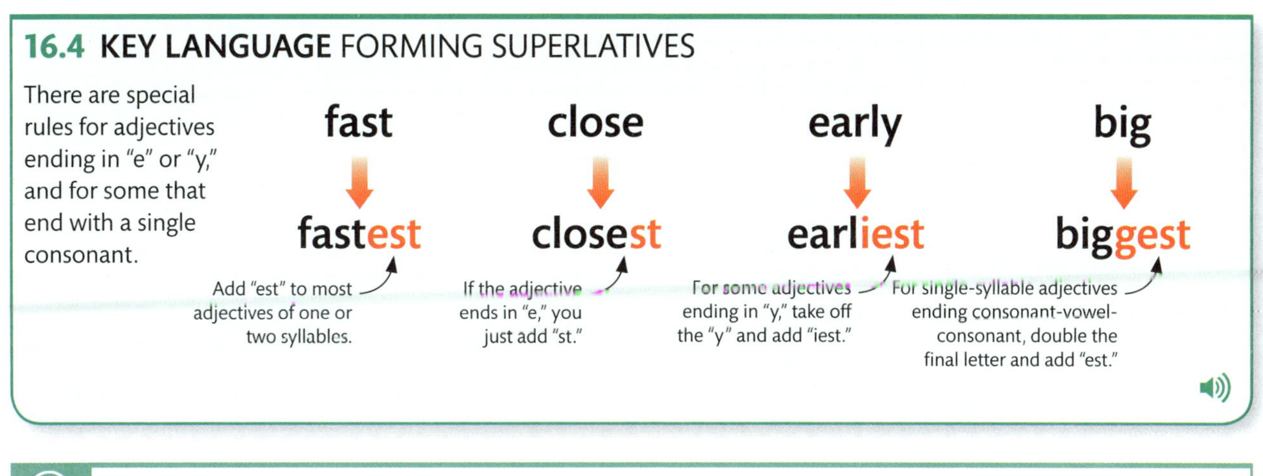

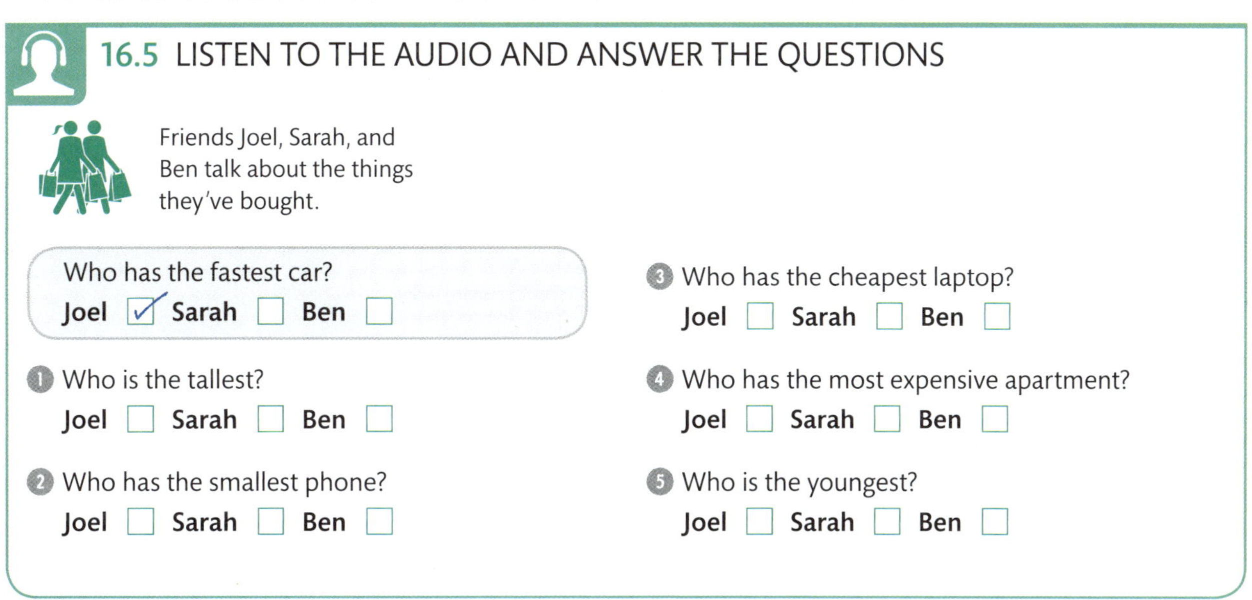

16.6 FILL IN THE GAPS BY PUTTING THE ADJECTIVES IN THE CORRECT FORM

The ___oldest___ (old) plane in the world is the Blériot XI.

1. The African elephant is the ______________ (heavy) animal on land.
2. The ______________ (fast) animal in the world is the peregrine falcon.
3. The ______________ (long) word in the English dictionary has 45 letters.
4. The Sahara is the ______________ (big) desert in the world.
5. The giraffe is the ______________ (tall) animal on Earth.

16.7 KEY LANGUAGE SUPERLATIVES WITH LONG ADJECTIVES

For some two-syllable adjectives and for adjectives of three syllables or more, use "the most" before the adjective. The form of the adjective doesn't change.

The Palace Hotel is more expensive than the Rialto, but the Biaritz is the most expensive hotel in the city.

Use "the most" with the adjective.

The adjective stays the same.

16.8 HOW TO FORM SUPERLATIVES WITH LONG ADJECTIVES

SUBJECT + VERB	"THE" + SUPERLATIVE	ADJECTIVE	REST OF SENTENCE
This is	the most	expensive	hotel in the city.

16.9 FURTHER EXAMPLES SUPERLATIVES WITH LONG ADJECTIVES

The science museum is the most interesting museum in town.

The Twister is the most exciting ride in the theme park.

This is the most comfortable chair in the room.

16.10 MATCH THE BEGINNINGS OF THE SENTENCES TO THE CORRECT ENDINGS

The Yangtze River is → the longest river in Asia.

1. Antarctica is
2. Mumbai is
3. Alaska is
4. The inland taipan is

- the largest state in the US.
- the coldest place on Earth.
- the most dangerous snake in the world.
- the longest river in Asia.
- the biggest city in India.

16.11 READ THE ARTICLE AND ANSWER THE QUESTIONS

The Hotel Blog

HOME | ENTRIES | ABOUT | CONTACT

POSTED FRIDAY, 28 AUGUST

The Rialto (height: 500 feet) is two miles from the beach. The average temperature is a hot 85°F, and it's in a three-star (***) area of natural beauty. *Room per night:* **$500**. *Number of rooms: 300.*

The Plaza (height: 600 feet) is one mile from the beach, and in a five-star (*****) area of natural beauty. The temperature is usually a warm 75°F. *Room per night:* **$400**. *Number of rooms: 500.*

The Grand (height: 300 feet) is less than a mile from the beach. It's in a four-star (****) area of natural beauty, and the temperature is a cool 65°F. *Room per night:* **$515**. *Number of rooms: 200.*

Which is the most expensive hotel?
The Rialto ☐ **The Plaza** ☐ **The Grand** ☑

1. Which hotel is the closest to the beach?
The Rialto ☐ **The Plaza** ☐ **The Grand** ☐

2. Which is the tallest hotel?
The Rialto ☐ **The Plaza** ☐ **The Grand** ☐

3. Which hotel is in the most beautiful area?
The Rialto ☐ **The Plaza** ☐ **The Grand** ☐

4. Which hotel has the fewest rooms?
The Rialto ☐ **The Plaza** ☐ **The Grand** ☐

5. Which hotel is in the warmest place?
The Rialto ☐ **The Plaza** ☐ **The Grand** ☐

16.12 SAY THE SENTENCES OUT LOUD, FILLING IN THE GAPS USING SUPERLATIVES

Mount Everest is a very high mountain. It is *the highest* mountain in the world.

1. Moscow is a very large city. It is ______________ city in Europe.

2. The Missouri River is 2,540 miles long. It is ______________ river in North America.

3. The cheetah is a very fast animal. It is ______________ land animal on Earth.

4. The Kali Gandaki Gorge is 3.46 miles deep. It is ______________ gorge in the world.

16 CHECKLIST

Superlative adjectives ☐ **Aa** Animals, facts, and places ☐ Talking about extremes ☐

17 Vocabulary

17.1 GEOGRAPHICAL FEATURES

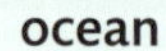
ocean

sea

coast

beach

island

cliff

rocks

cave

waterfall

countryside

field

hill

mountain

valley

canyon

sand dune

stream

river

pond

lake

woods

jungle

rainforest

swamp

desert

oasis

volcano

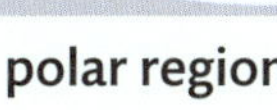

polar region

glacier

iceberg

18 Making choices

"Which," "what," "and," and "or" are all useful words to add to questions. You can use them to show whether a question is general or about specific options.

New language "Which" and "what"
Aa Vocabulary Geographical words
New skill Asking multiple-choice questions

18.1 KEY LANGUAGE "AND / OR"

Use "and" to ask about more than one thing, and "or" for choices and alternatives.

Use "or" if there is a choice.

Do you want to go to Germany or France?

France.

Do you want to go to Paris and Versailles?

Use "and" to join two things in one question.

Yes.

18.2 FURTHER EXAMPLES "AND / OR"

Would you like tea and cake?

Would you like tea or coffee?

Do you have a dog and a cat?

Do you want to play golf or tennis?

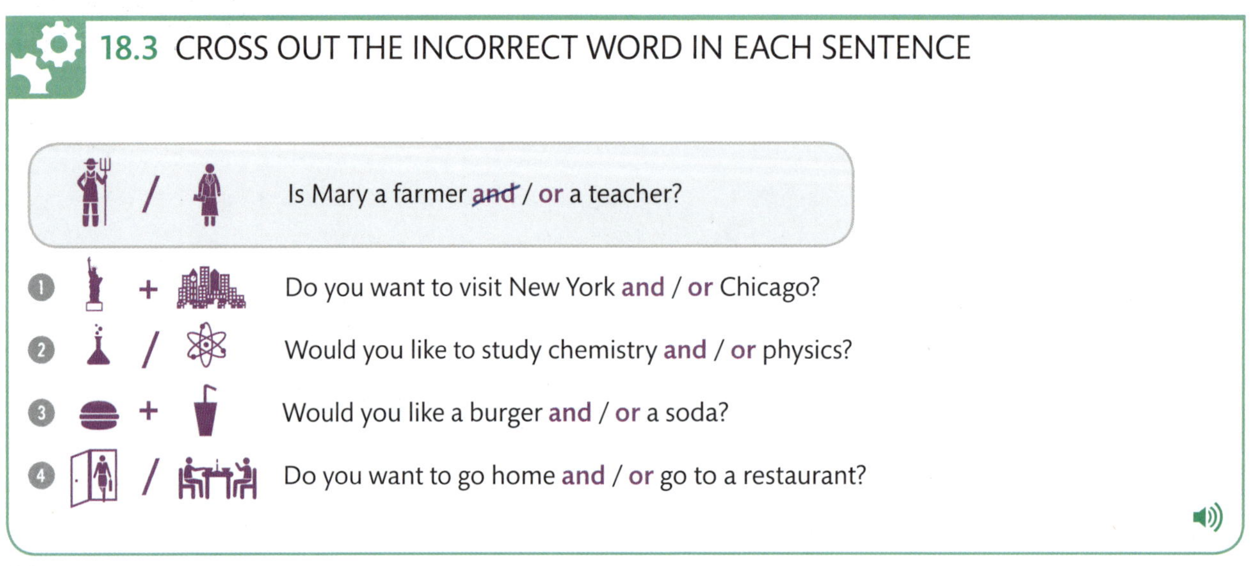

18.4 KEY LANGUAGE "WHICH / WHAT"

You use "which" when there are two or more possibilities in the question. Use "what" when the question is more general.

There are no choices in the question.

What is the tallest building in the world?

The question includes a choice of possible answers.

Which building is taller, Big Ben or the Eiffel Tower?

18.5 FURTHER EXAMPLES "WHICH / WHAT"

What is the highest mountain in the Himalayas?

Which mountain is higher, the Matterhorn or Mont Blanc?

What is the fastest animal in the world?

Which animal is the fastest, a lion, a rhino, or a cheetah?

18.6 FILL IN THE GAPS USING "WHICH" OR "WHAT"

Which country would you like to visit, India, China, or Thailand?

1 ______ is the biggest country in Africa?

2 ______ would you like to eat for your dinner?

3 ______ jacket do you want to wear, the blue one or the red one?

4 ______ is your favorite color, red, green, yellow, or blue?

18.7 KEY LANGUAGE IRREGULAR COMPARATIVES AND SUPERLATIVES

Some common adjectives have irregular comparatives and superlatives.

ADJECTIVE	COMPARATIVE	SUPERLATIVE
good	better	best
bad	worse	worst
far	farther (US) further (UK)	farthest (US) furthest (UK)

TIP
In US English, "further" and "furthest" are used to describe figurative (not physical) distances.

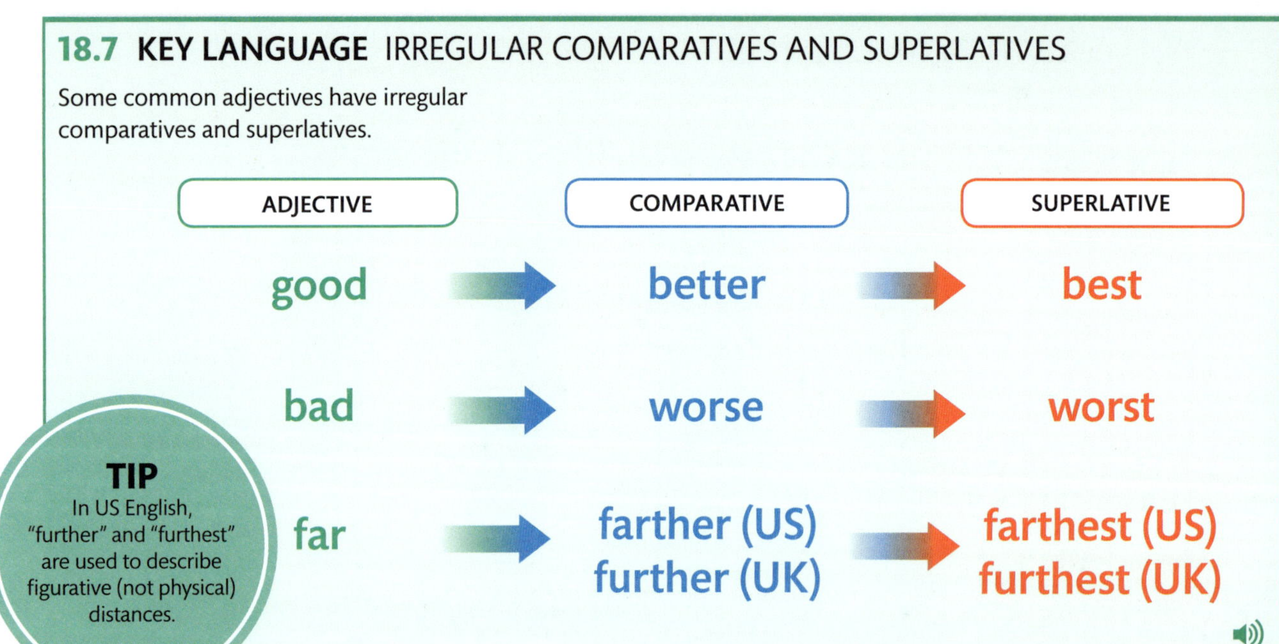

18.8 FURTHER EXAMPLES IRREGULAR COMPARATIVES AND SUPERLATIVES

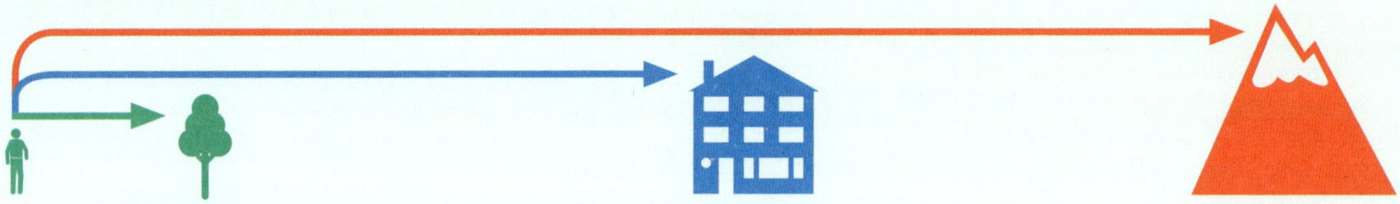

The tree is far away.

The house is farther away than the tree.

The mountain is the farthest away.

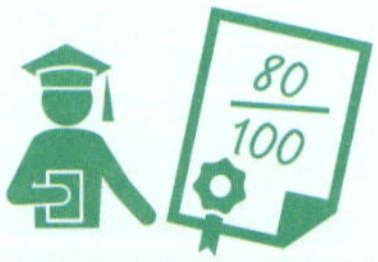

John got a good grade on his exam.

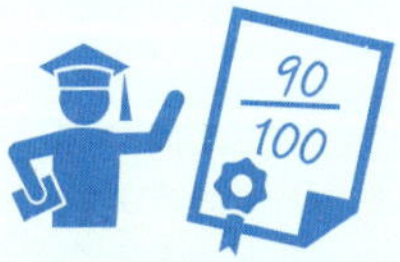

Jill got a better grade than John.

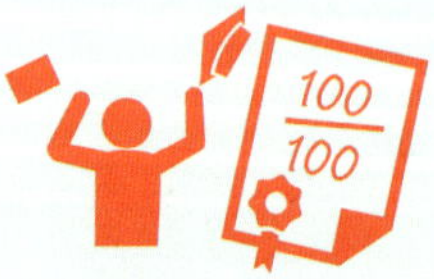

Aziz got the best grade.

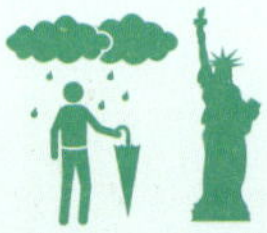

New York has bad weather today.

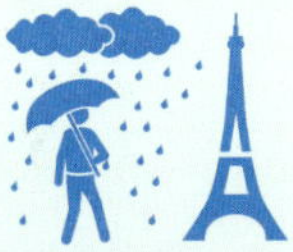

Paris has worse weather.

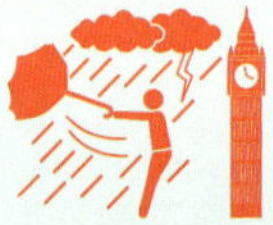

London has the worst weather.

18.9 READ THE ARTICLE AND ANSWER THE QUESTIONS

Which restaurant has the best service?
The Little Olive has the best service.

1. Which has the best music?
2. Which is the farthest from the beach?
3. Which has the best ice cream?
4. Which has the worst food?
5. Which has the best seafood?

GREAT FOOD MAGAZINE

PLACES TO EAT

Where to go for dinner this weekend

THE LITTLE OLIVE – This restaurant is five minutes from the beach. It has no live music, but the food is great and its seafood is the best in town. The service here is excellent.

JOHN'S BAR – This is a great place to listen to music. It's on the beach and has bands every night. The food and service are OK.

SEAVIEW CAFÉ – This café is two minutes from the beach. It doesn't have music, but the food and service aren't bad. Go here for the ice cream, it's the best in town.

THE BIG CAHUNA – They play OK music here, but the food and service are not good. It's more than ten minutes from the beach, but it has the best views in town.

18.10 LISTEN TO THE AUDIO AND ANSWER THE QUESTIONS

Rita Adams answers questions on a TV game show.

Which is the largest US state?
Texas ☐ **Virginia** ☐ **Alaska** ☑

1. Which city is farthest from the equator?
   Taipei ☐ **Bangkok** ☐ **Manila** ☐
2. Which is the smallest South American country?
   Brazil ☐ **Peru** ☐ **Suriname** ☐
3. Which is the biggest desert?
   Mojave ☐ **Sahara** ☐ **Kalahari** ☐
4. Which is the tallest building?
   Big Ben ☐ **Eiffel Tower** ☐ **Pisa Tower** ☐
5. Which is the highest mountain?
   K2 ☐ **Kilimanjaro** ☐ **Mont Blanc** ☐

18 CHECKLIST

"Which" and "what" ☐ **Aa** Geographical words ☐  Asking multiple-choice questions ☐

19 Using large numbers

You usually write numbers larger than 100 in figures. To say them, add "and" in front of the number signified by the last two digits, such as "one hundred and ten."

New language Large numbers
Vocabulary Thousands and millions
New skill Talking about large amounts

19.1 KEY LANGUAGE LARGE NUMBERS

You can say "one hundred" or "a hundred." Both are correct. Don't add "s" to "hundred," "thousand," or "million."

100 — one hundred / a hundred

1,000 — one thousand / a thousand

1,000,000 — one million / a million

Use commas to separate long rows of figures.

200 — two hundred

No "s" at the end.

3,000 — three thousand

4,000,000 — four million

19.2 FURTHER EXAMPLES LARGE NUMBERS

Add "and" before the last two numbers to say numbers higher than one hundred.

2,876 — two thousand, eight hundred and seventy-six

"And" goes before "seventy-six."

54,041 — fifty-four thousand and forty-one

296,308 — two hundred and ninety-six thousand, three hundred and eight

1,098,283 — one million, ninety-eight thousand, two hundred and eighty-three

Use commas to separate millions, thousands, and hundreds.

19.3 LISTEN TO THE AUDIO AND MARK THE NUMBERS YOU HEAR

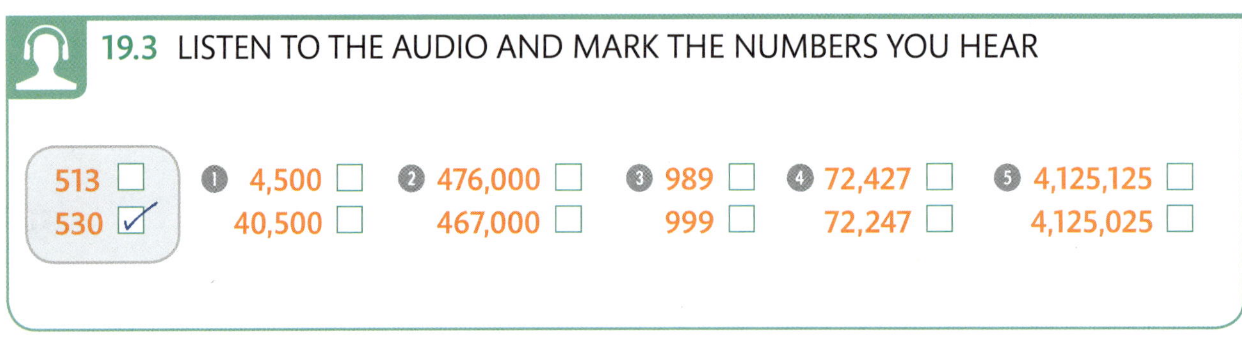

513 ☐
530 ☑

1. 4,500 ☐ / 40,500 ☐
2. 476,000 ☐ / 467,000 ☐
3. 989 ☐ / 999 ☐
4. 72,427 ☐ / 72,247 ☐
5. 4,125,125 ☐ / 4,125,025 ☐

19.4 SAY THE NUMBERS OUT LOUD

532 — *five hundred and thirty-two*

1. 3,107
2. 23,417
3. 345,972
4. 23,456,987

19 CHECKLIST

Large numbers ☐   Aa Thousands and millions ☐   Talking about large amounts ☐

REVIEW THE ENGLISH YOU HAVE LEARNED IN UNITS 15-19

NEW LANGUAGE	SAMPLE SENTENCE	☑	UNIT
COMPARATIVE ADJECTIVES	Greece is warmer than France.	☐	15.1, 15.3, 15.6
SUPERLATIVE ADJECTIVES	K2 is higher than Annapurna, but Everest is the highest mountain in the world.	☐	16.1, 16.4, 16.7
"AND" AND "OR"	Do you want to go to Germany or France? Do you want to go to Paris and Versailles?	☐	18.1, 18.2
"WHICH" AND "WHAT"	What is the tallest building? Which mountain is higher, the Matterhorn or Mont Blanc?	☐	18.4, 18.5
LARGE NUMBERS	Two thousand, eight hundred and seventy-six	☐	19.1, 19.2

20 Vocabulary

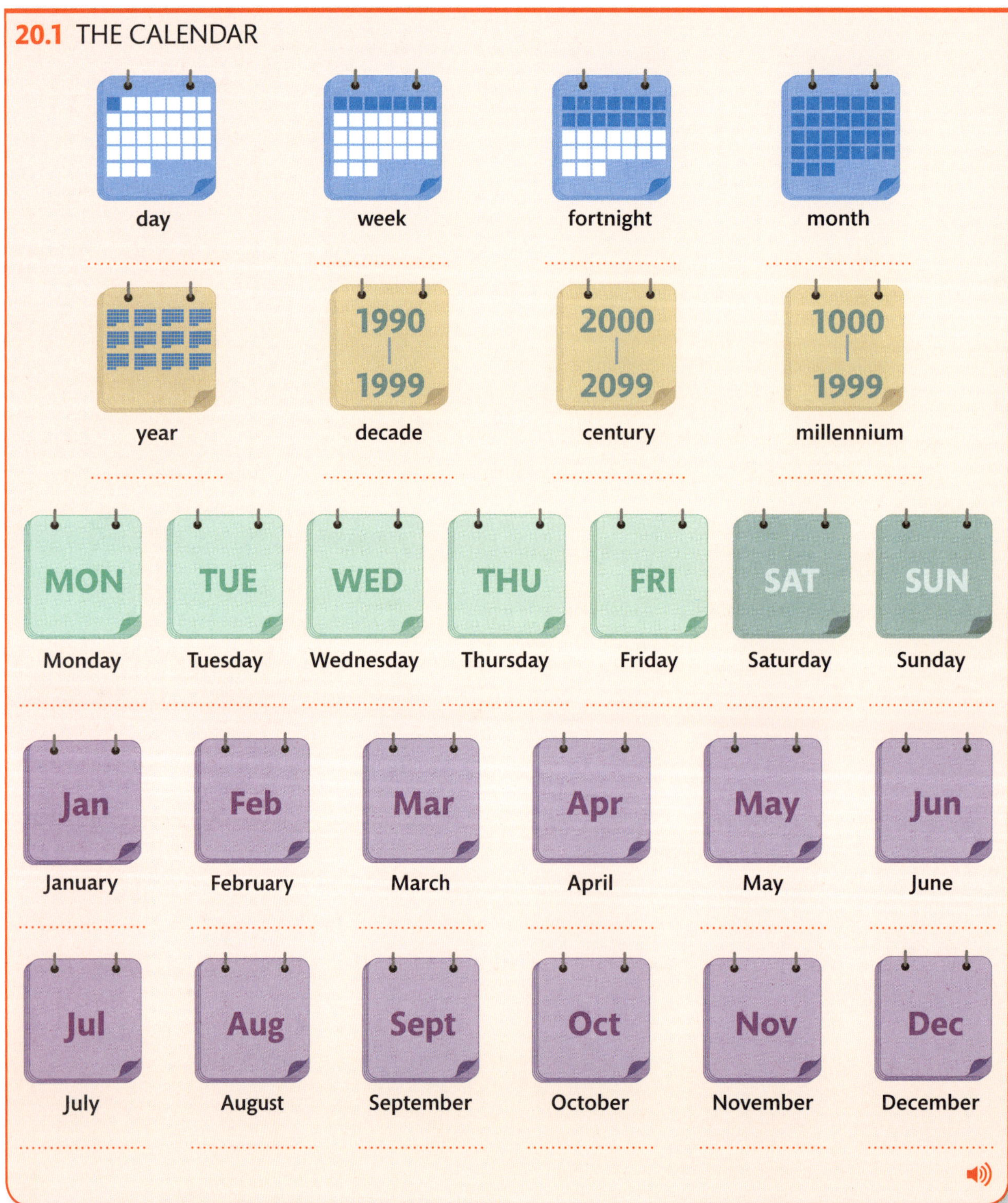

20.2 SEASONS

spring

summer

fall (US)
autumn (UK)

winter

20.3 ORDINAL NUMBERS

21 Talking about dates

There are two different ways of writing and saying dates. You use numbers along with the month to define the date you're talking about.

New language Dates, "was born," "ago"
Aa Vocabulary Numbers, months, and years
New skill Talking about dates

21.1 KEY LANGUAGE WRITING AND SAYING DATES

In the US, people often describe dates by writing cardinal numbers and saying ordinal numbers.

The number comes after the month.

His meeting is on May 10. — May tenth

My birthday is on May 18. — May eighteenth

The party is on May 31. — May thirty-first

21.2 ANOTHER WAY TO SAY IT WRITING AND SAYING DATES

In some other places, such as the UK, people use ordinal numbers to write and say dates.

His meeting is on the 10th of May. — the tenth of May

My birthday is on May the 18th. — May the eighteenth

The party is on the 31st of May. — the thirty-first of May

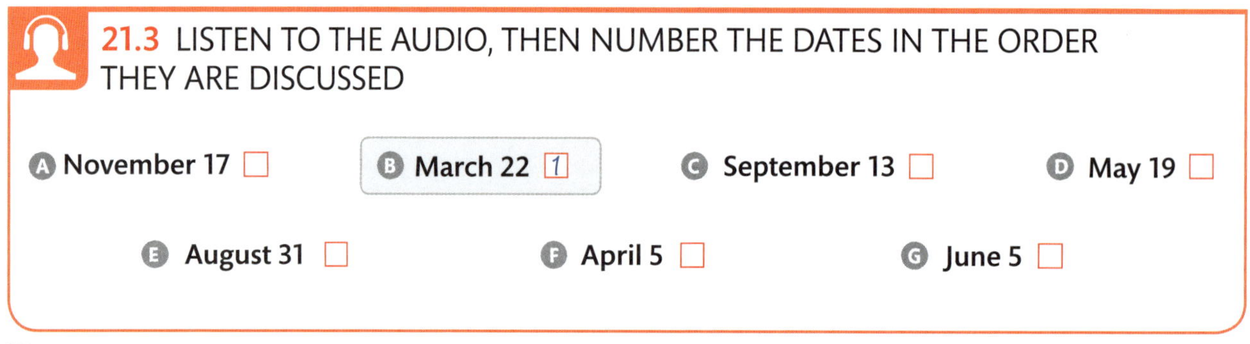

21.3 LISTEN TO THE AUDIO, THEN NUMBER THE DATES IN THE ORDER THEY ARE DISCUSSED

A November 17 ☐

B March 22 [1]

C September 13 ☐

D May 19 ☐

E August 31 ☐

F April 5 ☐

G June 5 ☐

21.4 KEY LANGUAGE USING "WAS BORN"

Use "was born" to talk about someone's date or year of birth.

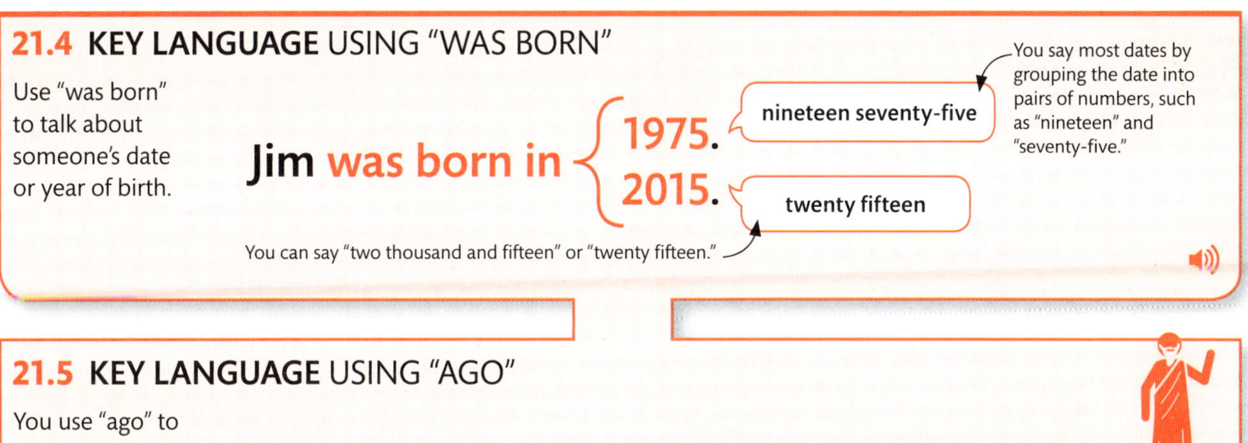

21.5 KEY LANGUAGE USING "AGO"

You use "ago" to say how many years before now something happened.

21.6 LISTEN TO THE AUDIO AND NOTE THE YEAR OF EACH EVENT

1971

1 ______ 2 ______ 3 ______ 4 ______ 5 ______

21.7 USE THE CHART TO CREATE 12 CORRECT SENTENCES AND SAY THEM OUT LOUD

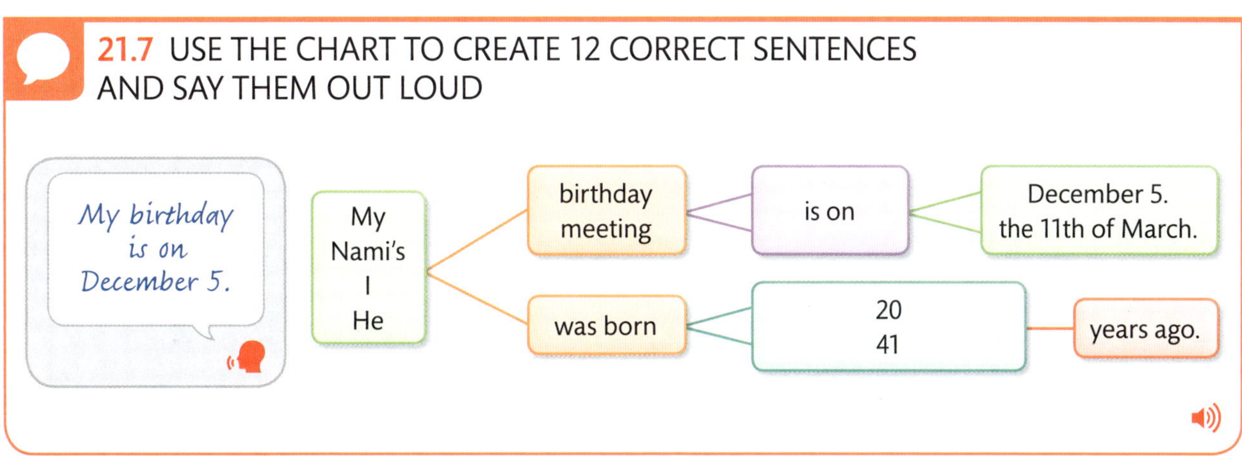

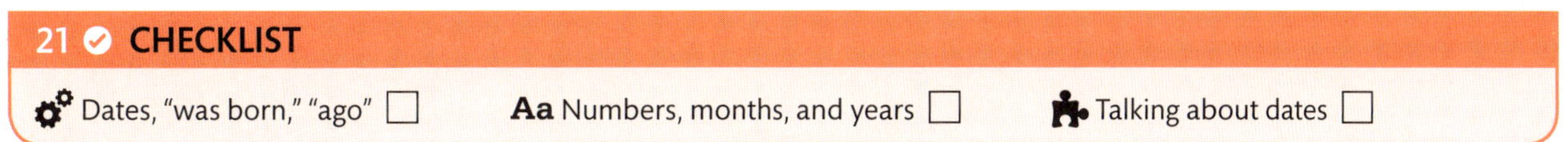

22 Talking about the past

The past simple describes events that happened at a definite time in the past, or the state of things at a particular point in time.

New language The past simple of "to be"
Aa Vocabulary Jobs, town, and life events
New skill Talking about past states

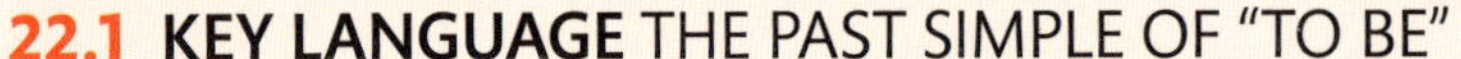

22.1 KEY LANGUAGE THE PAST SIMPLE OF "TO BE"

Any action that happened and was completed in the past can be described in the past simple. The past simple of "to be" is "was" or "were."

This is the present simple.

Jill is a businesswoman now.

She was a student in 1985.

This is the past simple.

This is a definite time in the past.

22.2 HOW TO FORM THE PAST SIMPLE OF "TO BE"

The past simple of "to be" changes with the subject.

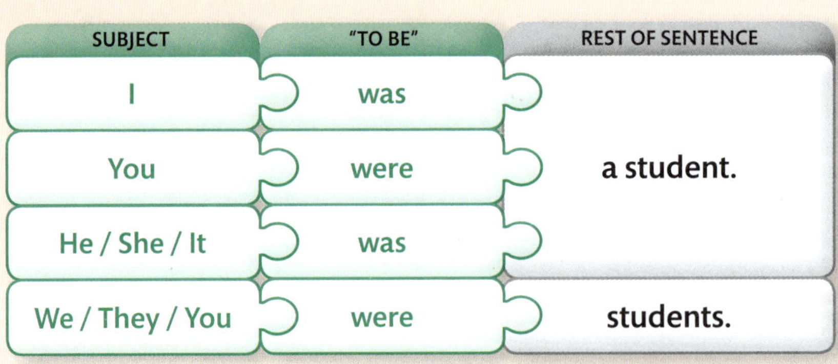

SUBJECT	"TO BE"	REST OF SENTENCE
I	was	a student.
You	were	
He / She / It	was	
We / They / You	were	students.

22.3 FURTHER EXAMPLES THE PAST SIMPLE OF "TO BE"

He was a doctor for 40 years. 

We were at the library yesterday. 

She was a Broadway star in the 1960s. 

There were lots of people at the party. 

There was a party last night. 

They were at the movies last week. 

22.4 CROSS OUT THE INCORRECT WORD IN EACH SENTENCE

She was / ~~were~~ a teacher.

1. You was / were at the museum last week.
2. There was / were five people here yesterday.
3. The students was / were there on Monday morning.
4. My mom was / were an artist in the 1990s.
5. I was / were in college in 1989.
6. Sal and I was / were at the theater last night.
7. My dad was / were a builder until 1995.

22.5 READ THE EMAIL AND ANSWER THE QUESTIONS

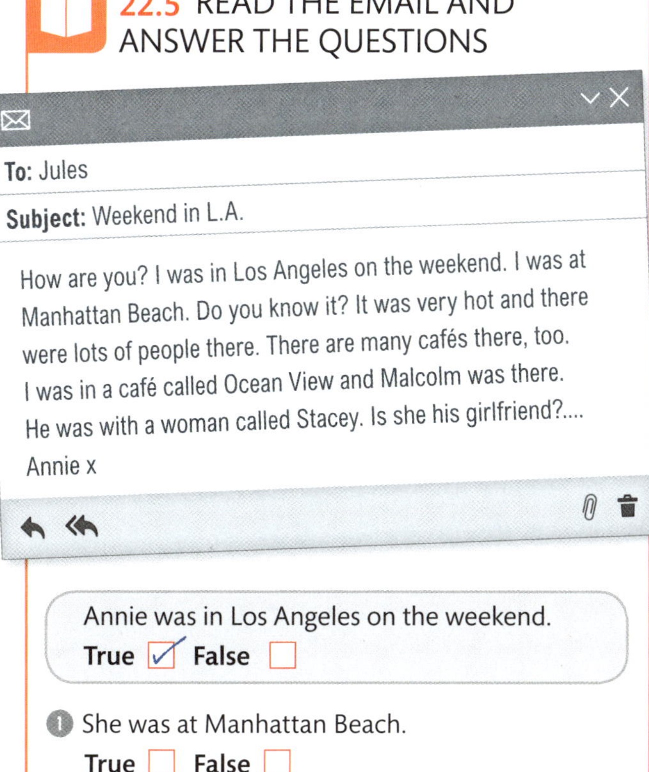

To: Jules

Subject: Weekend in L.A.

How are you? I was in Los Angeles on the weekend. I was at Manhattan Beach. Do you know it? It was very hot and there were lots of people there. There are many cafés there, too. I was in a café called Ocean View and Malcolm was there. He was with a woman called Stacey. Is she his girlfriend?....

Annie x

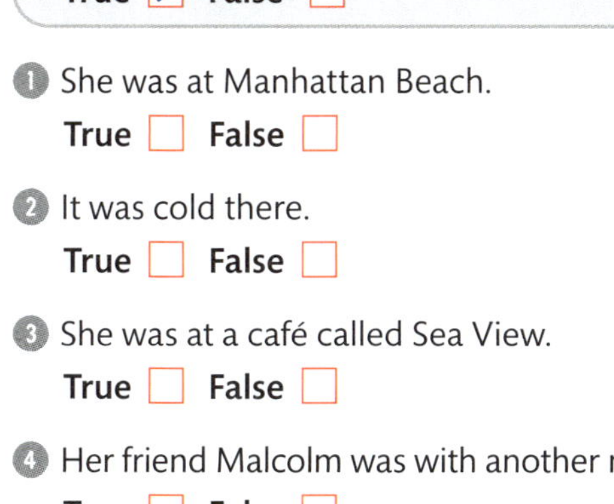

Annie was in Los Angeles on the weekend.
True ☑ False ☐

1. She was at Manhattan Beach.
True ☐ False ☐
2. It was cold there.
True ☐ False ☐
3. She was at a café called Sea View.
True ☐ False ☐
4. Her friend Malcolm was with another man.
True ☐ False ☐

22.6 LISTEN TO THE AUDIO AND MATCH THE EVENTS TO THE YEARS

Chat Radio give the answers to their "That Was The Day" quiz.

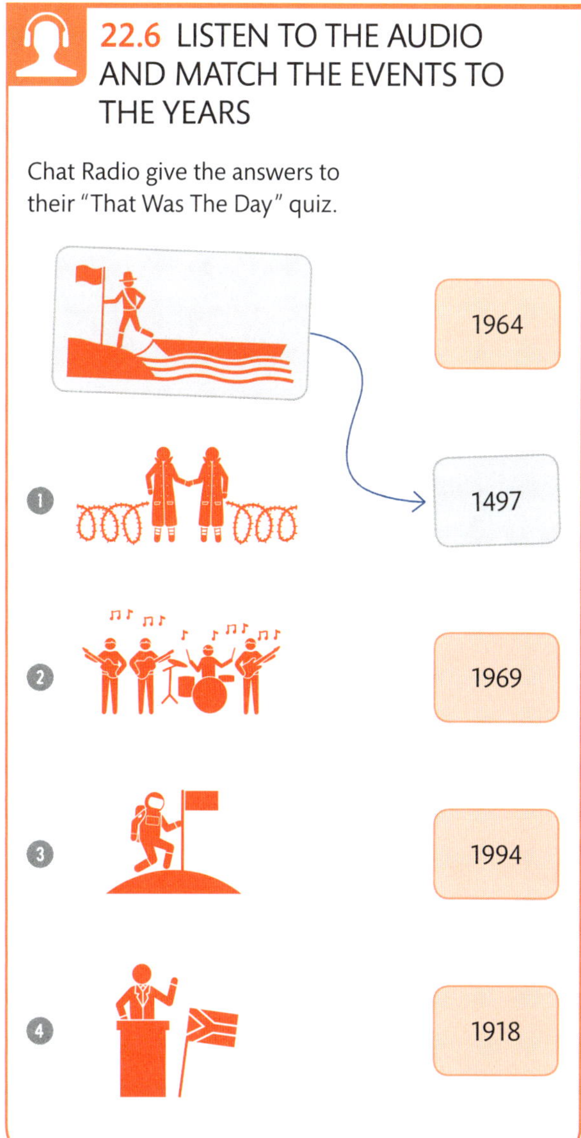

22.7 KEY LANGUAGE "WAS" / "WERE" NEGATIVES

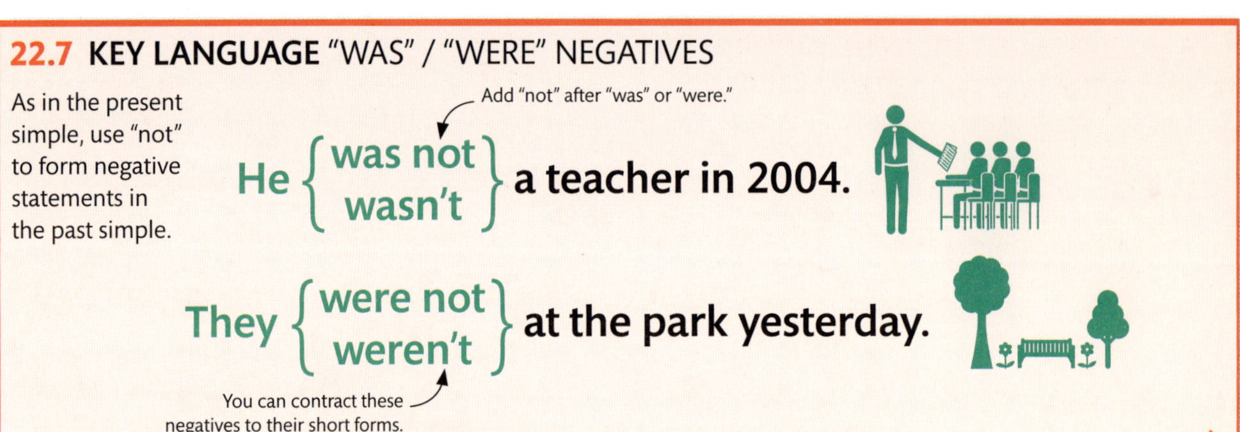

22.8 KEY LANGUAGE "WAS" / "WERE" QUESTIONS

To ask questions about the past using the verb "to be," swap the subject and verb.

He was in India.

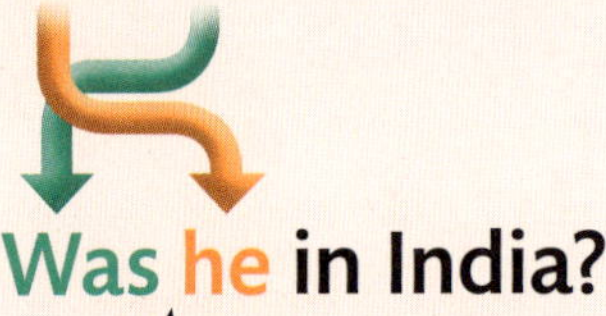

Was he in India?

Swap the subject and "to be."

They were late for school.

Were they late for school?

22.9 FURTHER EXAMPLES "WAS" / "WERE" NEGATIVES AND QUESTIONS

I wasn't a good waiter. 

Were there any cakes at the party? 

There weren't any boats. 

Was he good at playing tennis? 

22.10 CROSS OUT THE INCORRECT WORD IN EACH SENTENCE

He wasn't / ~~weren't~~ a doctor.

1. They wasn't / weren't very good at science.
2. I wasn't / weren't in Canada in 2002.
3. You wasn't / weren't at the party last night.
4. We wasn't / weren't in our house last year.
5. There wasn't / weren't a restaurant near the river.

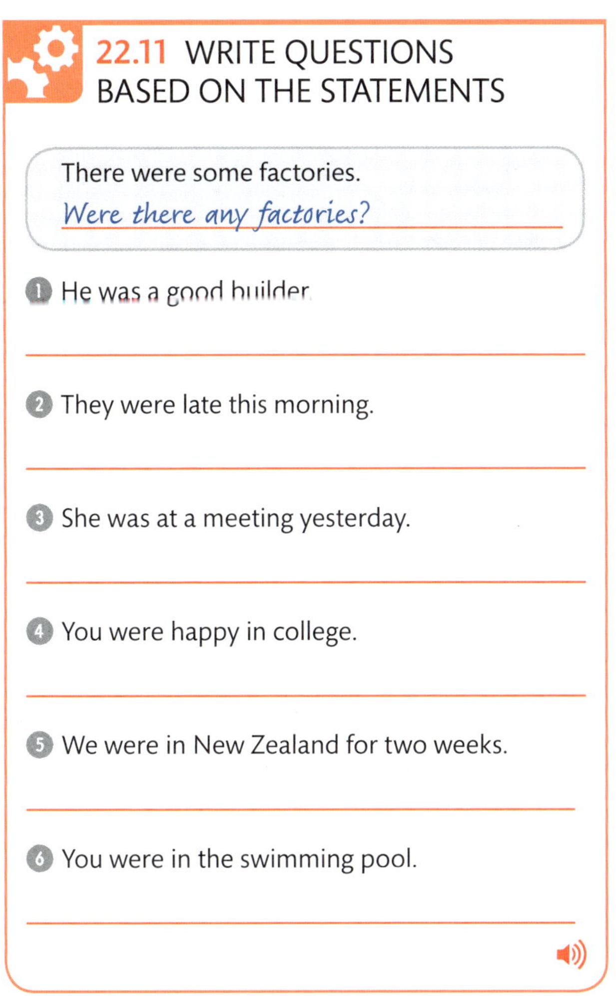

22.11 WRITE QUESTIONS BASED ON THE STATEMENTS

There were some factories.
Were there any factories?

1. He was a good builder.
2. They were late this morning.
3. She was at a meeting yesterday.
4. You were happy in college.
5. We were in New Zealand for two weeks.
6. You were in the swimming pool.

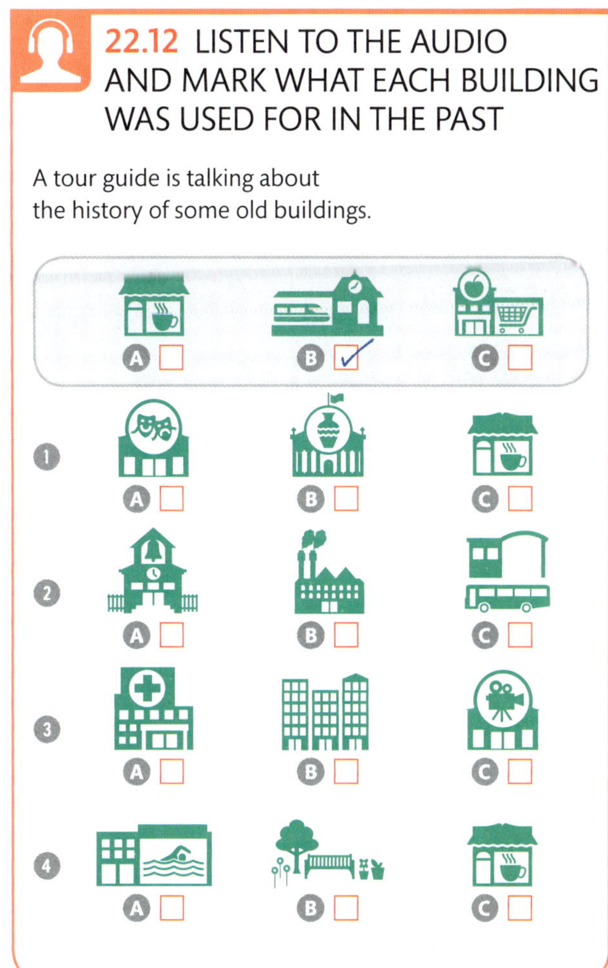

22.12 LISTEN TO THE AUDIO AND MARK WHAT EACH BUILDING WAS USED FOR IN THE PAST

A tour guide is talking about the history of some old buildings.

A ☐ B ☑ C ☐

1. A ☐ B ☐ C ☐
2. A ☐ B ☐ C ☐
3. A ☐ B ☐ C ☐
4. A ☐ B ☐ C ☐

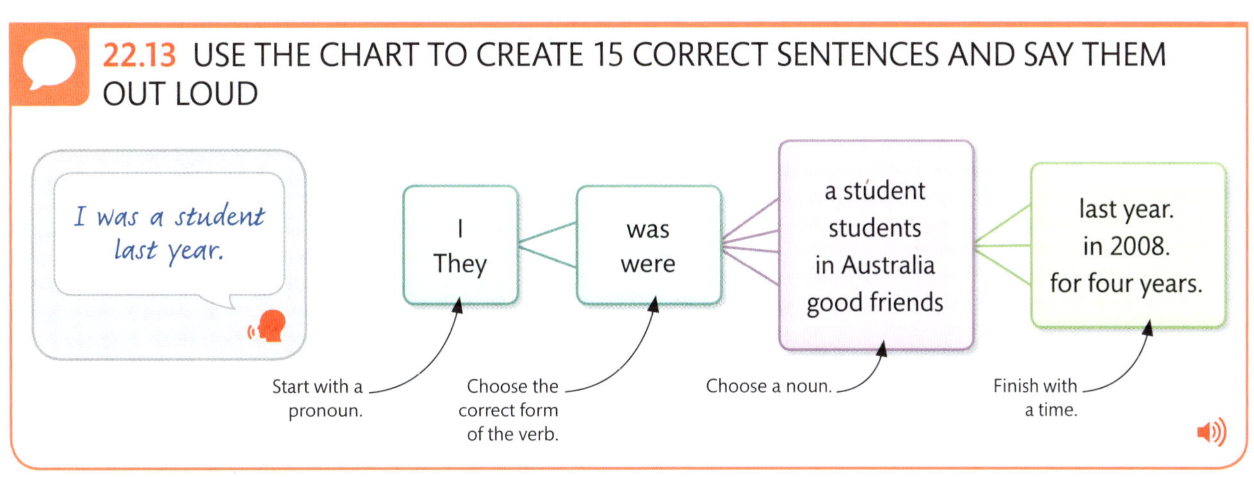

22.13 USE THE CHART TO CREATE 15 CORRECT SENTENCES AND SAY THEM OUT LOUD

22 CHECKLIST

The past simple of "to be" ☐ **Aa** Jobs, town, and life events ☐ Talking about past states ☐

23 Past events

Some verbs are regular in the past simple. You can use a lot of them to talk about the past week, the last year, or your life. Their past simple forms ends in "-ed."

New language Regular verbs in the past simple
Aa Vocabulary Pastimes and life events
New skill Talking about your past

23.1 KEY LANGUAGE REGULAR VERBS IN THE PAST SIMPLE

The past simple describes events that happened in the past. The past simple forms of regular verbs end in "-ed." The negative uses "did not" plus the base form.

The verb ends in "-ed."

I visited Luke last Friday.

He didn't play tennis last night.

23.2 HOW TO FORM REGULAR VERBS IN THE PAST SIMPLE

The past forms of most verbs do not change with the subject. Use the past simple of "do" plus the base verb to form negative statements.

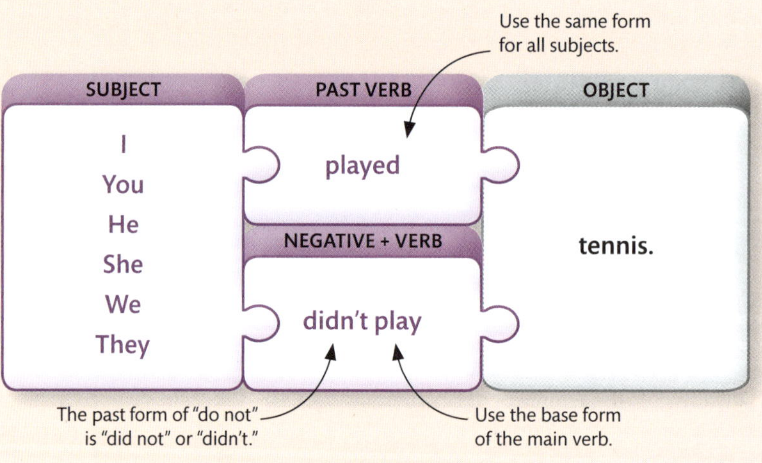

23.3 FURTHER EXAMPLES REGULAR VERBS IN THE PAST SIMPLE

He walked to the office.

Questions are formed using "did" + subject + the base form of the verb.

Did they work late?

She didn't walk downtown.

We didn't watch TV today.

23.4 FILL IN THE GAPS BY PUTTING THE VERBS IN THE PAST SIMPLE

Last Friday, I cooked (cook) a meal for my friends.

1. The music was good, but I ______________ (not dance) very much.
2. My friend ______________ (not listen) to the band on Saturday night.
3. Last week, I ______________ (clean) my brother's new car for him.
4. Did you ______________ (watch) a fun movie last night?
5. Ben and Franklin ______________ (play) tennis for five hours yesterday.

23.5 KEY LANGUAGE SPELLING RULES FOR THE PAST SIMPLE

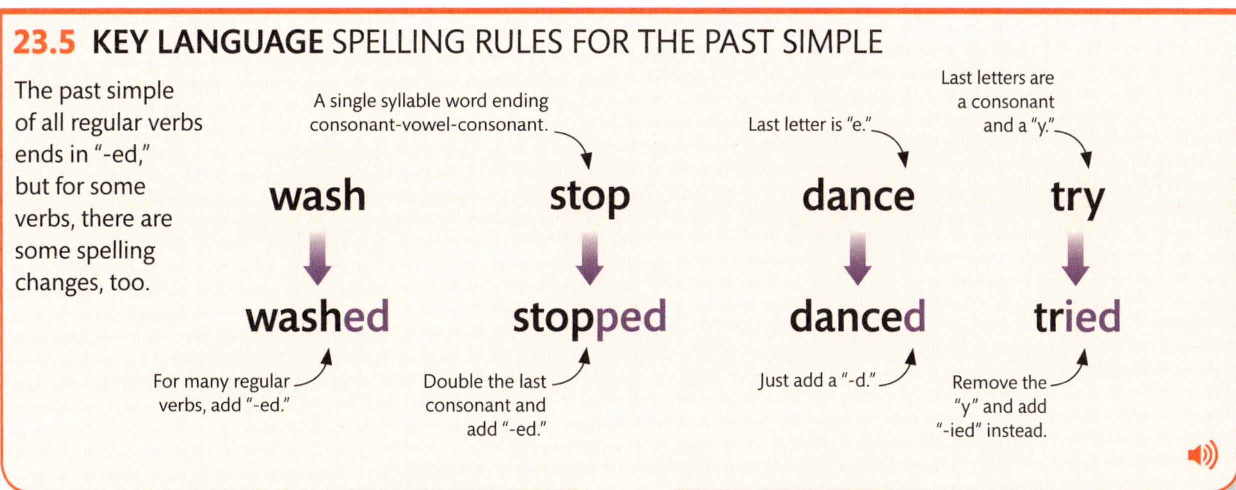

23.6 FURTHER EXAMPLES SPELLING RULES FOR THE PAST SIMPLE

He carried the bags for her. 

We arrived here at midnight. 

I studied English last year. 

They saved money for a vacation. 

23.7 LOOK AT JOYCE'S DIARY FROM LAST WEEK AND FILL IN THE GAPS TO COMPLETE THE SENTENCES

WEEKLY PLANNER

MONDAY
Evening: watch movie on TV

TUESDAY
Morning: play squash
Afternoon: phone my boss

WEDNESDAY
try sushi at Japanese restaurant

THURSDAY
Morning: clean the bathroom
Night: visit Aziz in hospital

FRIDAY
invite friends to my birthday party

SATURDAY
walk in the park

SUNDAY
cook dinner for my parents

On Monday evening, Joyce *watched* a movie on TV.

1. On Tuesday morning, she ______________ squash.
2. On Tuesday afternoon, she ______________ her boss.
3. On Wednesday, she ________ sushi at a Japanese restaurant.
4. On Thursday morning, she ______________ the bathroom.
5. On Thursday night, she ______________ Aziz in hospital.
6. On Friday, she ________ friends to her birthday party.
7. On Saturday, she ______________ in the park.
8. On Sunday, she ______________ dinner for her parents.

23.8 LISTEN TO THE AUDIO AND MATCH THE EVENTS TO THE YEARS

Arno describes his life so far.
He mentions important events and the years in which they happened.

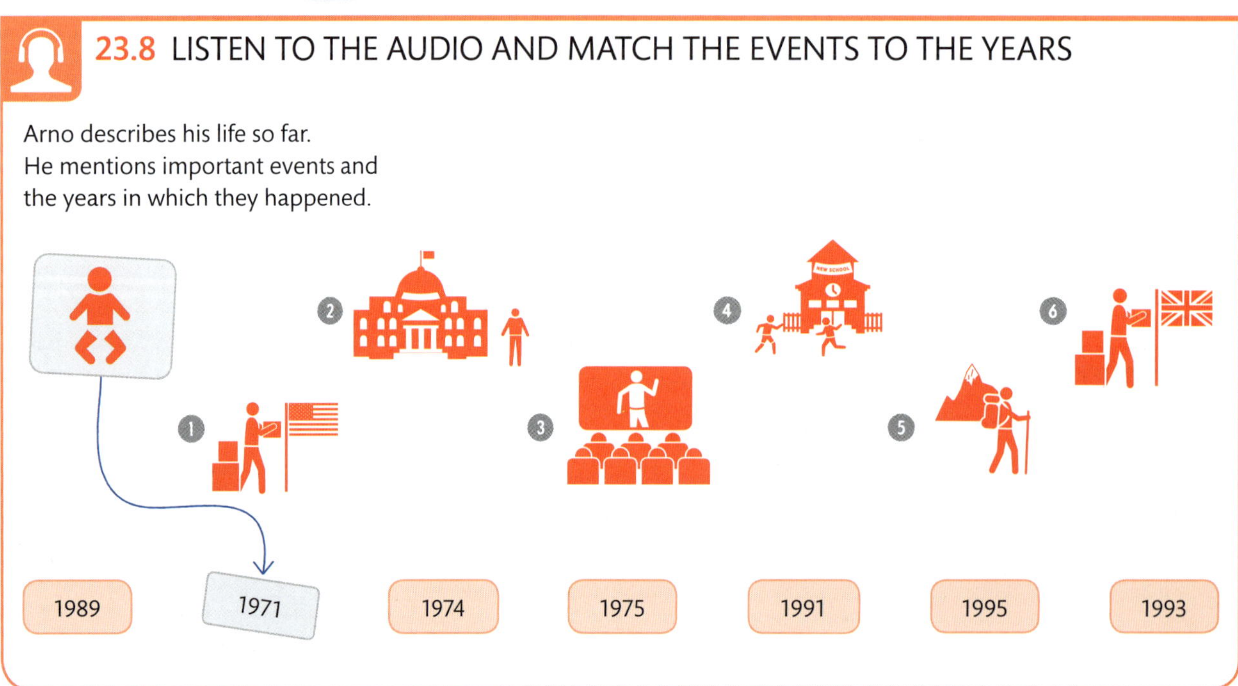

23.9 **KEY LANGUAGE** USING "WHEN" WITH THE PAST SIMPLE

To say when in someone's life something happened, you can either use "in" with the year, or "when" with the person's age.

This is the past simple action.

He moved to England in 1990.

He moved to England when he was 10 years old.

This describes when in the past it happened.

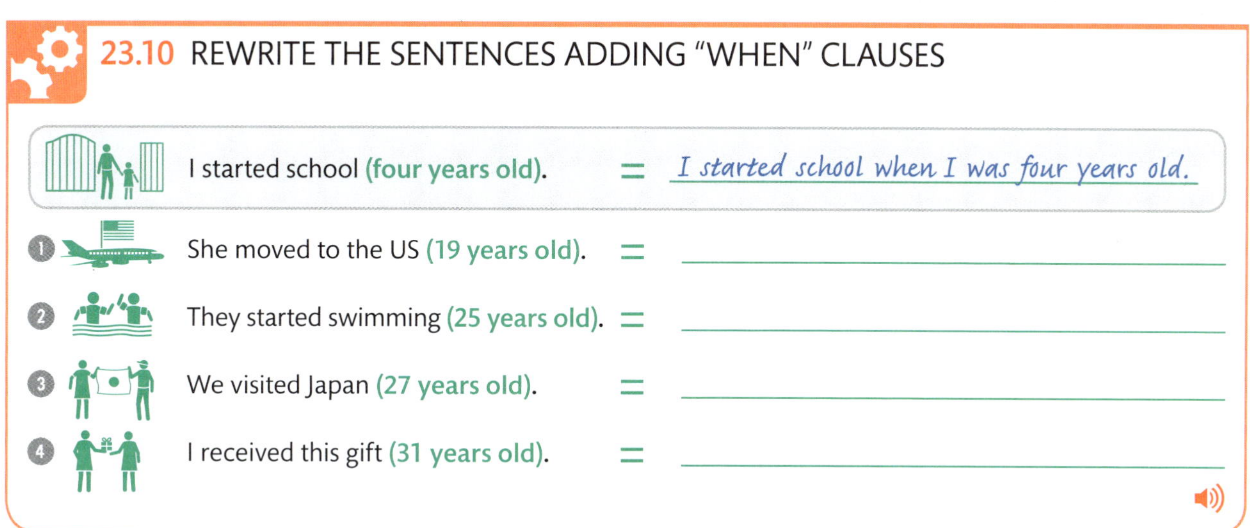

23.10 REWRITE THE SENTENCES ADDING "WHEN" CLAUSES

I started school (four years old). = *I started school when I was four years old.*

1. She moved to the US (19 years old). = ______
2. They started swimming (25 years old). = ______
3. We visited Japan (27 years old). = ______
4. I received this gift (31 years old). = ______

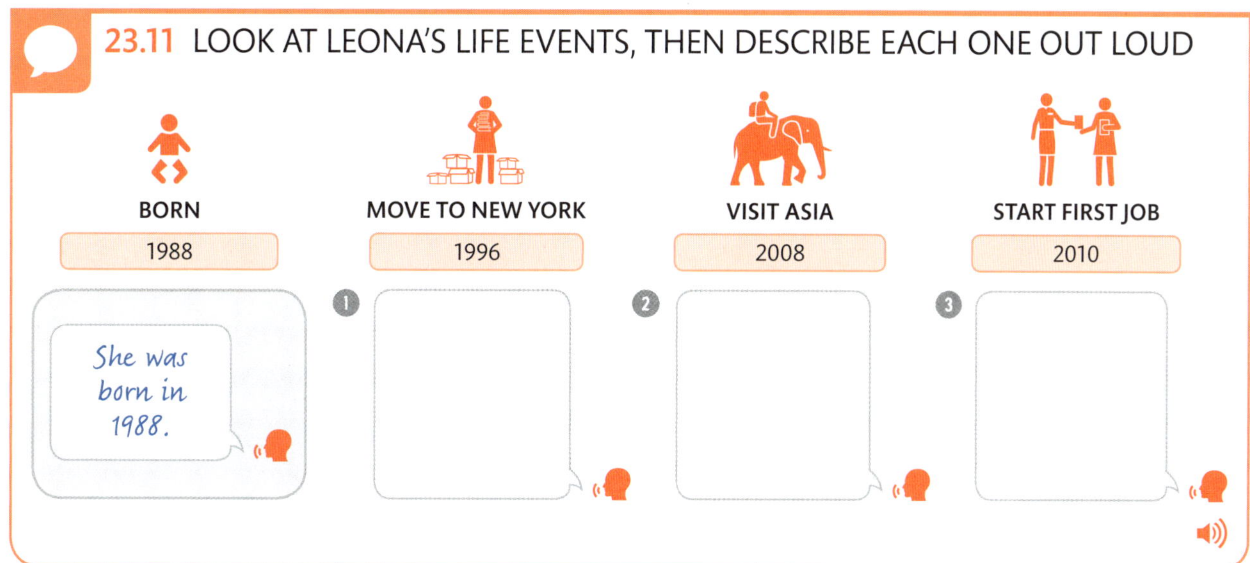

23.11 LOOK AT LEONA'S LIFE EVENTS, THEN DESCRIBE EACH ONE OUT LOUD

BORN	MOVE TO NEW YORK	VISIT ASIA	START FIRST JOB
1988	1996	2008	2010
She was born in 1988.	1	2	3

23 ✓ CHECKLIST

Regular verbs in the past simple ☐   **Aa** Pastimes and life events ☐   Talking about your past ☐

24 Past abilities

In the past simple, "can" becomes "could." You often use it to talk about things you "could" do in the past, but can't do now.

New language Using "could" in the past simple
Vocabulary Abilities and pastimes
New skill Talking about past abilities

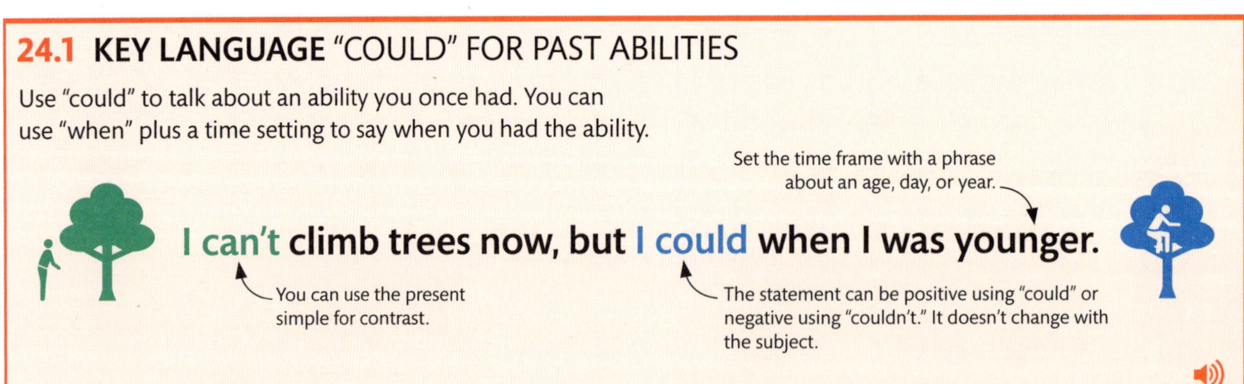

24.1 KEY LANGUAGE "COULD" FOR PAST ABILITIES

Use "could" to talk about an ability you once had. You can use "when" plus a time setting to say when you had the ability.

I can't climb trees now, but I could when I was younger.

You can use the present simple for contrast.

The statement can be positive using "could" or negative using "couldn't." It doesn't change with the subject.

Set the time frame with a phrase about an age, day, or year.

24.2 FURTHER EXAMPLES "COULD" FOR PAST ABILITIES

When I was a student, I could study all night before an exam.

I couldn't go to China last year because it was too expensive.

When Milo was eight, he could play the violin.

Last year, she couldn't run very far, but yesterday she ran a marathon.

24.3 HOW TO FORM "COULD" FOR PAST ABILITIES

"WHEN"	TIME SETTING	"COULD"	ABILITY
When	I was younger,	I could I couldn't	climb trees.
Begin with "when."	This phrase sets the time in the past when the action was possible.	The statement can be positive or negative.	Use the base form of the verb for the past ability.

24.4 REWRITE THESE SENTENCES IN THE PAST SIMPLE USING "COULD"

I **can** ski. — *I could ski.*

1. I **can** cook Italian food. ______
2. We **can't** play the piano. ______
3. She **can** paint a picture. ______
4. They **can't** make a cake. ______

24.5 LISTEN TO THE AUDIO AND MARK THE CORRECT ANSWERS

When Diana was five, she couldn't...
write music ☑
read music ☐
play the piano. ☐

1. When Louis was four, he could...
read ☐
write ☐
do mathematics. ☐

2. When Imelda was seven, she could...
ride a horse ☐
drive a car ☐
fly a plane. ☐

3. When Irina was four, she could speak...
one language ☐
two languages ☐
three languages. ☐

24.6 USE THE CHART TO CREATE 16 CORRECT SENTENCES AND SAY THEM OUT LOUD

When I was five, I couldn't play chess.

When I was When you were	five, seven,	I couldn't you could	play chess. ride a bike. swim. skate.
Start with a "when" phrase.	Choose an age.	Choose a positive or negative statement.	Finish with an ability.

24 CHECKLIST

Using "could" in the past simple ☐ **Aa** Abilities and pastimes ☐ Talking about past abilities ☐

25 Vocabulary

25.1 ENTERTAINMENT

movie (US)
film (UK)

novel

play

TV show

the news

newspaper

magazine

comedy

science fiction

thriller

documentary

action

horror

musical

romance

crime

hero

villain

audience

clap

movie star (US)
film star (UK)

actor

main character

director

author

plot

special effects

stunt

movie theater (US)
cinema (UK)

theater (US)
theatre (UK)

bookstore (US)
bookshop (UK)

exhibition

26 Irregular past verbs

In the past simple, some verbs are irregular. Their past simple forms are not formed using the normal rules, and sometimes look very different from the infinitive forms.

New language Irregular verbs in the past simple
Aa Vocabulary Sequence words
New skill Describing the past

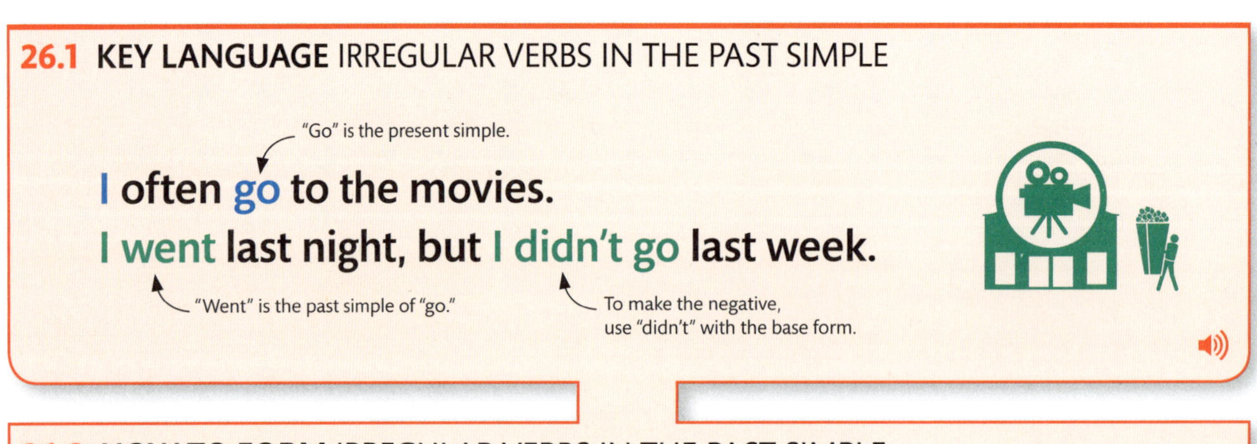

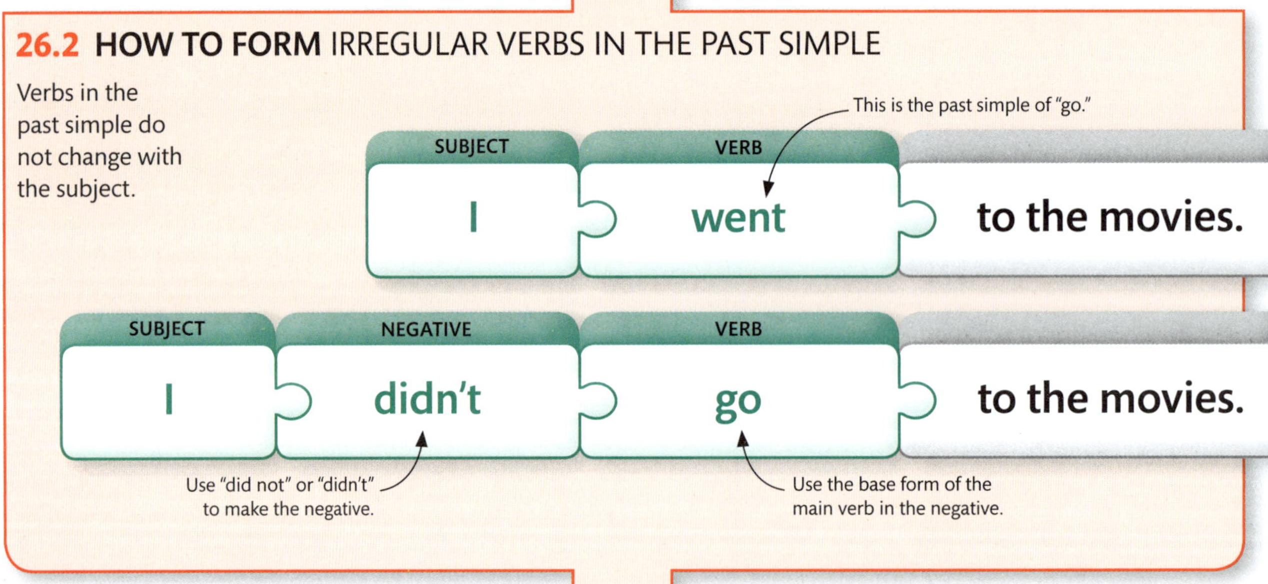

26.3 FURTHER EXAMPLES IRREGULAR VERBS IN THE PAST SIMPLE

They had a great vacation.

He didn't have any classes today.

I came to the US in 1980.

You didn't come to the party.

Aa 26.4 MATCH THE PAST SIMPLE FORMS OF THE VERBS TO THEIR BASE FORMS

	Past simple	Base form		Past simple	Base form
	put	break	5	bought	get
1	began	put	6	got	buy
2	broke	take	7	wrote	make
3	took	sell	8	made	sit
4	sold	begin	9	sat	write

(Example: put → put)

26.5 READ THE ARTICLE AND NUMBER THE PICTURES IN THE ORDER THEY ARE DESCRIBED

WILD ADVENTURES

A lucky escape!

A VERY WILD ADVENTURE IN THE FOREST

A few years ago I went camping in Redwood Park with my best friend, Jack. On our first day, we bought some food. We didn't want to stay on the campsite, so instead we walked through the forest to find somewhere else to camp. It got dark early and we were a bit lost so we decided to camp in the middle of the forest. That night, it was really dark and I felt a bit scared, but Jack and I made a fire and sang some songs. It was a quiet night and we slept well.

In the morning, we were hungry so we made our breakfast. But before we ate it, we went to the river. We had a wash and got some fresh water then walked back to our tent. When we got back to the tent, we saw a big brown bear. We didn't move or make a noise. We watched the bear as it sat in our tent and ate all of our breakfast. After that it walked off into the forest with our bags.

Jack and I were very hungry and cold, but we put our tent away and walked away quickly. Then, we ran and ran until finally we found the campsite. We were so happy. It was a very lucky escape!

A ☐

B ☐

C 1

D ☐

E ☐

F ☐

G ☐

26.6 FILL IN THE GAPS IN THIS JOURNAL USING THE WORDS IN THE PANEL

Wow! This morning a bear __ate__ my breakfast. We are in Redwood Park and last night we camped in the forest. We ________ a fire and it was very quiet, so my friend and I ________ well. The next morning, we ________ to the river to get water. When we got back to the tent, we ________ the bear. I ________ really scared. We ________ back to the campsite and we are safe now!

~~ate~~ slept made went felt saw ran

26.7 VOCABULARY SEQUENCE WORDS

You use certain words and phrases to help someone understand where you are in the story.

First he woke up.

Then he ate breakfast.

Next he had a shower.

After that he got dressed.

Finally he went to work.

26.8 FURTHER EXAMPLES SEQUENCE WORDS

First I got some money out of the bank.

Then I bought some food from the supermarket.

After that I had some coffee.

In the morning we watched the sun rise over the Serengeti.

Then we saw the birds fly off.

Finally the lions appeared.

26.9 REWRITE THE SENTENCES PUTTING THE SEQUENCE WORDS IN THE CORRECT PLACES

I won the game. I got a prize. (then)
I won the game. Then I got a prize.

1. Sheila put her best clothes on. (first)
____

2. Do your homework. Go out and play. (first, then)
____

3. Ben passed his test. He bought a car. (next)
____

4. Eat dinner. You can have some dessert. (after that)
____

5. He ate a large breakfast. (first)
____

26.10 FILL IN THE GAPS USING SEQUENCE WORDS, THEN SAY THE STORY OUT LOUD

First Harold and Jack bought some food. *Then* they went to the forest.

1. ______________ they got lost. Then they decided to camp and put the tent up.
2. They were scared of the sounds in the forest. But ______________ they went to sleep.
3. ______________ they washed in the river. They went back to their tent for food.
4. ______________ they saw a bear eating their food. After that it walked into the forest.
5. ______________ Harold and Jack arrived safely back at the campsite.

~~first~~ after that ~~then~~ finally
finally after that in the morning

26.11 KEY LANGUAGE IRREGULAR VERBS, QUESTIONS IN THE PAST SIMPLE

Use the past simple of "do" plus the base verb form to ask a question.

In the statement the main verb is in the past simple.

They bought a new car. → **Did they buy a new car?**

"Did" is in the past simple of "do."

The main verb is in its base form.

She saw the show last night. → **Did she see the show last night?**

26.12 FURTHER EXAMPLES IRREGULAR VERBS, QUESTIONS IN THE PAST SIMPLE

Did they have a good time?

Did she meet her friends in town?

Did you read a book on the beach?

Did he go to the gym?

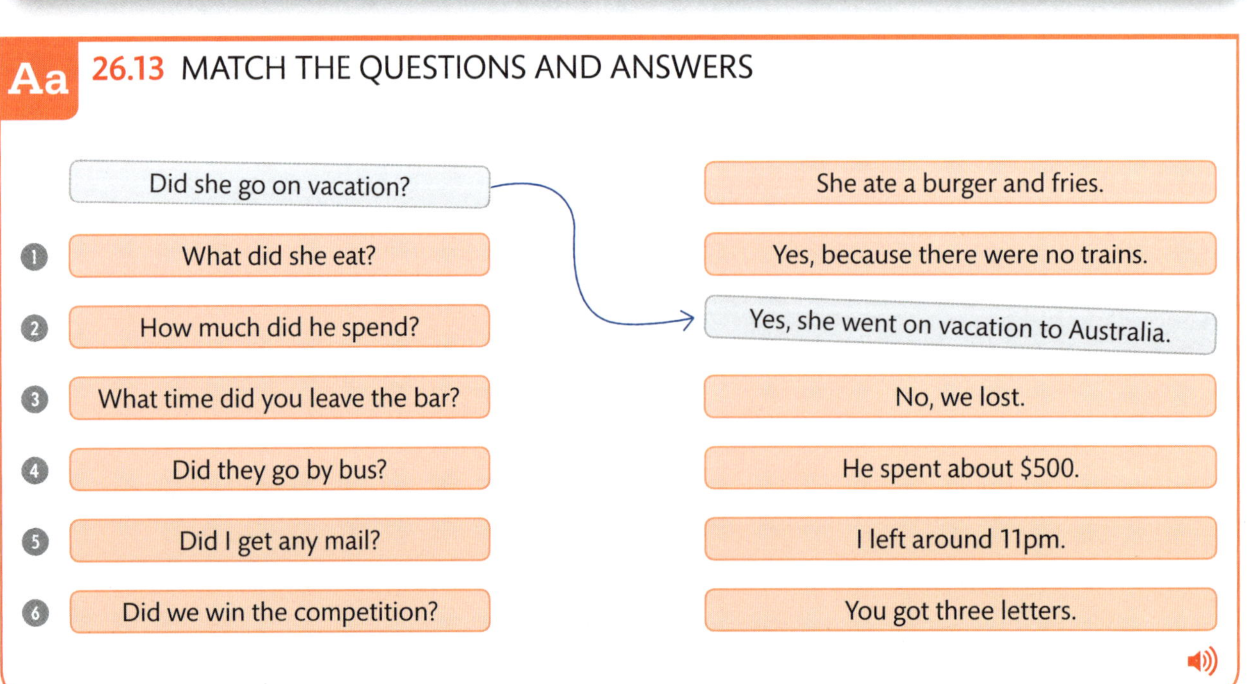

26.13 MATCH THE QUESTIONS AND ANSWERS

Did she go on vacation? → Yes, she went on vacation to Australia.

1. What did she eat?
2. How much did he spend?
3. What time did you leave the bar?
4. Did they go by bus?
5. Did I get any mail?
6. Did we win the competition?

- She ate a burger and fries.
- Yes, because there were no trains.
- Yes, she went on vacation to Australia.
- No, we lost.
- He spent about $500.
- I left around 11pm.
- You got three letters.

26.14 FILL IN THE GAPS TO WRITE QUESTIONS BASED ON THE SENTENCES

They sold 50 cakes.
How many *cakes did they sell?*

1. The movie began at 7:30pm.
When ______

2. He chose the red shirt.
Which ______

3. She ate pasta last night.
What ______

4. She read the magazine this morning.
What ______

5. Ala caught five fish at the lake.
How many ______

6. You saw Michelle at the party last night.
Who ______

7. He gave his brother a new sweater.
What ______

26.15 LISTEN TO THE AUDIO AND ANSWER THE QUESTIONS

Daniella and Marcus are talking about their friend's birthday party.

When did Daniella arrive at the party?
7pm ☐
8pm ☑
9pm ☐

1. What did she wear?
a red dress ☐
a green skirt ☐
her jeans ☐

2. What gift did she give her friend?
a watch ☐
flowers ☐
a book ☐

3. Who did she meet at the party?
Sam ☐
Lana ☐
Will ☐

4. What did she eat at the party?
burger ☐
pizza ☐
chicken ☐

5. Which music did she dance to?
jazz ☐
rock ☐
pop ☐

26 CHECKLIST

Irregular verbs in the past simple ☐ **Aa** Sequence words ☐ Describing the past ☐

27 Vocabulary

27.1 TOOLS

saw

drill

jigsaw

level (US)
spirit level (UK)

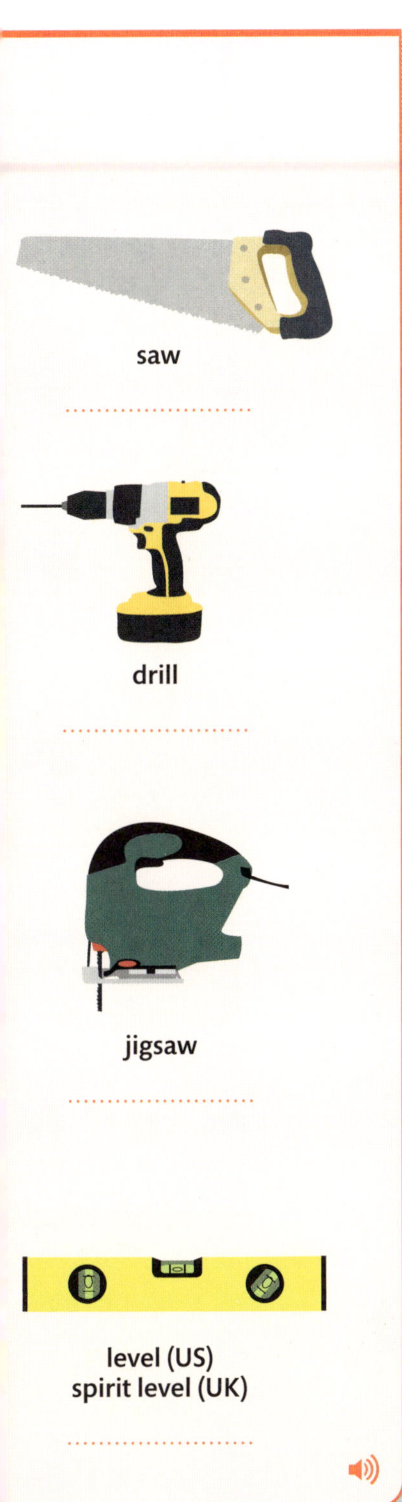

27.2 KITCHEN IMPLEMENTS

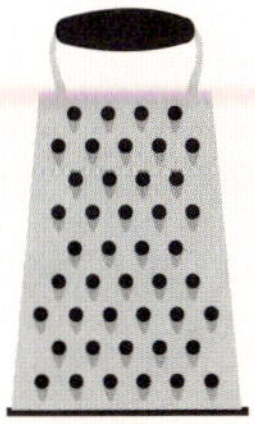

grater

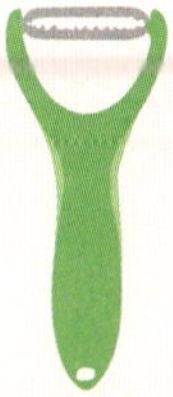

peeler

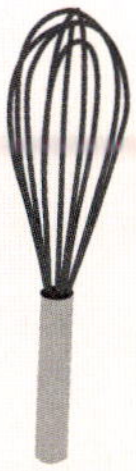

whisk

cutting board (US)
chopping board (UK)

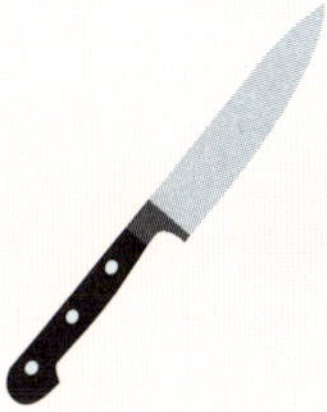

kitchen knife

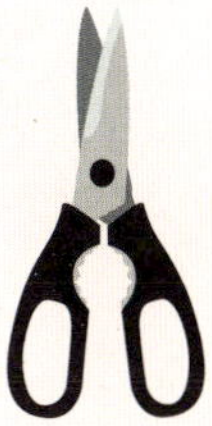

scissors

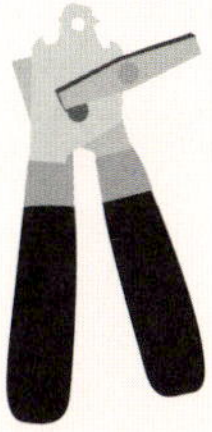

can opener (US)
tin opener (UK)

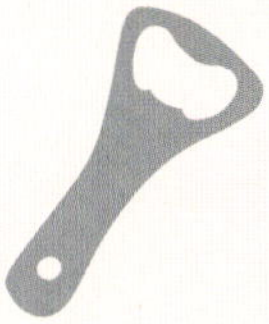

bottle opener

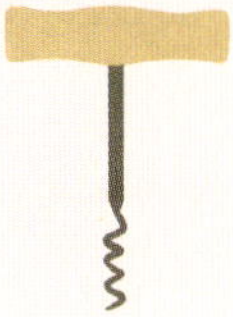

corkscrew

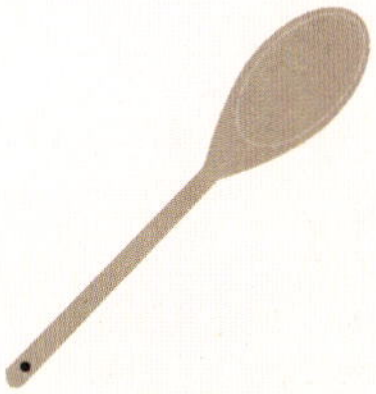

wooden spoon

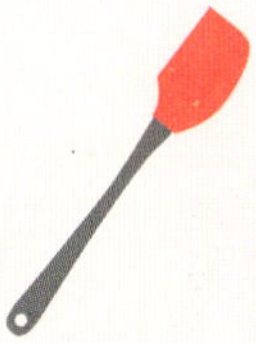

spatula

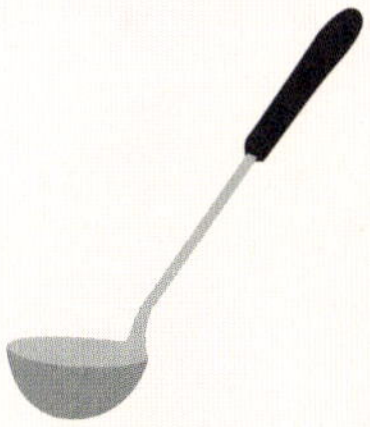

ladle

28 Telling a story

You can use "about" to describe the subject matter of movies, shows, and stories. Use adjectives to make a description more specific.

New language "About," opinions
Aa Vocabulary Opinions
New skill Describing media and culture

28.1 KEY LANGUAGE USING "ABOUT" TO DESCRIBE MEDIA AND CULTURE

Use "about" to give more information about a movie, play, show, story, or book.

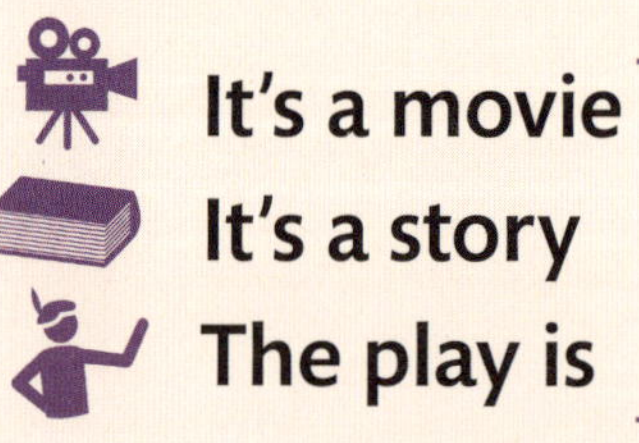

It's a movie / It's a story / The play is — about — **a mystery. / a lawyer. / two brothers.**

This introduces what the subject matter of the story is.

This is the additional information on the story.

28.2 FURTHER EXAMPLES USING "ABOUT" TO DESCRIBE MEDIA AND CULTURE

The movie is a thriller about two New York police officers.

It's a story about a young couple in the countryside.

The book is about a French city during the 1920s.

28.3 LISTEN TO THE AUDIO AND NUMBER THE MOVIES IN THE ORDER THEY ARE DESCRIBED

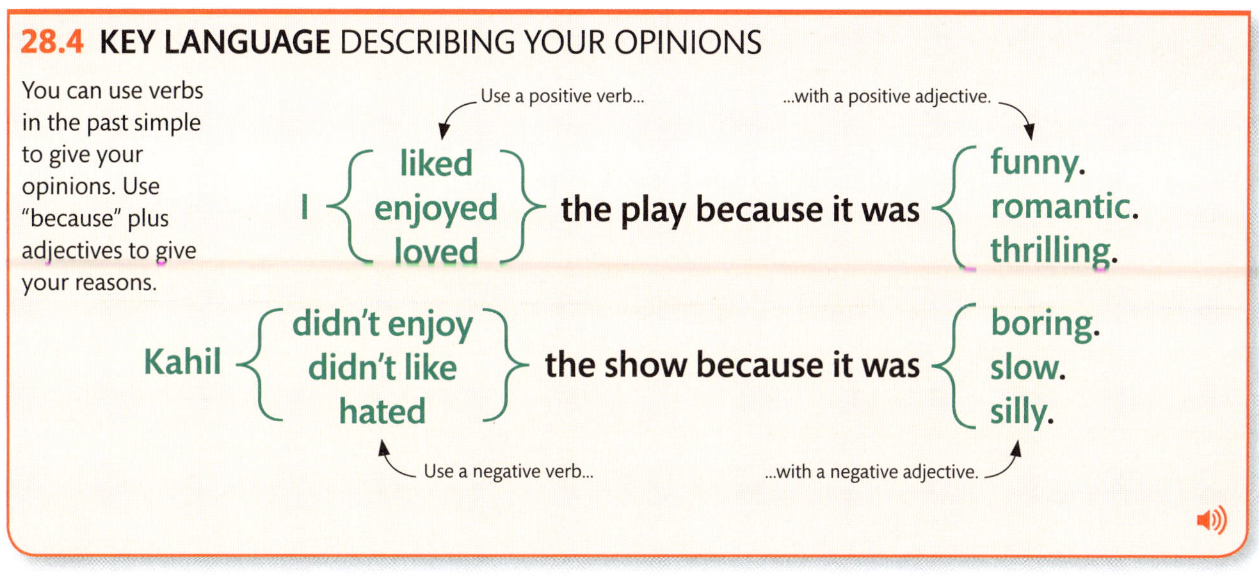

28.4 KEY LANGUAGE DESCRIBING YOUR OPINIONS

You can use verbs in the past simple to give your opinions. Use "because" plus adjectives to give your reasons.

Use a positive verb... / ...with a positive adjective.

I { liked / enjoyed / loved } the play because it was { funny. / romantic. / thrilling. }

Kahil { didn't enjoy / didn't like / hated } the show because it was { boring. / slow. / silly. }

Use a negative verb... / ...with a negative adjective.

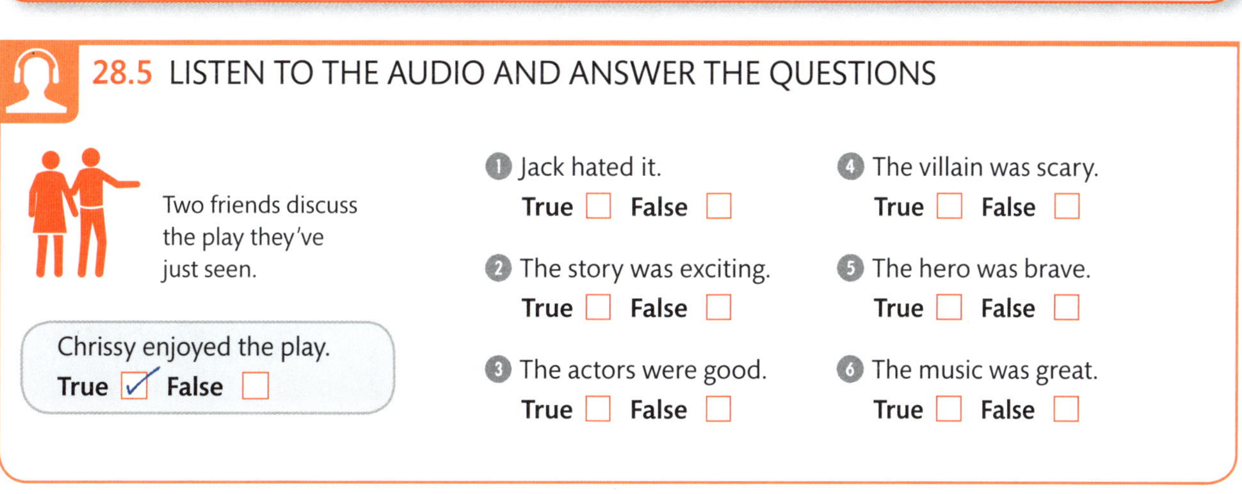

28.5 LISTEN TO THE AUDIO AND ANSWER THE QUESTIONS

Two friends discuss the play they've just seen.

Chrissy enjoyed the play.
True ☑ False ☐

1. Jack hated it.
True ☐ False ☐

2. The story was exciting.
True ☐ False ☐

3. The actors were good.
True ☐ False ☐

4. The villain was scary.
True ☐ False ☐

5. The hero was brave.
True ☐ False ☐

6. The music was great.
True ☐ False ☐

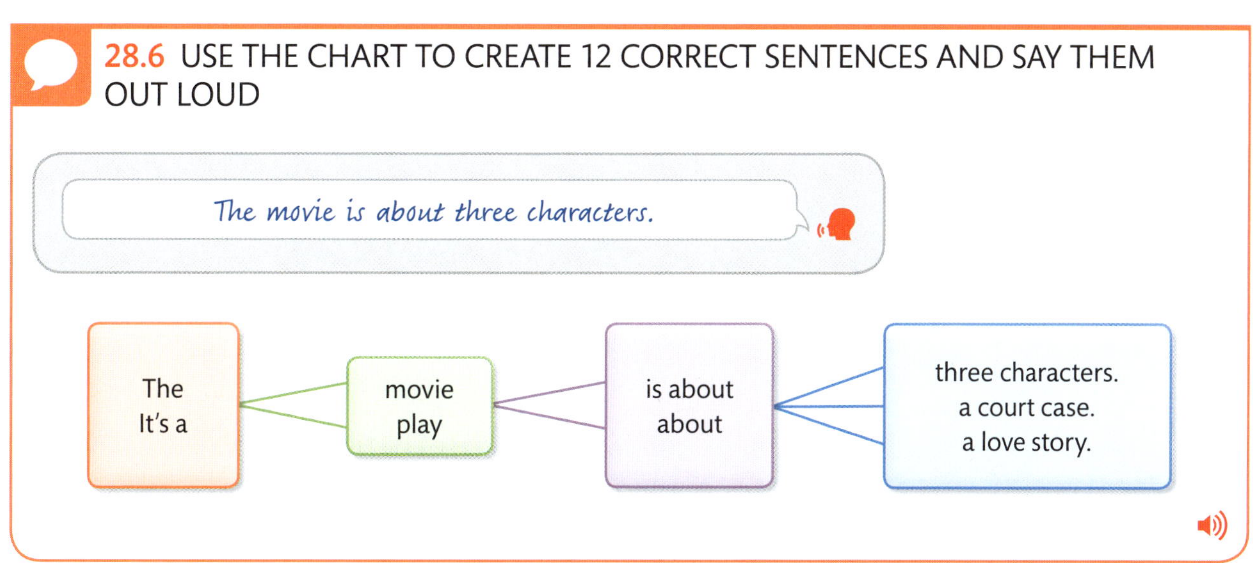

28.6 USE THE CHART TO CREATE 12 CORRECT SENTENCES AND SAY THEM OUT LOUD

The movie is about three characters.

The / It's a	movie / play	is about / about	three characters. / a court case. / a love story.

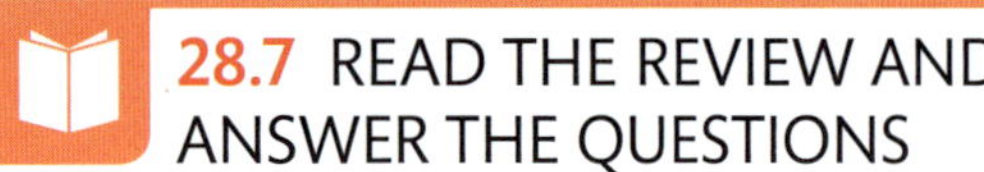

28.7 READ THE REVIEW AND ANSWER THE QUESTIONS

What type of show is it?
It is a musical.

1. What does Millie enjoy?

2. Where does she learn to sing?

3. What is the name of her music teacher?

4. Who is the villain?

5. Is Millie played by an adult?

STAGE REVIEW

Millie's Magic!

The latest show in town is a hit

Millie's Magical Music is a wonderful new show. The story is about a little girl called Millie. She loves singing. In her bedroom, she listens to songs and learns how to sing them. At school, she has a kind English teacher called Miss Graham and a terrible music teacher called Miss Cafferty, who is the villain of the story. Both Miss Graham and Miss Cafferty hear Millie's beautiful voice. Miss Graham wants everyone to hear Millie, but Miss Cafferty wants to stop her singing.

It's an enjoyable story about music, friendship, and hope.

Many of the actors in this musical are children and they are all excellent, especially Millie. The songs in the musical are very good, too.

I really liked the music. It's a hit!

28.8 REWRITE THESE SENTENCES USING NEGATIVE WORDS

The musical was **wonderful**.
The musical was awful.

1. Millie **loves** singing.

2. Millie has **beautiful** costumes.

3. Many of the actors were **excellent**.

4. The songs are very **good**.

5. I really **loved** the music.

bad	hated	~~awful~~	hates	terrible	ugly

Aa 28.9 READ THE CLUES AND WRITE THE ANSWERS IN THE GRID

1. The bad guy, the hero fights this person
2. A true story with real people, not actors
3. A funny story that makes people laugh
4. A story told in a theater
5. A person who writes novels
6. An exciting story

adventure | author | play
comedy | villain | documentary

1 villain
2
3
4
5
6

28 CHECKLIST

"About," opinions ☐ | Aa Opinions ☐ | Describing media and culture ☐

REVIEW THE ENGLISH YOU HAVE LEARNED IN UNITS 21–28

NEW LANGUAGE	SAMPLE SENTENCE	☑	UNIT
WRITING AND SAYING DATES	His birthday is on May 10. My meeting is on the 18th of May.	☐	21.1, 21.2
"TO BE" STATEMENTS AND QUESTIONS ABOUT THE PAST	She was a student in 1985. Was he in India last year? He wasn't in France.	☐	22.1, 22.7, 22.8
REGULAR VERBS IN THE PAST SIMPLE	I visited Luke last Friday. I didn't play tennis.	☐	23.1
USING "COULD" FOR PAST ABILITIES	I could climb trees when I was younger.	☐	24.1
IRREGULAR VERBS IN THE PAST SIMPLE	I went to the movies last night. I didn't go last week.	☐	26.1
GIVING OPINIONS ABOUT CULTURE	It's a movie about two brothers. I enjoyed it because it was thrilling.	☐	28.1, 28.4

29 Asking about the past

You can make questions in the past simple using "did." This is useful for asking about past events, such as travel and vacations.

New language Past simple questions
Aa Vocabulary Travel and activities
New skill Talking about vacations

29.1 KEY LANGUAGE "YES / NO" QUESTIONS IN THE PAST SIMPLE

Use the auxiliary verb "did" to make questions in the past simple that have "yes/no" answers.

"Did" goes before the subject.

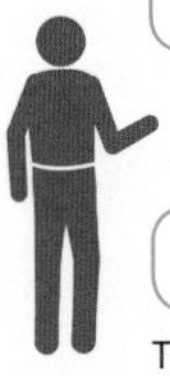

Did you have **a good holiday?**

Yes, we went to India.

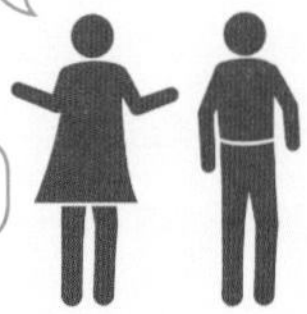

Did you visit **the Taj Mahal?**

The verb after "did" goes in its base form.

No, we didn't.

Use "did" or "didn't" for short answers.

29.2 FURTHER EXAMPLES "YES / NO" QUESTIONS IN THE PAST SIMPLE

Did you see **any tigers?**

Yes, I did.

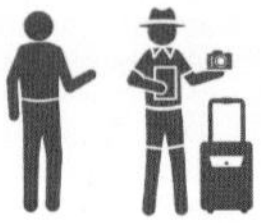

Did he stay **in the five-star hotel?**

"Did" doesn't change with the subject.

No, he didn't.

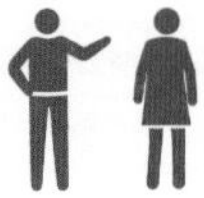

Did they buy **any ice cream?**

Yes, they did.

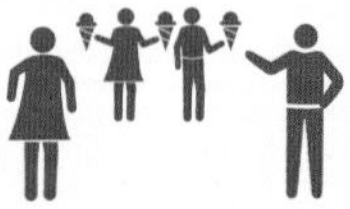

Did we bring **enough money with us?**

No, we didn't.

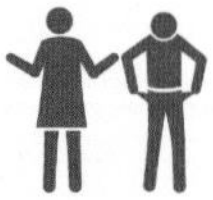

29.3 HOW TO FORM "YES / NO" QUESTIONS IN THE PAST SIMPLE

"DID"	SUBJECT	VERB	OBJECT
Did	you	visit	**the Taj Mahal?**

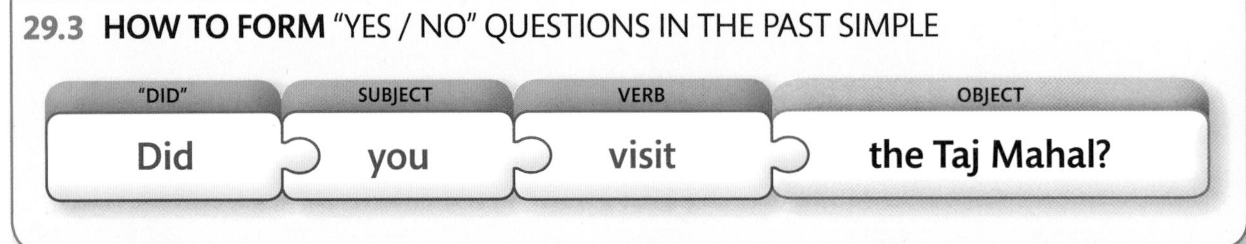

29.4 LISTEN TO THE AUDIO, THEN NUMBER THE PICTURES IN THE ORDER THEY ARE DESCRIBED

Bea talks about her vacation in India.

A ☐

B [1]

C ☐

D ☐

E ☐

29.5 MATCH THE QUESTIONS TO THE SHORT ANSWERS

	Did you get the job? → Yes, I did.	Yes, we did.
1	Did I have lunch today?	Yes, I did.
2	Did the dog eat its dinner?	No, you didn't.
3	Did they go to Venezuela?	Yes, it did.
4	Did we win the competition?	No, they didn't.

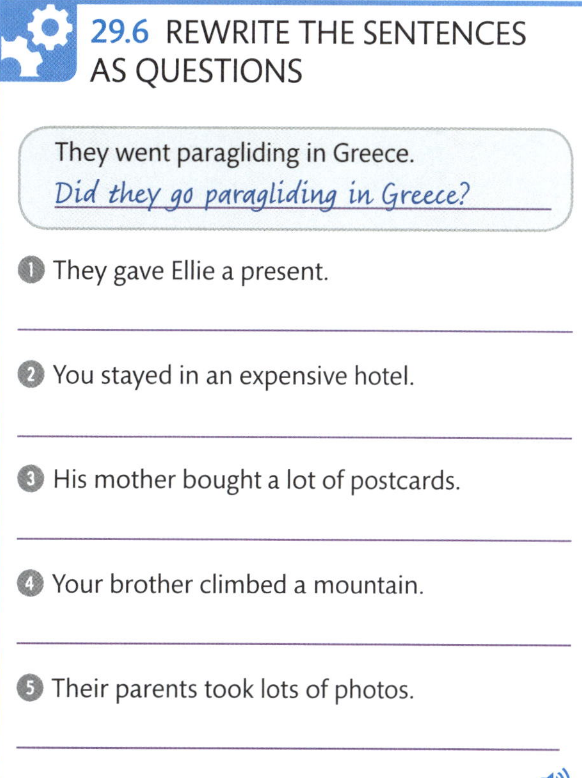

29.6 REWRITE THE SENTENCES AS QUESTIONS

They went paragliding in Greece.
Did they go paragliding in Greece?

1. They gave Ellie a present.
2. You stayed in an expensive hotel.
3. His mother bought a lot of postcards.
4. Your brother climbed a mountain.
5. Their parents took lots of photos.

29.7 KEY LANGUAGE QUESTION WORDS WITH THE PAST SIMPLE

The question word goes at the beginning of the question, followed by "did" and the subject.

The question word goes at the beginning.

When did you arrive at the hotel?

Yesterday.

How did you get here?

By taxi.

The verb after "did" goes in its base form.

29.8 FURTHER EXAMPLES QUESTION WORDS WITH THE PAST SIMPLE

Where did you go on vacation?

We went to Paris.

What did you see in Paris?

The Eiffel Tower.

What did you do on vacation?

We went hiking.

When did you come home?

This morning.

29.9 MATCH THE QUESTIONS WITH THE CORRECT ANSWERS

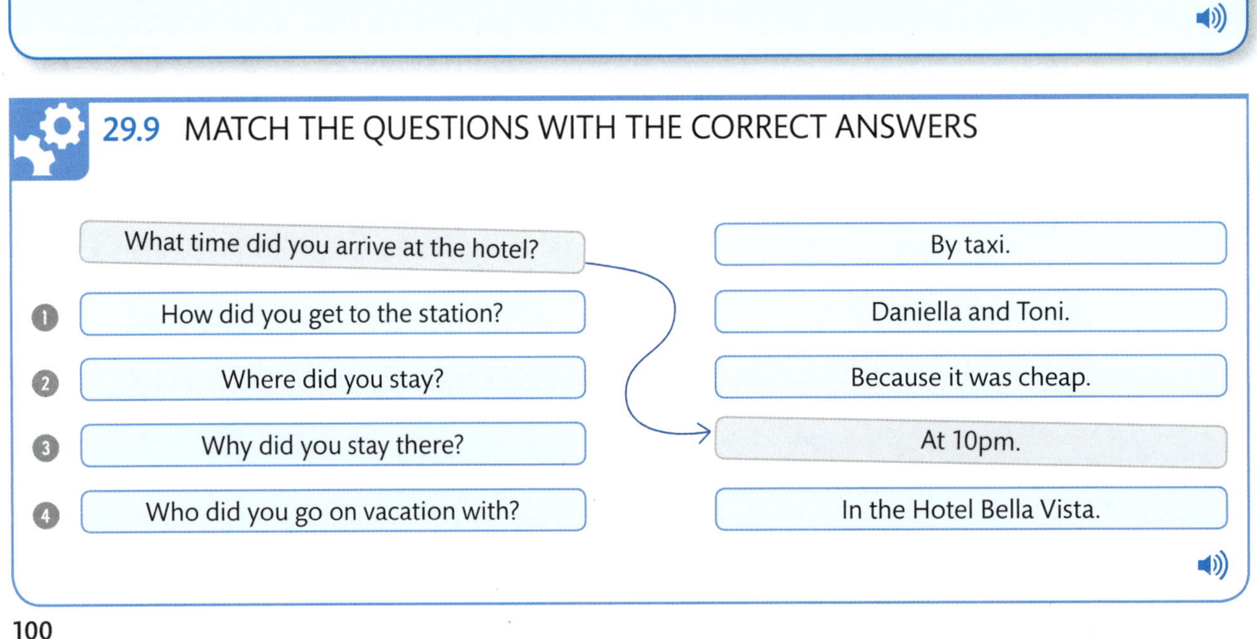

What time did you arrive at the hotel? → At 10pm.

1 How did you get to the station?

2 Where did you stay?

3 Why did you stay there?

4 Who did you go on vacation with?

By taxi.

Daniella and Toni.

Because it was cheap.

At 10pm.

In the Hotel Bella Vista.

29.10 READ THE EMAIL AND ANSWER THE QUESTIONS

When did she arrive in New York?
On Monday ☐ **On Thursday** ☐ **On Friday** ☑

1. How did she get to Staten Island?
By taxi ☐ **By boat** ☐ **By bus** ☐

2. When did she see the Statue of Liberty?
On Friday ☐ **On Saturday** ☐ **Yesterday** ☐

3. Which store did she go to?
Macy's ☐ **Bloomingdale's** ☐ **Saks Fifth Avenue** ☐

4. What did she buy there?
Some shoes ☐ **Some perfume** ☐ **Some clothes** ☐

5. What did Sue eat in Grand Central Station?
A hamburger ☐ **Oysters** ☐ **Steak and salad** ☐

To: Sam

Subject: Trip to New York

Hi Sam,

We're having a great time in New York. There's so much to do. We arrived on Friday and went up the Empire State Building. Then, on Saturday, we took the boat to Staten Island and saw the Statue of Liberty. I was surprised because it looked quite small. Yesterday, I went to a store called Macy's and bought some nice clothes. Then we went to a famous restaurant in Grand Central Station and ate oysters.

Love from Sue xx

29.11 SAY THE QUESTIONS OUT LOUD, FILLING IN THE GAPS

When *did you visit China* ?
We visited China in 2011.

1. Who ________________ ?
I went on vacation with Jo.

2. Where ________________ ?
We stayed in a hotel in London.

3. What ________________ ?
We ate fried rice in Chinatown.

4. How ________________ for?
We went abroad for six months.

5. When ________________ ?
We left the US on June 29th.

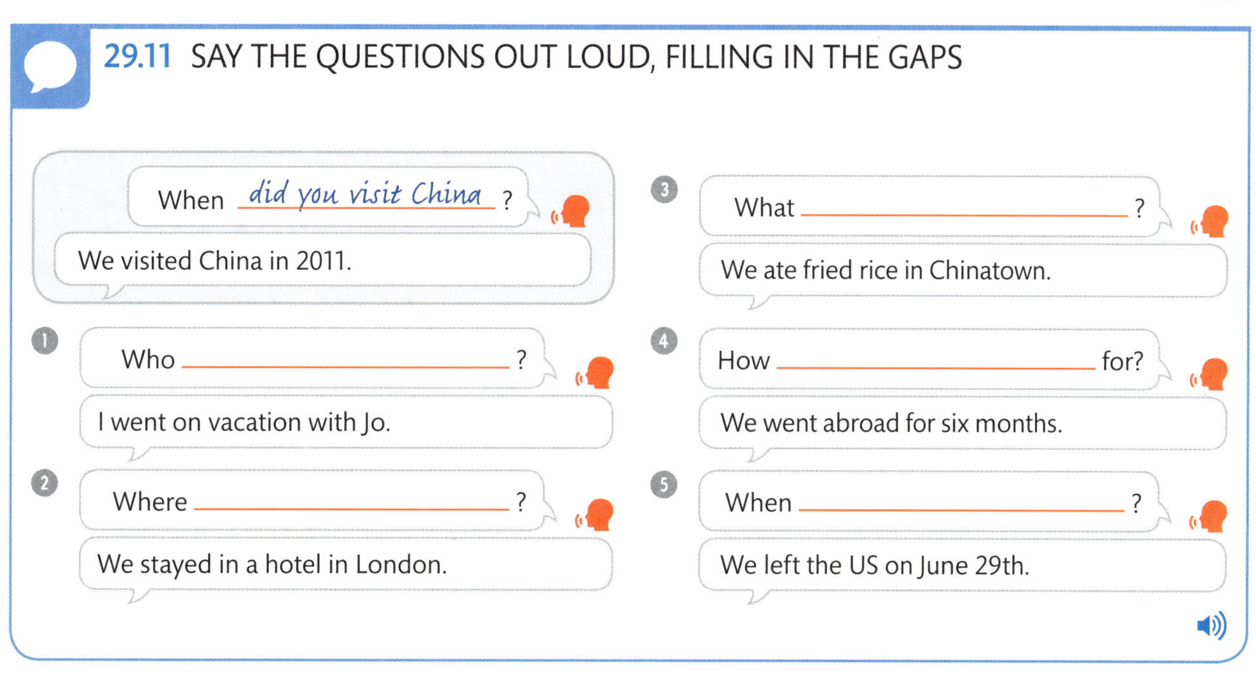

29 CHECKLIST

Past simple questions ☐ **Aa** Travel and activities ☐ Talking about vacations ☐

30 Applying for a job

If you want to find a job, you need to understand the English words and phrases used in advertisements and on recruitment websites.

New language Interview responses
Aa Vocabulary Job words and phrases
New skill Dealing with job applications

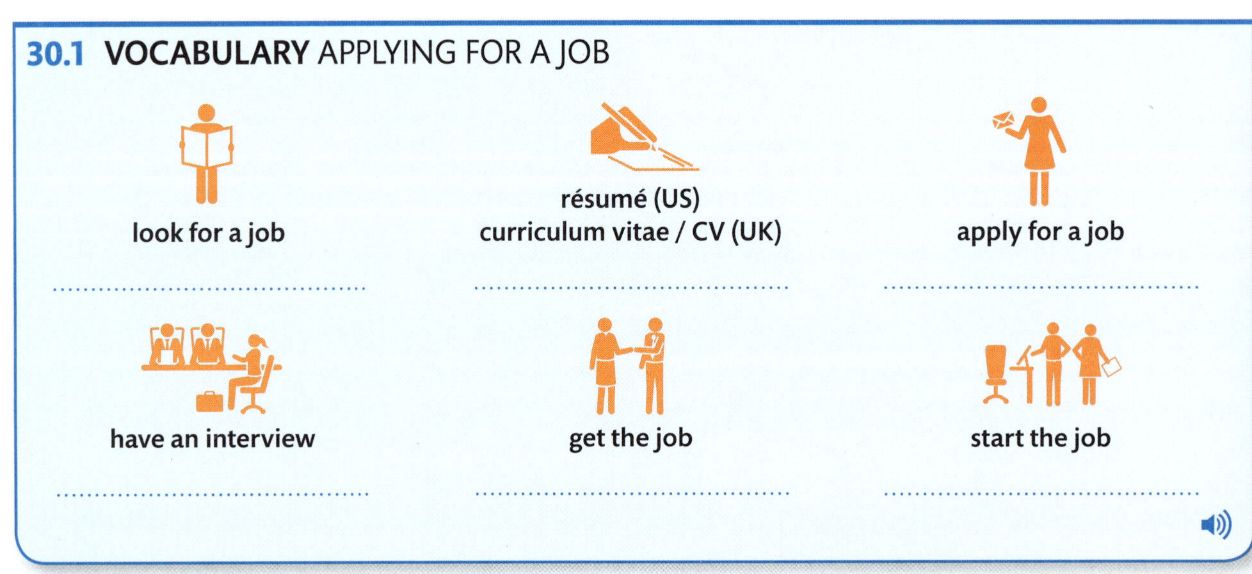

30.2 READ THE JOB ADVERTISEMENTS AND ANSWER THE QUESTIONS

26 BUSINESS TODAY

JOBS

WANTED: Assistant chef at Marie's Cakes, Ohio. Can you cook? Do you love cake? We need an assistant chef on Saturdays and Sundays (6am to 2pm), $10 per hour.

WANTED: Teacher at summer school, Alaska. Do you like children? You can teach kids aged 11 to 14 this summer (June to August). Some experience needed.

WANTED: Gardener at St. Bernard's College, Idaho. We need a gardener to work part-time in our beautiful gardens. Experience needed. 20 hours per week.

The job at Marie's Cakes is for Fridays and Saturdays.
True ☐ False ☑

1. The job at Marie's Cakes is in Ohio.
True ☐ False ☐

2. The teaching job starts in August.
True ☐ False ☐

3. You will teach children aged 11 to 14 years old.
True ☐ False ☐

4. The gardening job is full-time.
True ☐ False ☐

5. The gardening job is at a castle.
True ☐ False ☐

30.3 VOCABULARY WORDS IN YOUR RÉSUMÉ

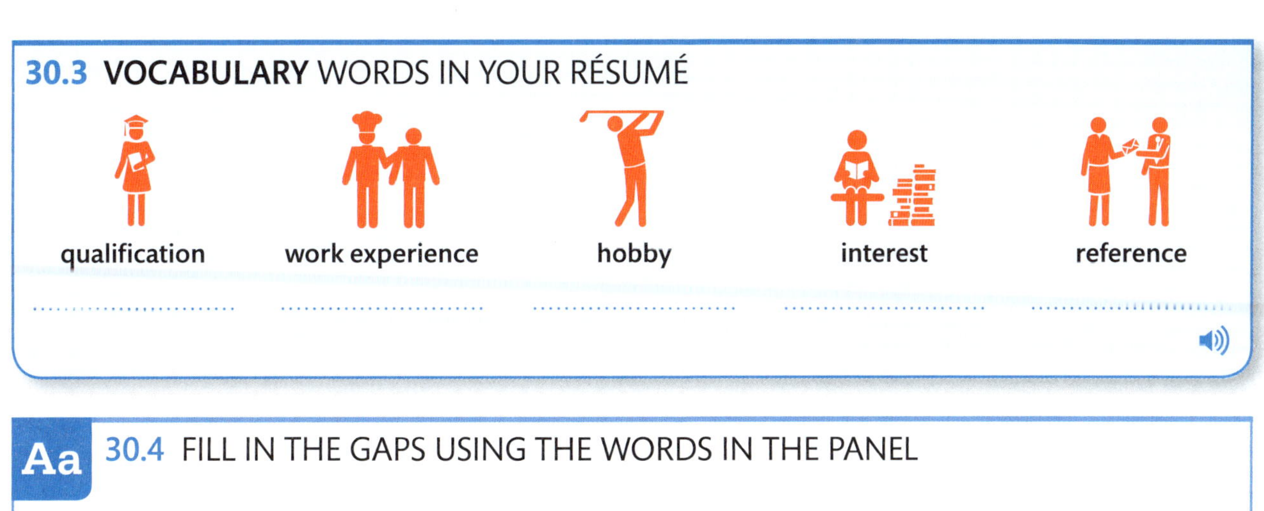

30.4 FILL IN THE GAPS USING THE WORDS IN THE PANEL

I need to give the interviewer a *reference* from my last boss.

1. My ______________ include degrees in biology and chemistry.
2. The interview at the bank went really well. I've ______________ .
3. The manager read my ______________ and said it was really good.
4. I can ______________ the job in January.
5. You need to ______________ before you can get the job.

have an interview | ~~reference~~ | qualifications | résumé | got the job | start

30.5 LISTEN TO THE AUDIO, THEN NUMBER THE QUESTIONS IN THE ORDER THAT YOU HEAR THEM

Tom Willis is being interviewed for a job.

A. Why do you want this job? ☐
B. What did you do at the store? ☐
C. Why did you study English at college? 1
D. When can you start work? ☐
E. Why did you leave the music store? ☐
F. Are you good at working with people? ☐

30 CHECKLIST

Interview responses ☐ Aa Job words and phrases ☐ Dealing with job applications ☐

31 Types of questions

There are two kinds of question: subject questions and object questions. You form them in different ways in order to ask about different things.

New language Subject and object questions
Aa Vocabulary Workplace words
New skill Asking different kinds of question

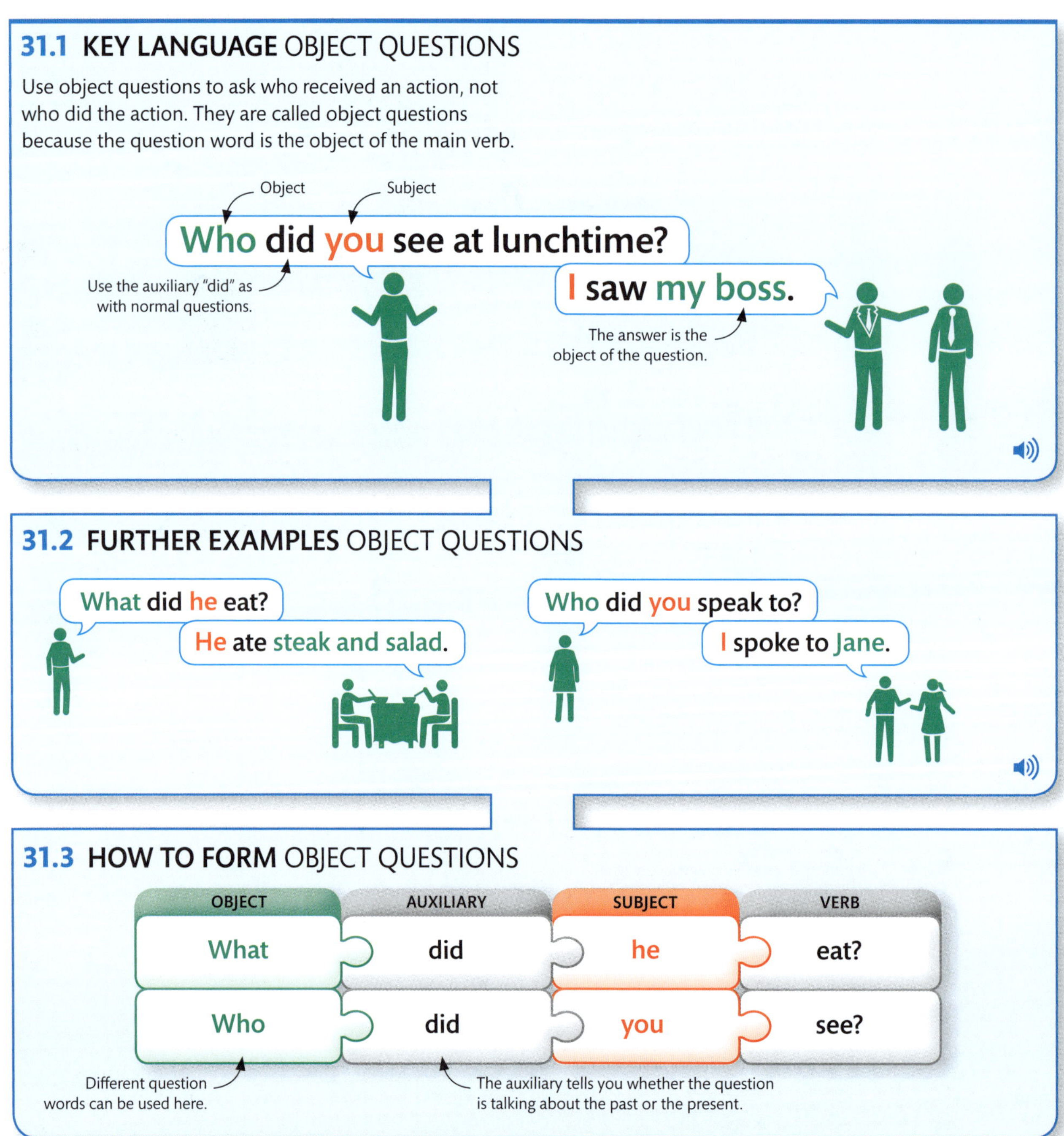

31.4 VOCABULARY IN THE WORKPLACE

customer	boss	manager	salary	pay
....	....	....	....	....
staff	**company**	**nine-to-five job**	**part-time**	**full-time**
....	....	....	....	....

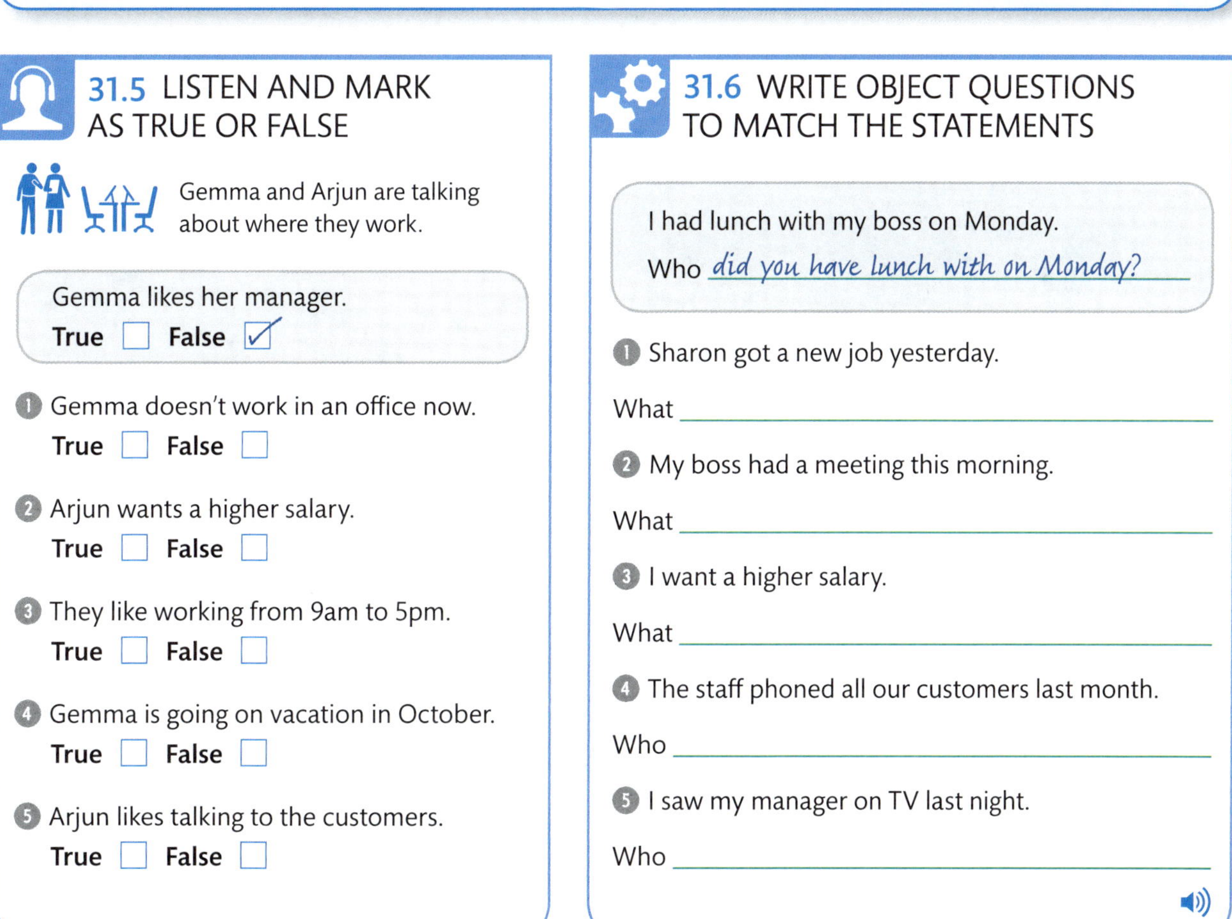

31.5 LISTEN AND MARK AS TRUE OR FALSE

Gemma and Arjun are talking about where they work.

Gemma likes her manager.
True ☐ **False** ☑

1. Gemma doesn't work in an office now.
   True ☐ **False** ☐
2. Arjun wants a higher salary.
   True ☐ **False** ☐
3. They like working from 9am to 5pm.
   True ☐ **False** ☐
4. Gemma is going on vacation in October.
   True ☐ **False** ☐
5. Arjun likes talking to the customers.
   True ☐ **False** ☐

31.6 WRITE OBJECT QUESTIONS TO MATCH THE STATEMENTS

I had lunch with my boss on Monday.
Who *did you have lunch with on Monday?*

1. Sharon got a new job yesterday.
   What ______________________
2. My boss had a meeting this morning.
   What ______________________
3. I want a higher salary.
   What ______________________
4. The staff phoned all our customers last month.
   Who ______________________
5. I saw my manager on TV last night.
   Who ______________________

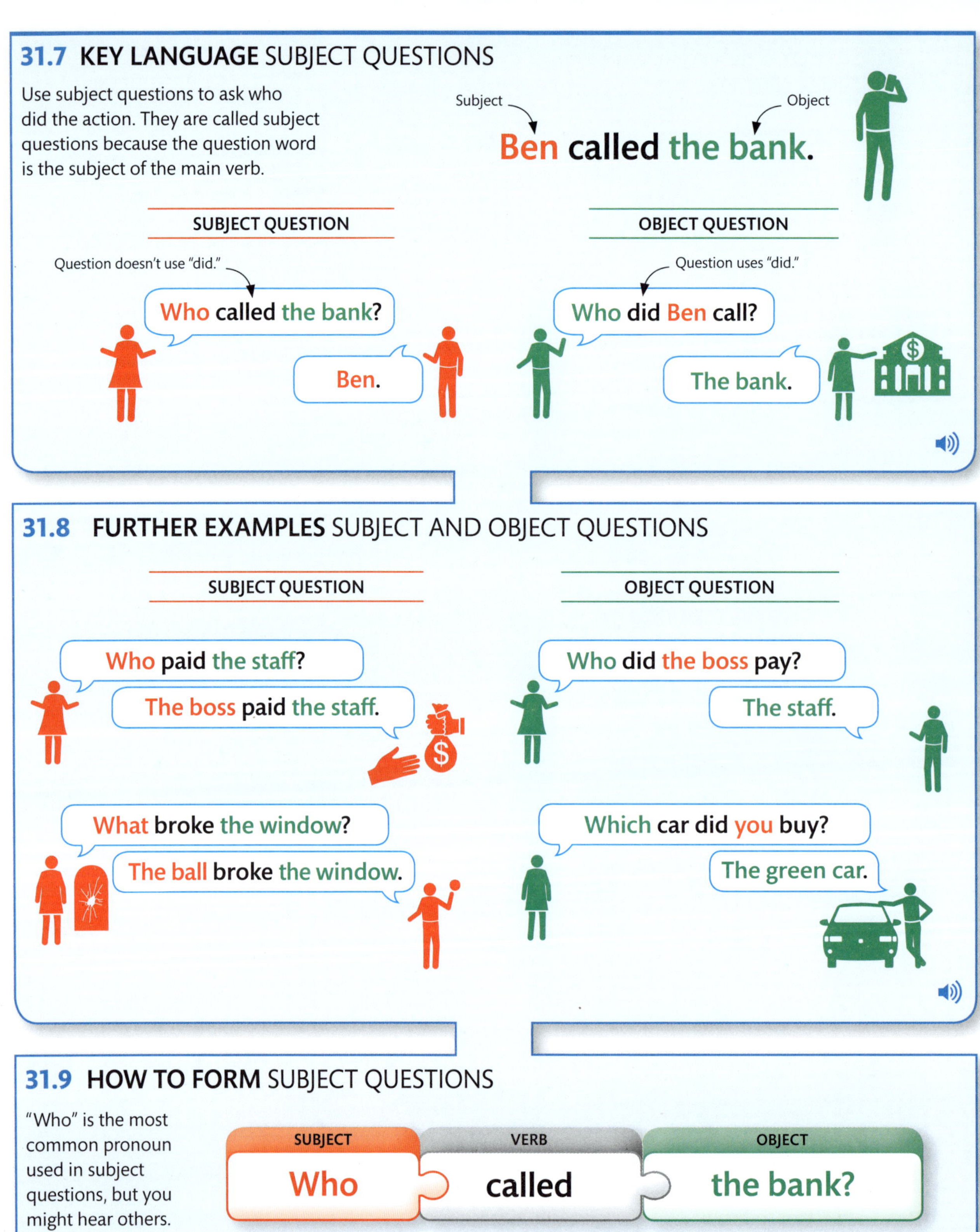

31.7 KEY LANGUAGE SUBJECT QUESTIONS

Use subject questions to ask who did the action. They are called subject questions because the question word is the subject of the main verb.

SUBJECT QUESTION

OBJECT QUESTION

31.8 FURTHER EXAMPLES SUBJECT AND OBJECT QUESTIONS

SUBJECT QUESTION

OBJECT QUESTION

31.9 HOW TO FORM SUBJECT QUESTIONS

"Who" is the most common pronoun used in subject questions, but you might hear others.

SUBJECT	VERB	OBJECT
Who	called	the bank?

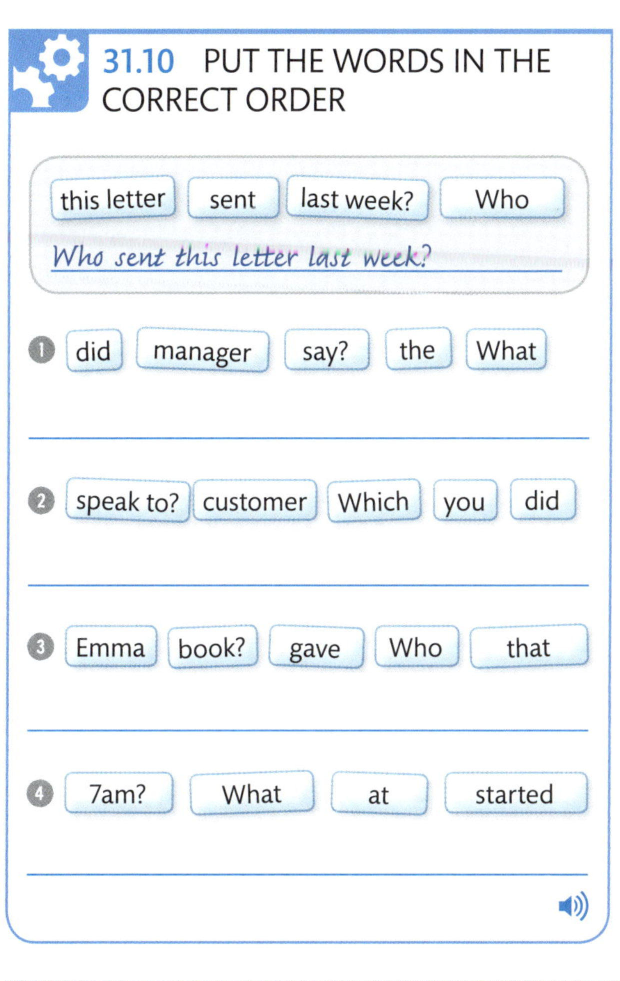

31.10 PUT THE WORDS IN THE CORRECT ORDER

this letter | sent | last week? | Who

Who sent this letter last week?

1. did | manager | say? | the | What

2. speak to? | customer | Which | you | did

3. Emma | book? | gave | Who | that

4. 7am? | What | at | started

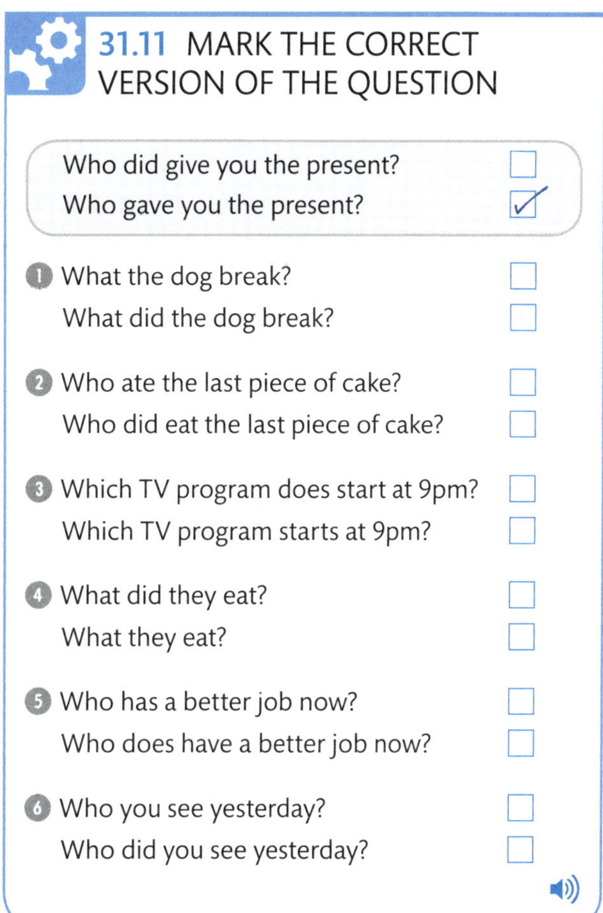

31.11 MARK THE CORRECT VERSION OF THE QUESTION

Who did give you the present? ☐
Who gave you the present? ☑

1. What the dog break? ☐
   What did the dog break? ☐
2. Who ate the last piece of cake? ☐
   Who did eat the last piece of cake? ☐
3. Which TV program does start at 9pm? ☐
   Which TV program starts at 9pm? ☐
4. What did they eat? ☐
   What they eat? ☐
5. Who has a better job now? ☐
   Who does have a better job now? ☐
6. Who you see yesterday? ☐
   Who did you see yesterday? ☐

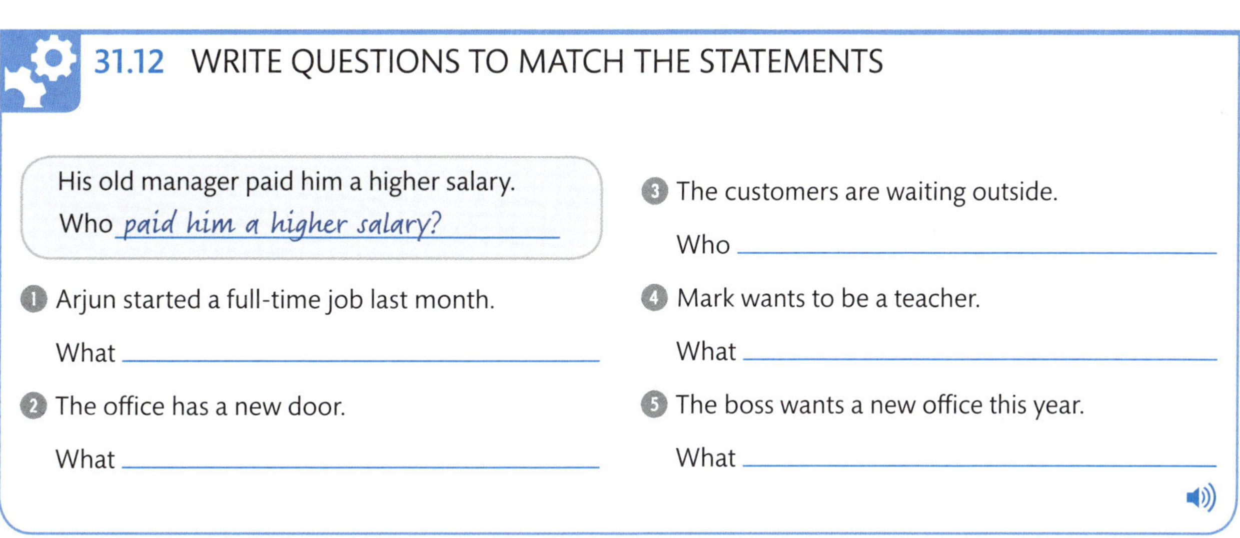

31.12 WRITE QUESTIONS TO MATCH THE STATEMENTS

His old manager paid him a higher salary.
Who *paid him a higher salary?*

1. Arjun started a full-time job last month.
   What ______
2. The office has a new door.
   What ______
3. The customers are waiting outside.
   Who ______
4. Mark wants to be a teacher.
   What ______
5. The boss wants a new office this year.
   What ______

31 CHECKLIST

Subject and object questions ☐ **Aa** Workplace words ☐ Asking different kinds of question ☐

32 Someone, anyone, everyone

Use indefinite pronouns, such as "anyone," "someone," and "everyone," to refer to a person or a group of people without explaining who they are.

New language Indefinite pronouns
Aa Vocabulary Office words
New skill Talking about people in general

32.1 KEY LANGUAGE "ANYONE / SOMEONE"

Use "someone" or "somebody" to refer to a person in a positive statement, and "anyone" or "anybody" for a question or a negative statement.

Did anyone call me this morning?

You can also use "anybody." Both words mean: any person.

Yes, someone called you at 11 o'clock.

You can also use "somebody." Both words mean: a person.

32.2 FURTHER EXAMPLES "ANYONE / SOMEONE"

Someone is working late.

Somebody left this letter on my desk.

Did anyone buy a gift for Mrs. Tan?

I didn't give anybody your name.

The statement is negative, so use "anybody/anyone."

32.3 CROSS OUT THE INCORRECT WORD IN EACH SENTENCE

I saw ~~anyone~~ / someone at reception this morning.

1. Please ask anyone / someone to phone Mr. Richards immediately.
2. Mrs. Turner didn't give anyone / someone any work to do this week.
3. Can I give anyone / someone a lift to the station tomorrow morning?
4. Mr. Phillips needs anyone / someone to go with him to the hospital.
5. I'm sorry, but there isn't anyone / someone in the office at the moment.

32.4 KEY LANGUAGE "EVERYONE / NO ONE"

Use "everyone" or "everybody" to refer to the whole group in a statement or question. "No one" or "nobody" means none of the group.

32.5 LISTEN TO THE AUDIO AND CROSS OUT THE INCORRECT WORD IN EACH SENTENCE

~~Everybody~~ / Somebody wants to have a meeting this afternoon.

1. Nobody / Somebody in room 212 needs a new computer.
2. Theodore tells everyone / someone the good news about the business.
3. Everyone / Anybody is going for lunch at the restaurant to celebrate Daniella's birthday.
4. Nobody / Somebody closed the window last night before they left the office.
5. Everyone / Anyone knows that we have a new office.

32.6 USE THE CHART TO CREATE 12 CORRECT SENTENCES AND SAY THEM OUT LOUD

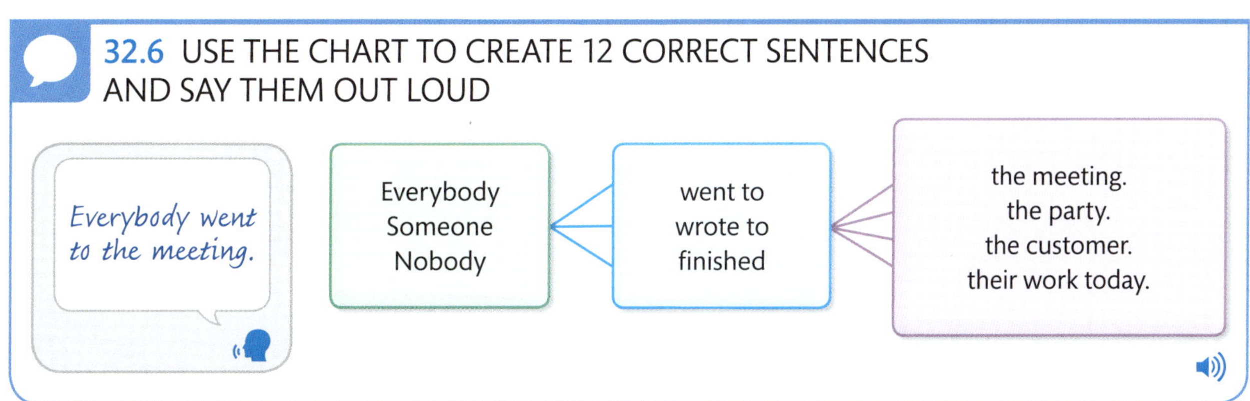

33 Making conversation

Short questions are a way of showing interest when you are talking with someone. Use them to keep the conversation going.

New language Short questions
Aa Vocabulary Question words
New skill Asking short questions

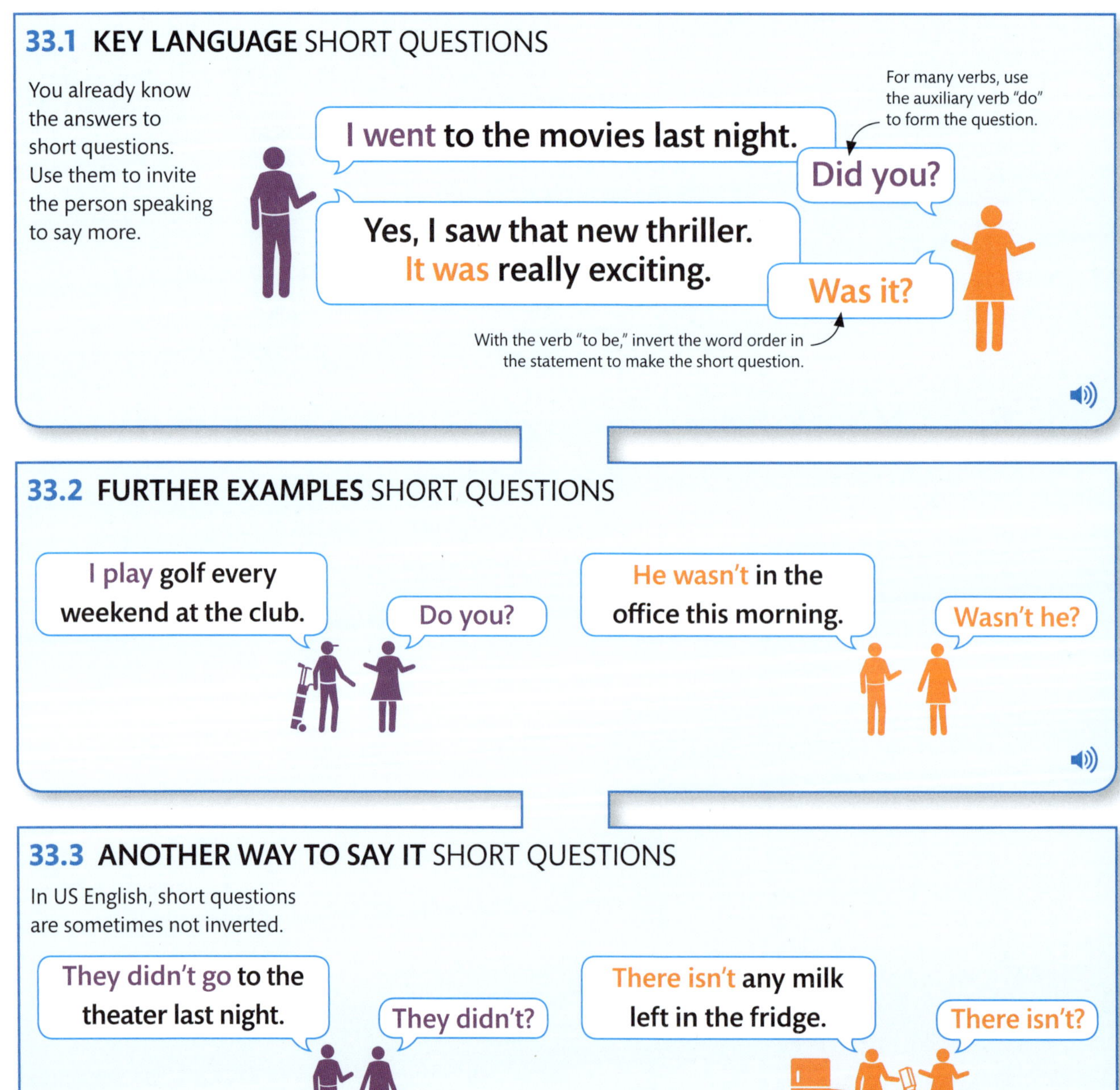

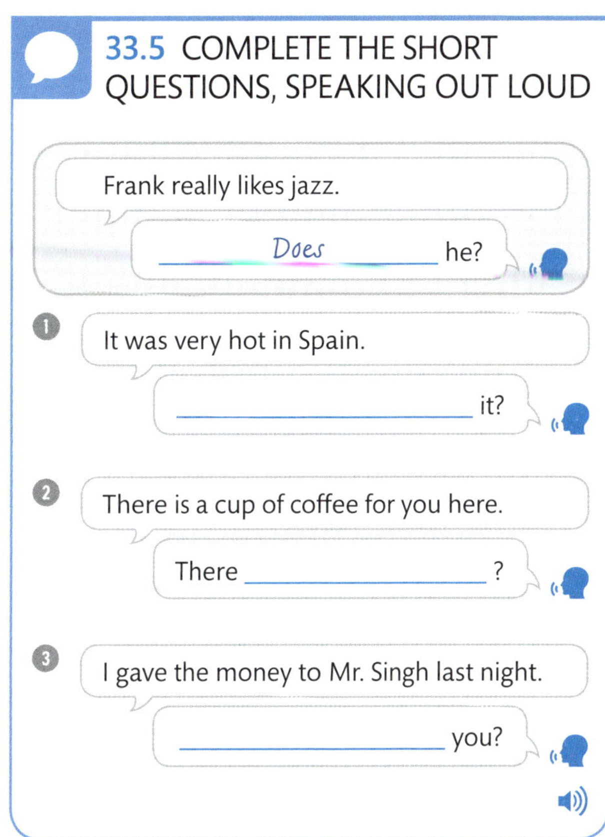

33 CHECKLIST

Short questions ☐ **Aa** Question words ☐ Asking short questions ☐

REVIEW THE ENGLISH YOU HAVE LEARNED IN UNITS 29-33

NEW LANGUAGE	SAMPLE SENTENCE	☑	UNIT
QUESTIONS IN THE PAST SIMPLE	"Did you have a good vacation?" "Yes, we went to India."	☐	29.1, 29.3, 29.7
SUBJECT AND OBJECT QUESTIONS	Who called the bank? Who did Ben call?	☐	31.1, 31.7, 31.8
"SOMEONE" AND "ANYONE"	"Did anyone call me this morning?" "Yes, someone called at 11 o'clock."	☐	32.1, 32.2
"EVERYONE" AND "NO ONE"	"Why is there no one in the office?" "Everyone is at the big meeting."	☐	32.4
SHORT QUESTIONS	"I went to the movies last night." "Did you?" "It was really exciting." "Was it?"	☐	33.1, 33.2

34 Vocabulary

34.1 GOING OUT

art gallery

book club

night club

concert hall

fun fair

circus

restaurant

bar

menu

waiter

waitress

check (US)
bill (UK)

ballet

opera

band

orchestra

musician

festival

concert

show

audience

applause

meet friends

go clubbing

go dancing

go to a party

go to a restaurant

go to the movies (US)
go to the cinema (UK)

see a play

do karaoke

go bowling

buy a ticket

35 Future arrangements

You can use the present continuous to talk about things that are happening now. You can also use it to talk about arrangements for the future.

New language Future with present continuous
Aa Vocabulary Excuses
New skill Talking about future arrangements

35.1 KEY LANGUAGE PRESENT CONTINUOUS WITH FUTURE EVENTS

Use time phrases to show whether a verb in the present continuous refers to the present or the future.

"At the moment" refers to the present.

Present continuous refers to Dave's present activity.

At the moment Dave is working, but tomorrow he is playing golf.

Time clause "tomorrow" refers to the future.

Present continuous refers to a future event that is planned.

35.2 FURTHER EXAMPLES PRESENT CONTINUOUS WITH FUTURE EVENTS

Jack's playing soccer now, then later he's seeing a movie.

Sue is studying now, but this evening she's visiting a friend.

Today, I'm playing tennis, but I'm playing golf tomorrow.

You can use the time word or phrase at the start or end of a clause.

I'm reading at the moment, but I'm going running later.

35.3 KEY LANGUAGE "ON / IN" WITH DAYS, MONTHS, AND DATES

Use the preposition "on" in front of days of the week and specific dates. Use "in" with months and years.

I'm working on Tuesday.

I'm working on May 9th.

I'm retiring in June.

I'm retiring in 2035.

35.4 FILL IN THE GAPS BY PUTTING THE VERBS IN THE PRESENT CONTINUOUS

I *am watching* (watch) TV with my friends tonight.

1. John's cousins ______ (come) to the party tomorrow.
2. I ______ (go) to the dentist tomorrow morning.
3. My family and I ______ (visit) my grandma on Saturday.
4. The managers in my office ______ (have) a meeting this afternoon.
5. A famous band ______ (play) in Central Park this weekend.
6. He ______ (study) for his test tomorrow.

35.5 LISTEN TO THE AUDIO, THEN NUMBER THE PICTURES IN THE ORDER YOU HEAR THEM

A ☐

B ☐

C 1

D ☐

E ☐

F ☐

G ☐

35.6 KEY LANGUAGE MAKING EXCUSES

Sometimes you need to say why you can't do something. To be polite, use an expression like "Sorry, I can't" before saying what your other plans are.

Would you like to go to the movies tonight?

Sorry, I can't. I'm working late.

To be polite, apologize first.

Use the present continuous to say what you are doing instead.

35.7 FURTHER EXAMPLES MAKING EXCUSES

I'd like to, but I'm going to the dentist.

That would be fun, but I'm visiting family.

I'd love to, but I'm meeting friends.

That sounds nice, but I'm playing baseball.

35.8 REWRITE THE SENTENCES, PUTTING THE WORDS IN THE CORRECT ORDER

tonight. | fun, but | theater | That | the | I'm | going to | would be

That would be fun, but I'm going to the theater tonight.

1. my | parents | I'm | Sorry, I can't. | visiting | this | evening.

2. this | like to, | but | weekend. | I'd | France | going to | I'm

3. sounds | but | I'm going | That | on Tuesday. | nice, | swimming

4. love to, | I'm | looking after | I'd | my nephew | tomorrow. | but

35.9 ANSWER EACH INVITATION OUT LOUD, USING AN EXCUSE FROM THE DIARY

September 2020

21 SATURDAY

9am – Play soccer with Eva.
Noon – Go to lunch with Aziz.
1:30–3pm – Look after Sandy's baby.
4pm – Go to yoga class.
6pm – Go to dinner with Marco and Olivia.
7:30pm – Go to the theater to see a musical.

Would you like to come swimming at 9am?
I'd love to, but *I'm playing soccer with Eva.*

1. Would you like to come to dinner tonight?
I'd like to, but ______________________

2. Would you like to go to lunch today?
Sorry, I can't. ______________________

3. Would you like to play tennis at 7:30pm?
That would be fun, but ______________________

4. Would you like to go shopping at 2pm?
That sounds nice, but ______________________

5. Would you like to go to a dance class at 4pm?
I'd like to, but ______________________

35 CHECKLIST

Future with present continuous ☐ **Aa** Excuses ☐ Talking about future arrangements ☐

36 Plans and intentions

You can use "going to" to talk about what you want to do in the future. Use it also to talk about specific plans, such as when and where you're going to do something.

New language Future tense
Aa Vocabulary Time words and phrases
New skill Talking about your plans

36.1 KEY LANGUAGE "GOING TO" FOR FUTURE PLANS

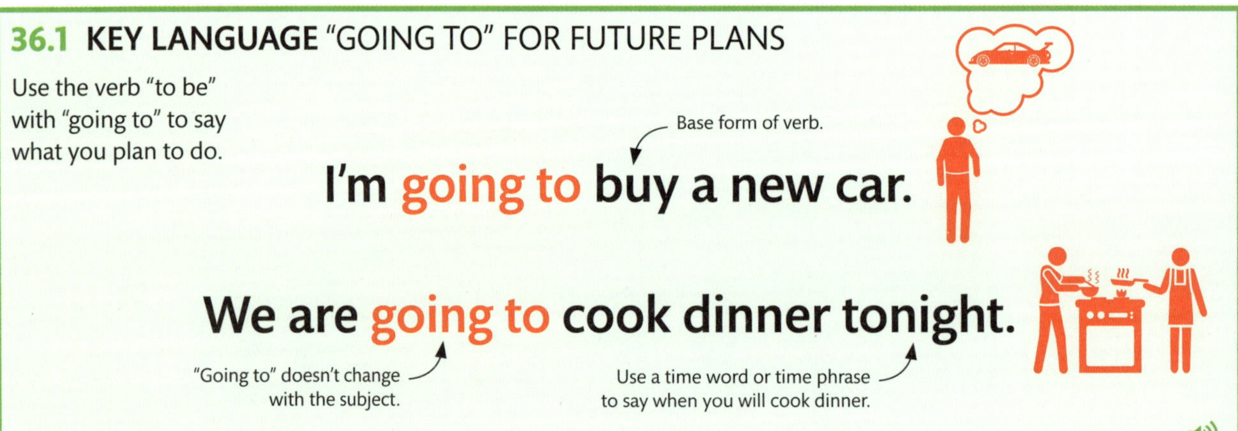

Use the verb "to be" with "going to" to say what you plan to do.

Base form of verb.

I'm going to buy a new car.

We are going to cook dinner tonight.

"Going to" doesn't change with the subject.

Use a time word or time phrase to say when you will cook dinner.

36.2 FURTHER EXAMPLES "GOING TO" FOR FUTURE PLANS

I'm going to start this book soon.

Sam's going to get fit before his next birthday.

We're going to cycle from Boston to Cape Cod next weekend.

I'm not going to eat any chocolate this month.

Add "not" after the verb "to be" to make the negative.

36.3 HOW TO FORM "GOING TO" FOR FUTURE PLANS

SUBJECT	"TO BE"	"GOING TO"	BASE FORM OF VERB	REST OF SENTENCE
He	is	going to	buy	a new car.

36.4 FILL IN THE GAPS PUTTING THE VERBS IN THE FUTURE WITH "GOING TO"

Darren and Miki *are going to watch* (watch) a movie tonight.

1. I ______________________ (not eat) sushi for dinner.
2. Debra ______________________ (get) a new job soon.
3. My friends ______________________ (cook) a meal for me next week.
4. Manuel ______________________ (learn) how to scuba dive this summer.
5. We ______________________ (travel) to Dubai in December.

36.5 READ THE ARTICLE AND ANSWER THE QUESTIONS

14 The Weekly You

WHAT ARE YOUR RESOLUTIONS?

Exercise more or stop eating chocolate? It's a question many of us ask ourselves as the year ends.

Betty from California makes one resolution every year. "I'm not going to give up smoking," she tells us, "because I did that last time. This year, I'm going to get fit!"

In the US only 8 percent of people keep to their resolutions. Many give up by the end of January.

A lot of people make resolutions, but Australian Joanna Gee makes one resolution for every day of the year. That's 365 resolutions every year.

"I love making resolutions," Joanna says. "This year I'm going to do more unusual things. On June 23 I'm going to climb a mountain, and then on September 30 I'm going to swim with sharks."

Betty has one resolution this year.
True ☑ False ☐

1. Betty is going to give up smoking this year.
   True ☐ False ☐
2. Only 8% of Americans keep to their resolutions.
   True ☐ False ☐
3. Joanna has a resolution for every day of the year.
   True ☐ False ☐
4. Joanna is going to climb a mountain on July 23.
   True ☐ False ☐
5. Joanna is going to swim with dolphins.
   True ☐ False ☐

36.6 KEY LANGUAGE "BY" WITH TIME WORDS AND PHRASES

"By" followed by a noun or time phrase means something will happen at some point before that time.

"Going to" follows the verb "to be."

I am going to paint the house by June.

NOW — JUNE

36.7 FURTHER EXAMPLES "BY" WITH TIME WORDS AND PHRASES

You are going to write to the person between now and next weekend.

I am going to write to you by next weekend.

I am going to get fit by this time next year.

You are going to get fit by the same date the following year.

36.8 READ JACK'S RESOLUTIONS, THEN WRITE ABOUT THEM USING "GOING TO"

Jack's January Resolutions

- Tidy my house by the weekend.
- Paint my bedroom by the end of this month.
- Join a gym by this time next month.
- Book a vacation by the end of March.
- Get fit by the summer.
- Buy a new car by December.

He is going to tidy his house by the weekend.

1 ____________________

2 ____________________

3 ____________________

4 ____________________

5 ____________________

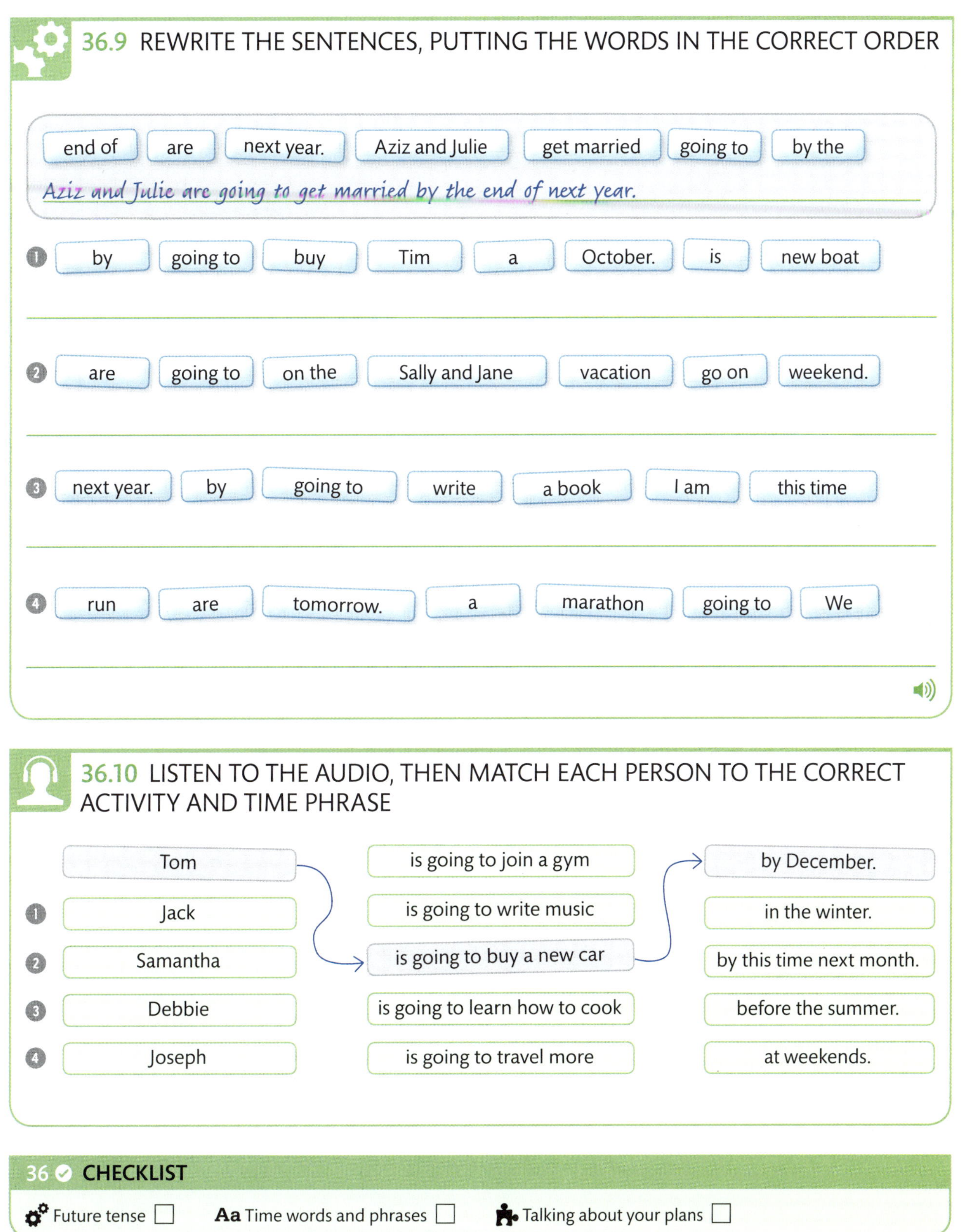

36.9 REWRITE THE SENTENCES, PUTTING THE WORDS IN THE CORRECT ORDER

end of | are | next year. | Aziz and Julie | get married | going to | by the

Aziz and Julie are going to get married by the end of next year.

1. by | going to | buy | Tim | a | October. | is | new boat

2. are | going to | on the | Sally and Jane | vacation | go on | weekend.

3. next year. | by | going to | write | a book | I am | this time

4. run | are | tomorrow. | a | marathon | going to | We

36.10 LISTEN TO THE AUDIO, THEN MATCH EACH PERSON TO THE CORRECT ACTIVITY AND TIME PHRASE

Tom	is going to join a gym	by December.
1 Jack	is going to write music	in the winter.
2 Samantha	is going to buy a new car	by this time next month.
3 Debbie	is going to learn how to cook	before the summer.
4 Joseph	is going to travel more	at weekends.

36 CHECKLIST

Future tense ☐ **Aa** Time words and phrases ☐ Talking about your plans ☐

37 What's going to happen

Use the future with "going to" to make a prediction about the future when there is evidence in the present moment to back up that prediction.

New language The future with "going to"
Vocabulary Prediction verbs
New skill Predicting future events

37.1 KEY LANGUAGE "GOING TO" FOR FUTURE EVENTS

This form of the future is formed using "to be" + "going to" + the base form of the verb.

Use "going to" to give your prediction.

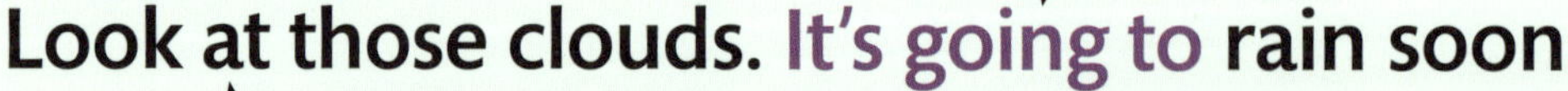

Look at those clouds. It's going to rain soon.

Evidence in the present moment means that you can make a prediction.

37.2 FURTHER EXAMPLES "GOING TO" FOR FUTURE EVENTS

Oh no! She's going to slip and fall over.

The hill is too steep. Jon is going to crash!

She studies a lot. She's going to pass her exam.

Look! The waiter is going to drop those plates.

They're going to break a window.

Joe fell asleep in the exam. He's going to fail.

He's wearing a raincoat, so he's not going to get wet.

37.3 FILL IN THE GAPS PUTTING THE VERBS IN THE FUTURE WITH "GOING TO"

Kim doesn't study very hard. She *is going to fail* (fail) her exams.

1. Watch out! You ______________________ (step into) that puddle.
2. The dog ______________________ (not eat) its food. I think it's sick.
3. Oh no! She ______________________ (fall off) the ladder.
4. John is terrible at golf! He ______________________ (not win) the tournament.
5. It's very windy! His umbrella ______________________ (blow away).
6. You're carrying too much. You ______________________ (drop) everything.

37.4 REWRITE THE SENTENCES, CORRECTING THE ERRORS

The traffic is moving very slowly. I **are** going to be late for work.
The traffic is moving very slowly. I am going to be late for work.

1. John and Jill are putting their coats on. They **is** going to leave now.

____

2. I saw the weather forecast. It **are** going to snow this afternoon.

____

3. It's my birthday, so I **is** going to get a present from my husband.

____

4. Larry and John have gone home to get their tennis rackets. They **is** going to play tennis.

____

37.5 READ THE SCHOOL REPORT, THEN FILL IN THE GAPS USING "GOING TO" OR "NOT GOING TO"

Marco is *going to* pass his history exam.

1. He is ________________ be in the next Olympics.
2. Marco is ________________ study art at college.
3. He is ________________ be the main character in a musical.
4. Marco is ________________ fail his English exam.
5. He is ________________ play soccer next weekend.

Report: Marco Di Stefano

English 33%	Marco needs to work harder at English. He is predicted not to pass this exam.
History 95%	This is Marco's best subject. He doesn't have any problems and will do well in the exam.
Music 25%	Marco doesn't like to sing and doesn't play a musical instrument.
Art 92%	Marco loves this subject and is very good at it. He has an offer from Rome Art College and wants to study art.
Gym 55%	This is not Marco's best subject, but he is a member of the soccer team. They play every weekend.

37.6 READ THE CLUES AND WRITE THE ANSWERS IN THE CORRECT PLACES ON THE GRID

1. Pick up those toys. Someone is going to *fall over* them.
2. You're going to ________________ someone if you skateboard on the sidewalk.
3. Jo left her exam too early. She's going to ________________ .
4. Ben is clever. He's going to easily ________________ his test.
5. That wall is too high. He is going to ________________ his leg if he jumps off it.

~~fall over~~ fail crash into break pass

37.7 LOOK AT THE PICTURES, THEN FILL IN THE GAPS USING THE WORDS IN THE PANEL, SPEAKING OUT LOUD

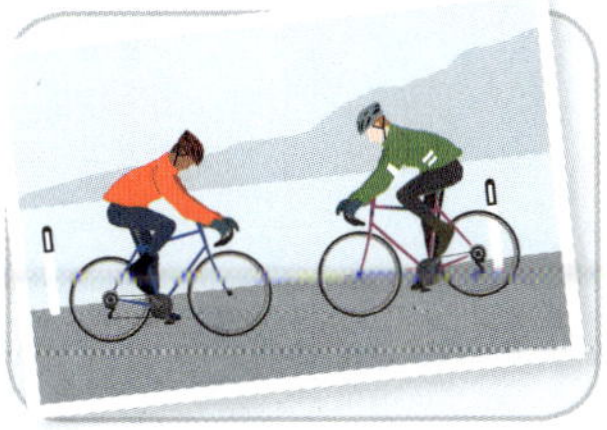

The cyclists are going to *crash into* each other.

1

The man is going to ________ the pond.

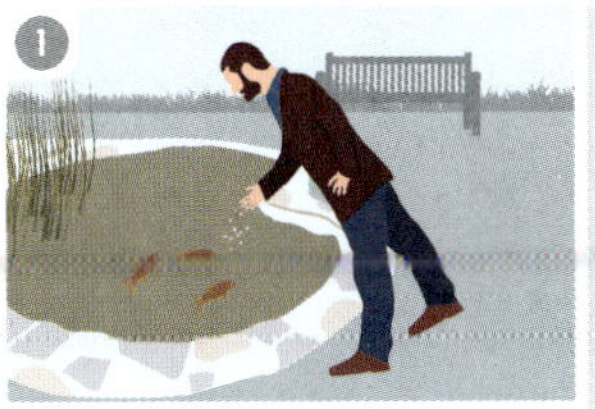

2

The snowman is going to ________.

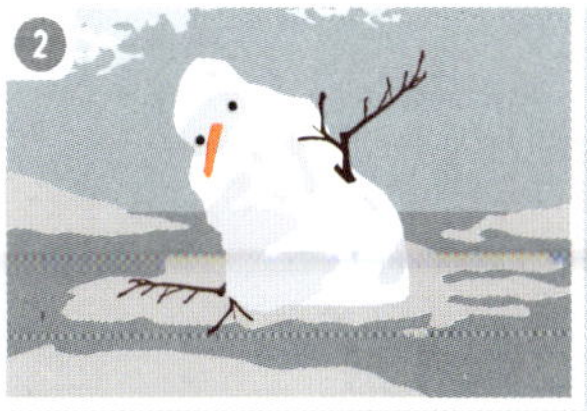

3

It is going to ________ later today.

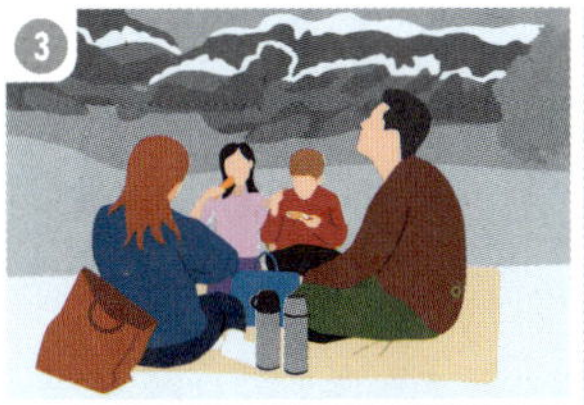

4

The boy in the blue shirt is going to ________.

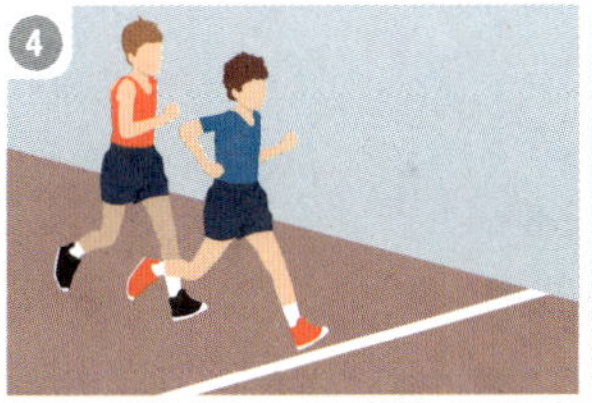

5

The store is going to ________ now.

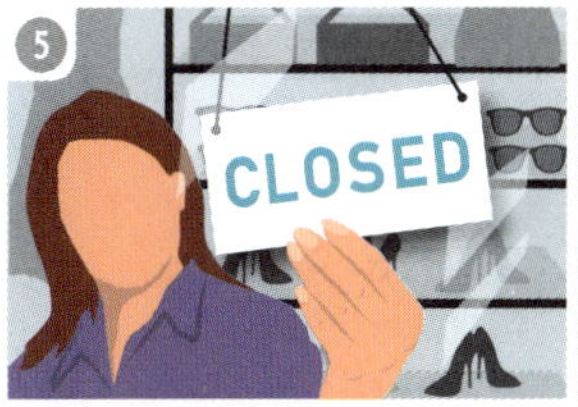

fall over | close | rain | ~~crash into~~ | fall into | win

37.8 USE THE CHART TO CREATE 12 CORRECT SENTENCES AND SAY THEM OUT LOUD

I am going to be late for work.

I Sheila We They	am is are	going to	be late for work. make a fruit cake. play soccer.

37 CHECKLIST

Future tense with "going to" ☐   **Aa** Prediction verbs ☐   Predicting future events ☐

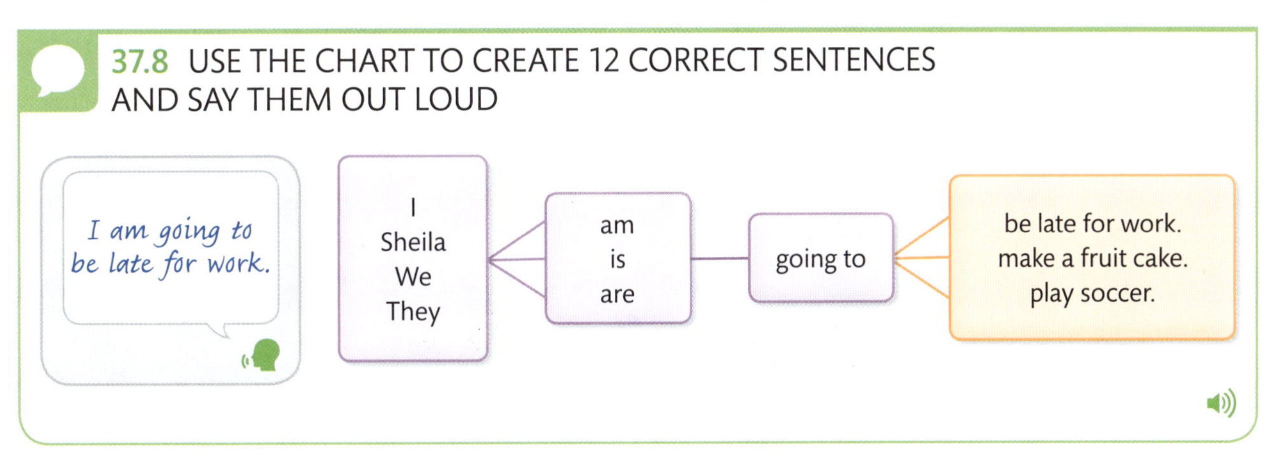

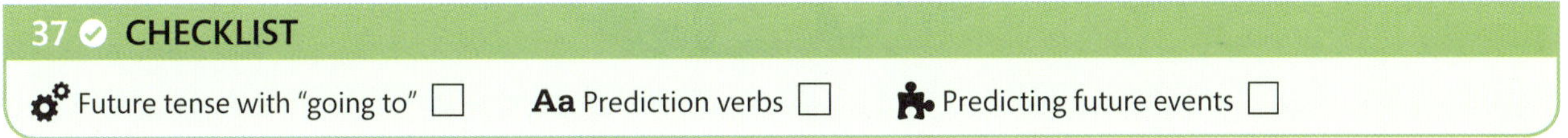

38 Vocabulary

38.1 ANIMALS

insect

fish

bird

bear

rhino

buffalo

camel

lion

tiger

elephant

monkey

giraffe

kangaroo

bull

cow

mouse

rat

eagle

snake

lizard

frog

shark

whale

dolphin

crab

octopus

turtle

crocodile

bee

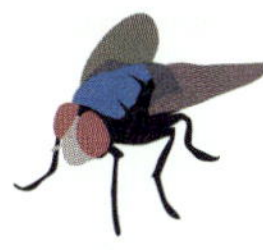
fly

spider

butterfly

39 Making predictions

You can use the verb "will" to talk about future events in English. This form of the future tense has a slightly different meaning from futures using "going to."

New language The future with "will"
Aa Vocabulary Prediction words
New skill Saying what you think will happen

39.1 KEY LANGUAGE THE FUTURE WITH "WILL"

Use "will" to say what you think will happen in the future when you don't have firm evidence for your prediction.

That new movie is great. They will love it.

You think the other people will love the movie, but you don't have firm evidence.

39.2 FURTHER EXAMPLES THE FUTURE WITH "WILL"

Jane will like the new house. It's really nice.

It'll rain every day this summer.

In negative sentences, "not" goes between "will" and the base form of the verb.

We will not get home before midnight.

You can also say "he'll not," but "won't" is more common in US English.

He won't be late for work again this year.

In spoken English, you normally use the contracted form of "will."

They'll enjoy their holiday in Venice.

She'll be really angry when she finds out.

39.3 HOW TO FORM THE FUTURE WITH "WILL"

"Will" is a modal verb, so its form doesn't change with the subject.

SUBJECT	"WILL"	BASE FORM OF VERB	REST OF SENTENCE
She	will	love	the new movie.

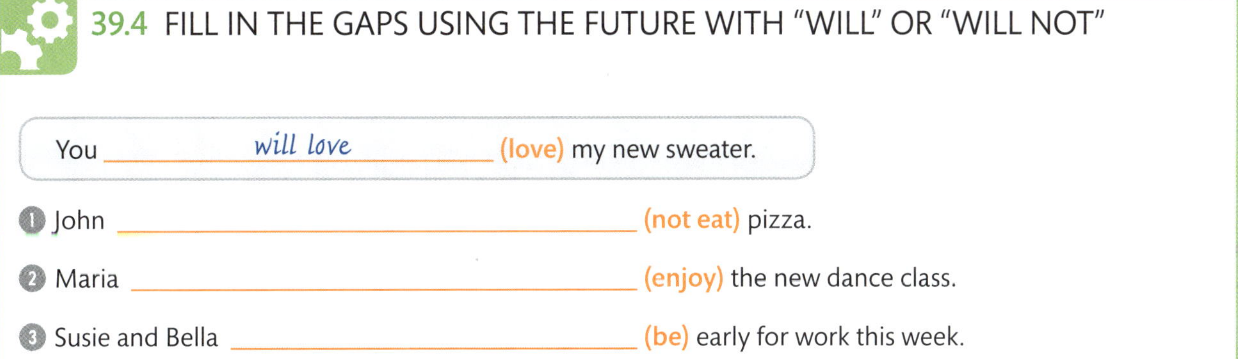

39.4 FILL IN THE GAPS USING THE FUTURE WITH "WILL" OR "WILL NOT"

You *will love* (love) my new sweater.

1. John ______ (not eat) pizza.
2. Maria ______ (enjoy) the new dance class.
3. Susie and Bella ______ (be) early for work this week.
4. The children ______ (not understand) this information.

39.5 READ THE NOTE AND REWRITE THE HIGHLIGHTED PHRASES USING PRONOUNS AND CONTRACTED "WILL" WITH FUTURE VERBS

He'll buy pizzas.

1. ______
2. ______
3. ______
4. ______
5. ______

Hi Jim,
What do you want us to bring to movie night? **Ben will buy pizzas** because he always does. **John will bring chocolates** and **Mary will make a salad**. As usual, **David won't bring anything**. **I will bring drinks**, and **Lillian and Jo will buy cheese**. Is that OK?
Sandy

39.6 LISTEN TO THE AUDIO AND MATCH THE QUESTIONS TO THE CORRECT ANSWERS

Who will clean the house? → Jenny's sister will do it.

1. Who will find the party music?
2. Who will bring the party games?
3. Who will bake a birthday cake?
4. Who will cook the food?

Jenny's brother will do it.
Jenny's mother will do it.
Jenny's sister will do it.
Sam will do it.
Marsha will do it.

39.7 KEY LANGUAGE "THINK" WITH "WILL"

If you're not sure about something, you can begin a sentence with "I think." This shows you are giving your opinion.

You're not certain.

"That" is not essential to the sentence, and it's often left out.

We think that he'll like the play.

39.8 HOW TO FORM "THINK" WITH "WILL"

SUBJECT	"THINK"	"THAT"	SUBJECT + "WILL"	VERB	REST OF SENTENCE
We	think	that	he'll	like	the play.

"That" is often left out.

39.9 FURTHER EXAMPLES SENTENCES WITH "THINK" AND "WILL"

I think that we'll have enough food for the party.

He thinks it'll be a great show tonight.

It's cold outside, but we don't think it'll snow today.

To make the sentence negative, add "do not" or "don't" before "think."

She doesn't think she'll get that job at the bank.

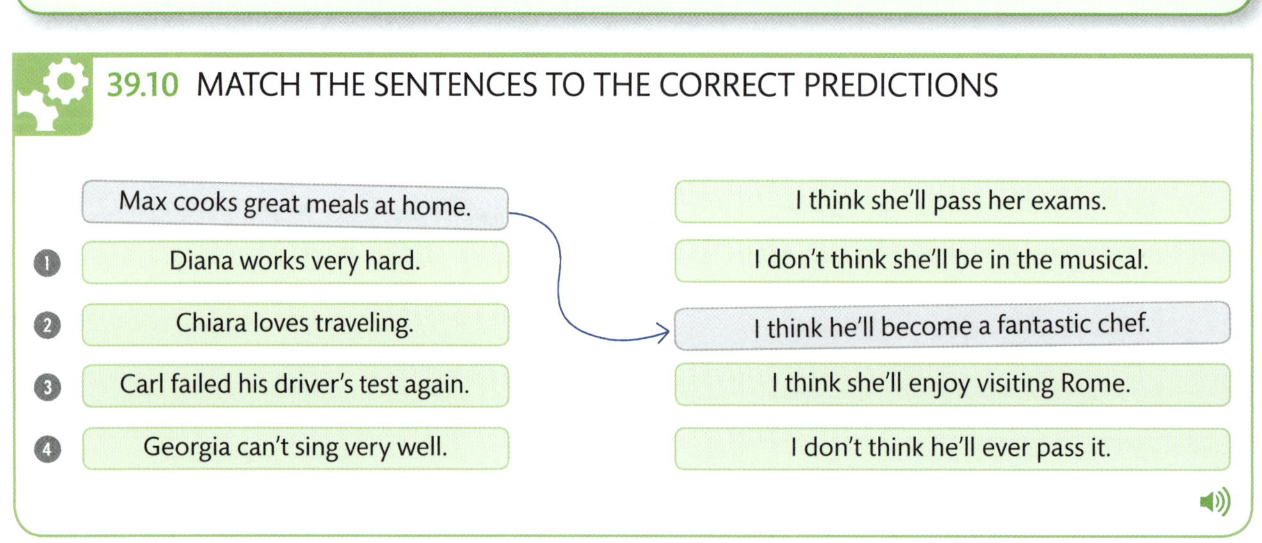

39.10 MATCH THE SENTENCES TO THE CORRECT PREDICTIONS

Max cooks great meals at home. → I think he'll become a fantastic chef.

1. Diana works very hard.
2. Chiara loves traveling.
3. Carl failed his driver's test again.
4. Georgia can't sing very well.

I think she'll pass her exams.

I don't think she'll be in the musical.

I think he'll become a fantastic chef.

I think she'll enjoy visiting Rome.

I don't think he'll ever pass it.

39.11 KEY LANGUAGE "GOING TO" AND "WILL"

Use "going to" when you have evidence for a prediction. Use "will" when a prediction is an opinion without evidence.

You are predicting this, but you don't have firm evidence.

I think Number 5 will win.

Look, Number 5 is going to win.

You are predicting this based on firm evidence.

39.12 LOOK AT THE PICTURES, THEN SAY THE SENTENCES OUT LOUD, FILLING IN THE GAPS USING THE PHRASES IN THE PANEL

Lily is going to *jump* the fence.

1 Bob is going to ______ all his dinner.

2 It is going to ______ this afternoon.

3 The dog will ______ these leftovers.

4 The car is going to ______ left.

5 John thinks he will ______ tonight.

eat | ~~jump~~ | turn | go out | eat | snow

39 CHECKLIST

The future with "will" ☐ | **Aa** Prediction words ☐ |  Saying what you think will happen ☐

40 Making quick decisions

You can use “will” to talk about the future in two ways: when you make a prediction without evidence, and when you make a quick decision to do something.

New language Quick decisions with “will”
Aa Vocabulary Decision words
New skill Talking about future actions

40.1 KEY LANGUAGE QUICK DECISIONS WITH “WILL”

If you suddenly decide to do something while you’re speaking, use “will” to say what you’re going to do.

Oh, it’s raining!
I’ll take my umbrella.

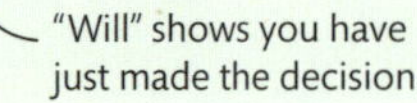

“Will” shows you have just made the decision.

40.2 FURTHER EXAMPLES QUICK DECISIONS WITH “WILL”

Contracted form of “will not.”

It’s midnight, so I won’t walk home through the park.

This apple is delicious. I’ll have another one.

40.3 KEY LANGUAGE “SO / IN THAT CASE”

Use “so” or the expression “in that case” to link a situation and the decision you make as a result of that situation.

SITUATION — DECISION

There’s no juice, so I’ll have water.

The car won’t start. In that case we’ll walk.

SITUATION — DECISION

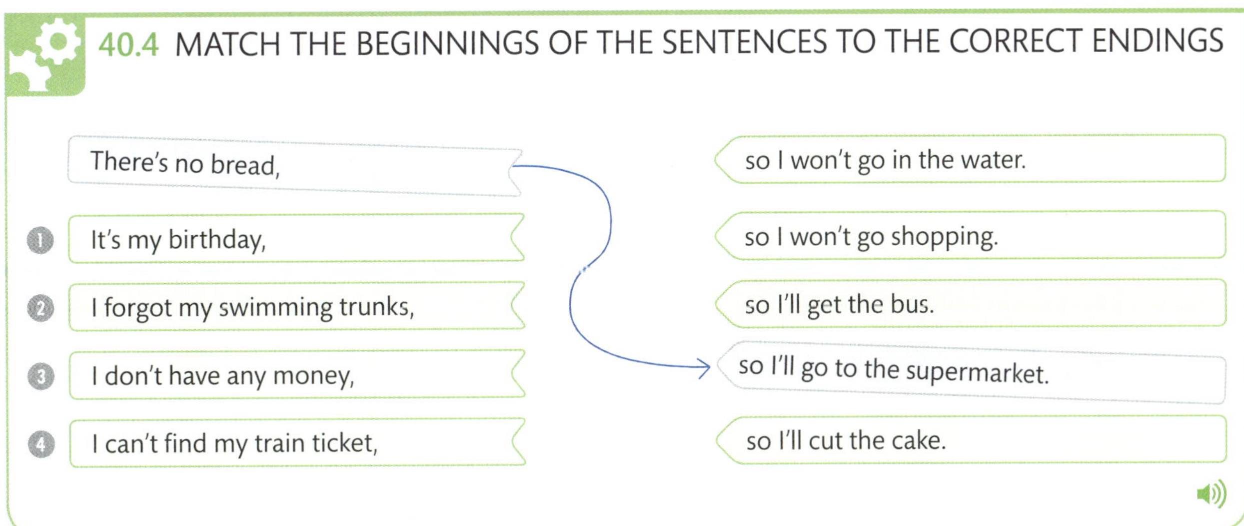

40.4 MATCH THE BEGINNINGS OF THE SENTENCES TO THE CORRECT ENDINGS

There's no bread, → so I'll go to the supermarket.

1. It's my birthday,
2. I forgot my swimming trunks,
3. I don't have any money,
4. I can't find my train ticket,

- so I won't go in the water.
- so I won't go shopping.
- so I'll get the bus.
- so I'll go to the supermarket.
- so I'll cut the cake.

40.5 LISTEN TO THE AUDIO, THEN NUMBER THE PICTURES IN THE ORDER THEY ARE DESCRIBED

A ☐

B ☐

C 1

D ☐

E ☐

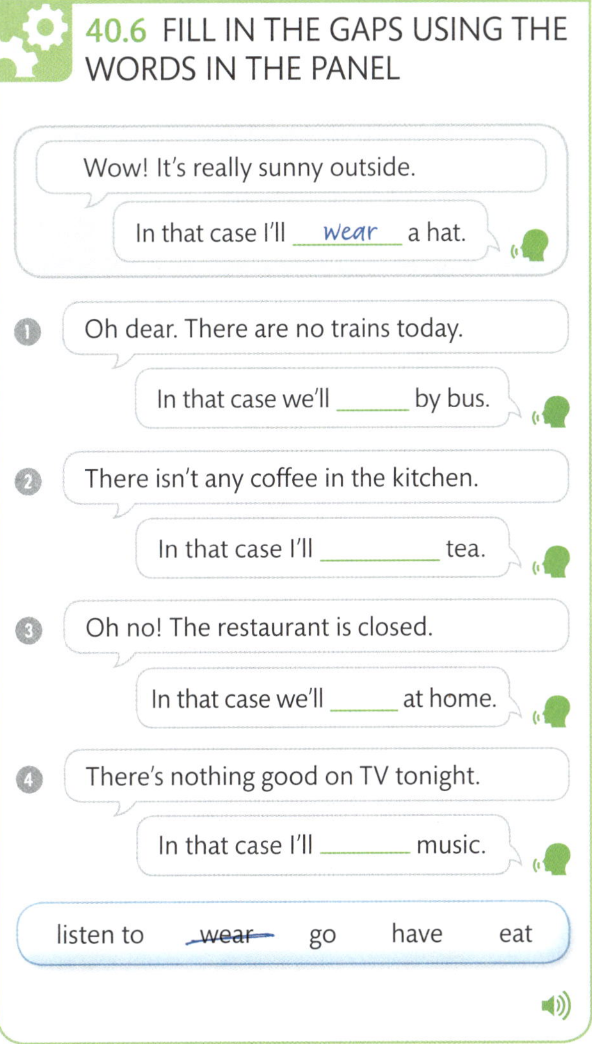

40.6 FILL IN THE GAPS USING THE WORDS IN THE PANEL

Wow! It's really sunny outside.
In that case I'll __wear__ a hat.

1. Oh dear. There are no trains today.
   In that case we'll ______ by bus.
2. There isn't any coffee in the kitchen.
   In that case I'll ______ tea.
3. Oh no! The restaurant is closed.
   In that case we'll ______ at home.
4. There's nothing good on TV tonight.
   In that case I'll ______ music.

listen to | ~~wear~~ | go | have | eat

40.7 KEY LANGUAGE "THINK" WITH "WILL"

You can use "think" with "will" to show that your decision is something you are considering.

I'm tired. I think I'll go to bed.

You are deciding now. You're not completely sure.

40.8 FURTHER EXAMPLES "THINK" WITH "WILL"

There are lots of options on the menu. I think we'll have the fish.

There are lots of bands to see, but I think I'll watch the rock band.

This movie is terrible. I think I'll leave before the end.

It's getting really hot outside. I think I'll put my shorts on.

40.9 READ THE TEXT MESSAGES AND ANSWER THE QUESTIONS

Two friends will buy her flowers.
True ☐ False ☑

1. One friend will take her to a restaurant.
True ☐ False ☐

2. One friend will have a party for her.
True ☐ False ☐

3. One friend will get her ballet tickets.
True ☐ False ☐

4. Two friends will take her shopping.
True ☐ False ☐

5. One friend will make her a birthday cake.
True ☐ False ☐

6. One friend will buy her a DVD.
True ☐ False ☐

40.10 SAY THE SENTENCES OUT LOUD, FILLING IN THE GAPS USING THE PHRASES IN THE PANEL

The TV is broken. What will you do tonight?
I think I'll *read a book*.

1 There's no juice. What do you want to drink?
I think I'll ______.

2 What time are you leaving work?
I think I'll ______.

3 Jo is busy, so who will you play tennis with?
I think I'll ______.

4 Which TV show do you want to see?
I think I'll ______.

5 Where do you want to go now?
I think I'll ______.

play with Cassie | have milk | ~~read a book~~ | leave at 6:30pm | go home | watch the news

40 CHECKLIST

Quick decisions with "will" ☐ Aa Decision words ☐ Talking about future actions ☐

REVIEW THE ENGLISH YOU HAVE LEARNED IN UNITS 35–40

NEW LANGUAGE	SAMPLE SENTENCE	☑	UNIT
FUTURE TENSE WITH PRESENT CONTINUOUS	At the moment, Dave is working, but tomorrow he is playing golf.	☐	35.1, 35.3, 35.6
"GOING TO" FOR FUTURE PLANS	I'm going to buy a new car. We are going to exercise tonight.	☐	36.1, 36.6
FUTURE TENSE WITH "GOING TO"	Look at those clouds. It's going to rain soon.	☐	37.1, 37.2
FUTURE TENSE WITH "WILL"	That new movie is great. They will love it.	☐	39.1, 39.7, 39.11
QUICK DECISIONS WITH "WILL"	Oh, it's raining! I'll take my umbrella.	☐	40.1, 40.2, 40.7

41 Future possibilities

Use "might" to show you're not sure if you'll do something. It's a possibility and you don't want to say that you "will" or you "won't."

New language Using "might"
Aa Vocabulary Activities, food, and pastimes
New skill Talking about future possibilities

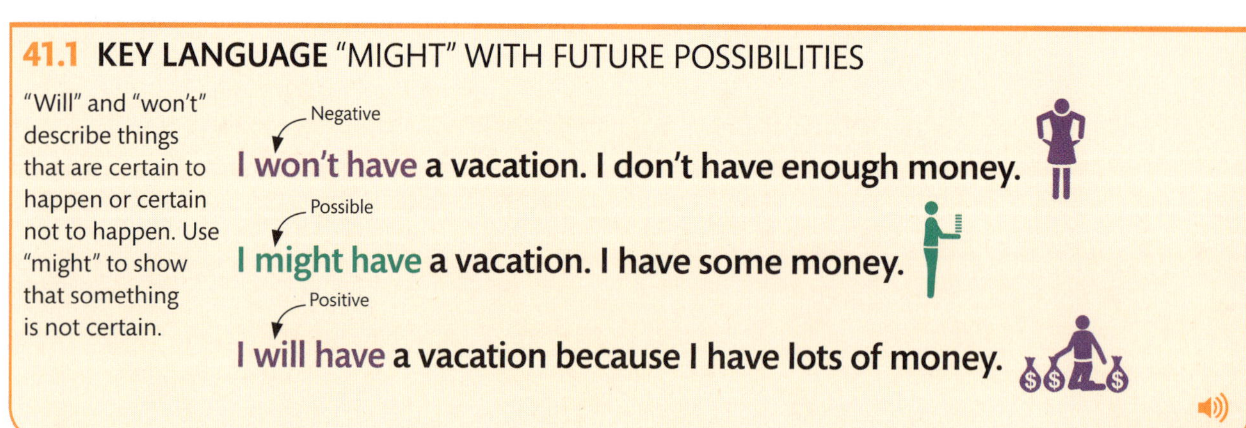

41.1 KEY LANGUAGE "MIGHT" WITH FUTURE POSSIBILITIES

"Will" and "won't" describe things that are certain to happen or certain not to happen. Use "might" to show that something is not certain.

Negative
I won't have a vacation. I don't have enough money.

Possible
I might have a vacation. I have some money.

Positive
I will have a vacation because I have lots of money.

41.2 FURTHER EXAMPLES "MIGHT" WITH FUTURE POSSIBILITIES

To form the negative, add "not" between "might" and the verb. In UK English, it can be shortened to "mightn't."

He might not go to Rome this year. He doesn't know yet.

I might speak English at the party tonight as there are British people coming.

TIP
"Might" isn't normally used in questions.

41.3 HOW TO FORM "MIGHT" WITH FUTURE POSSIBILITIES

SUBJECT	"MIGHT"	MAIN VERB	REST OF SENTENCE
I / You He / She / It We / They	might might not mightn't	have	a vacation.

As with all modal verbs, "might" doesn't change with the subject.

Use the base form of the main verb.

41.4 REWRITE THE SENTENCES, PUTTING THE WORDS IN THE CORRECT ORDER

She | to | might | party. | my | come

She might come to my party.

1. dad | My | me | give | some money. | might

2. might | Helen | test. | driving | pass | her

3. bar. | might | I | not | a chocolate | eat

4. They | not | have | party. | a | might

41.5 REWRITE THE HIGHLIGHTED PHRASES, CORRECTING THE ERRORS

Hi Bill,

I'm excited about our hiking trip on Saturday. **It might rains** in the afternoon so **we wills go** in the morning. **I'll brings** some water, but **I willn't bring** any food. **We mights wanting** to stop at one of the pubs on our walk. What do you think?

See you this weekend,

Matt

It might rain

1.

2.

3.

4.

41.6 FILL IN THE GAPS USING "WON'T," "MIGHT," AND "WILL"

	NEGATIVE	POSSIBLE	POSITIVE
	I **won't** buy a computer.	*I might buy a computer.*	*I will buy a computer.*
1			They **will** make dinner.
2		He **might** be late again.	
3	You **won't** remember that.		
4		She **might** become a teacher.	
5			We **will** win the game!
6	The dog **won't** eat this food.		

41.7 KEY LANGUAGE "MIGHT" WITH UNCERTAINTY

You can use other phrases along with "might" to emphasize that you are uncertain about something.

I might go to town. I'm not sure.

I don't know. I might have more pizza.

Aa 41.8 MATCH THE QUESTIONS TO THE ANSWERS

When are you going to clean your room? → I might do it this afternoon. I'm not sure.

1. Where will you live next year?
2. What will you do before you start college?
3. How much money are you taking on vacation?

- I don't know. I might live in Boston.
- I might get a summer job. I'm not sure.
- I might do it this afternoon. I'm not sure.
- I'm not sure. I might take about $300.

41.9 LISTEN TO THE AUDIO AND ANSWER THE QUESTIONS

Will John go to work today?
- **Yes, he will.** ☐
- **He might.** ☑
- **No, he won't.** ☐

1. Is Mel going to the party this evening?
   - **Yes, she is.** ☐
   - **She might.** ☐
   - **No, she isn't.** ☐

2. Are Donna and Elise going swimming today?
   - **Yes, they are.** ☐
   - **They might.** ☐
   - **No, they're not.** ☐

3. Will Elliot be late for the concert?
   - **Yes, he will.** ☐
   - **He might.** ☐
   - **No, he won't.** ☐

4. Will Elsa study English?
   - **Yes, she will.** ☐
   - **She might.** ☐
   - **No, she won't.** ☐

5. Will Delilah travel by bus today?
   - **Yes, she will.** ☐
   - **She might.** ☐
   - **No, she won't.** ☐

41.10 SAY THE SENTENCES OUT LOUD USING "WILL," "MIGHT," AND "WON'T"

	POSITIVE	POSSIBLE	NEGATIVE
ABAN	go on vacation this year	1 learn French	2 run a marathon
NADIYA	3 become a doctor	4 write a book	5 do a bungee jump
JACK	6 get a dog	7 buy a motorcycle	8 move house

Aban will go on vacation this year.

1

2

3

4

5

6

7

8

41 CHECKLIST

Using "might" ☐ **Aa** Activities, food, and pastimes ☐ Talking about future possibilities ☐

42 Giving advice

If someone has a problem, one of the ways that you can give advice is by using the modal verb "should."

New language "Should"
Aa Vocabulary Advice
New skill Giving advice

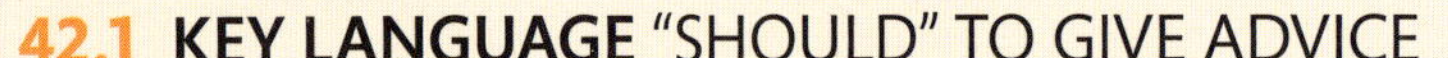

42.1 KEY LANGUAGE "SHOULD" TO GIVE ADVICE

"Should" shows that you think this is the best thing to do.

It's very sunny. You should wear a hat.

"Should" comes before the advice.

42.2 FURTHER EXAMPLES "SHOULD" TO GIVE ADVICE

It might rain. You should take your umbrella.

For a negative, add "not" between "should" and the main verb.

There's ice on the roads. You should not drive tonight.

"Should not" can be shortened to "shouldn't."

You're sick. You shouldn't go to work today.

42.3 HOW TO FORM "SHOULD" TO GIVE ADVICE

SUBJECT	"SHOULD"	MAIN VERB	REST OF SENTENCE
You	should	wear	a hat.

"Should" is a modal verb, so it stays the same no matter what the subject is.

"Should" is followed by the base form of the verb.

42.4 REWRITE THE SENTENCES, CORRECTING THE ERRORS

Kim should arrives on time.
Kim should arrive on time.

1. You shouldn't opens this door.
______

2. She shoulds to play the guitar every day.
______

3. He shouldn't wears that tie with that shirt.
______

4. You should to take a tablet twice a day.
______

5. They shouldn't to rides their bikes here.
______

42.5 LOOK AT THE PICTURES AND CROSS OUT THE INCORRECT WORDS IN THE SENTENCES TO GIVE GOOD ADVICE

Kim ~~should~~ / should not try to get on the train.

1. We should / shouldn't swim at this beach.

2. People should / should not be quiet in the library.

3. Shoppers should / shouldn't email.

4. They should / should not walk on the ice.

5. You should / shouldn't drive too fast.

42.6 MATCH THE PROBLEMS TO THE ADVICE

My plants are dying. → You should water them.

1. I've got too many clothes.
2. I eat too much junk food.
3. I don't know my neighbors.
4. I feel tired all the time.
5. I need more exercise.
6. I'm so lonely.
7. I've nothing to wear tonight.

- You should sell some of them.
- You should get more sleep.
- You should eat more fruit.
- You should water them.
- You should join a gym.
- You should have a block party.
- You should go shopping.
- You should get a dog.

42.7 LISTEN TO THE AUDIO AND MARK THE CORRECT PIECE OF ADVICE FOR EACH PROBLEM

To get to work tomorrow, James should...
leave early ☐
take the bus ☐
walk. ☑

1. On the trip, people should...
bring $10 ☐
complete a form ☐
be on time. ☐

2. Maya says Matt should first...
clean up ☐
finish his work ☐
eat dinner. ☐

3. Sheila's busy at work. Martin says she should...
go to bed later ☐
work on the weekend ☐
get up earlier. ☐

4. Atif's sister thinks he should...
buy a new computer ☐
use a friend's computer ☐
write emails on his phone. ☐

5. In the exam, students should...
be quiet ☐
read all the information ☐
speak clearly. ☐

42.8 SAY THE SENTENCES OUT LOUD, FILLING IN THE GAPS USING "SHOULD" OR "SHOULDN'T"

He *shouldn't* go climbing in the rain.

3 You ______ eat anything in a laboratory.

1 People ______ visit the library more often.

4 You ______ go through that blue door.

2 People ______ have a shower before swimming.

5 Students ______ speak during their exams.

42 ✓ CHECKLIST

"Should" ☐ Aa Advice ☐ Giving advice ☐

43 Making suggestions

You can use the modal verb "could" to offer suggestions. "Could" is not as strong as "should." It communicates gentle advice.

New language "Could" for suggestions
Aa Vocabulary Advice
New skill Making suggestions

43.1 KEY LANGUAGE "COULD" FOR SUGGESTIONS

"Could" is often used to suggest a solution to a problem. It introduces possibilities but not preferences.

I hate my car!

Well, you could get a new one!

"Could" means that the action is a possibility; a choice that might solve the problem.

43.2 FURTHER EXAMPLES "COULD" FOR SUGGESTIONS

You could study science in college.

We could learn English in Canada next year.

They could buy a bigger house with a yard.

You could get a job at that new restaurant in town.

43.3 HOW TO FORM "COULD" FOR SUGGESTIONS

SUBJECT	"COULD"	VERB	REST OF SENTENCE
You	could	get	a new car.

"Could" is a modal verb, so it doesn't change with the subject.

The main verb goes in its base form.

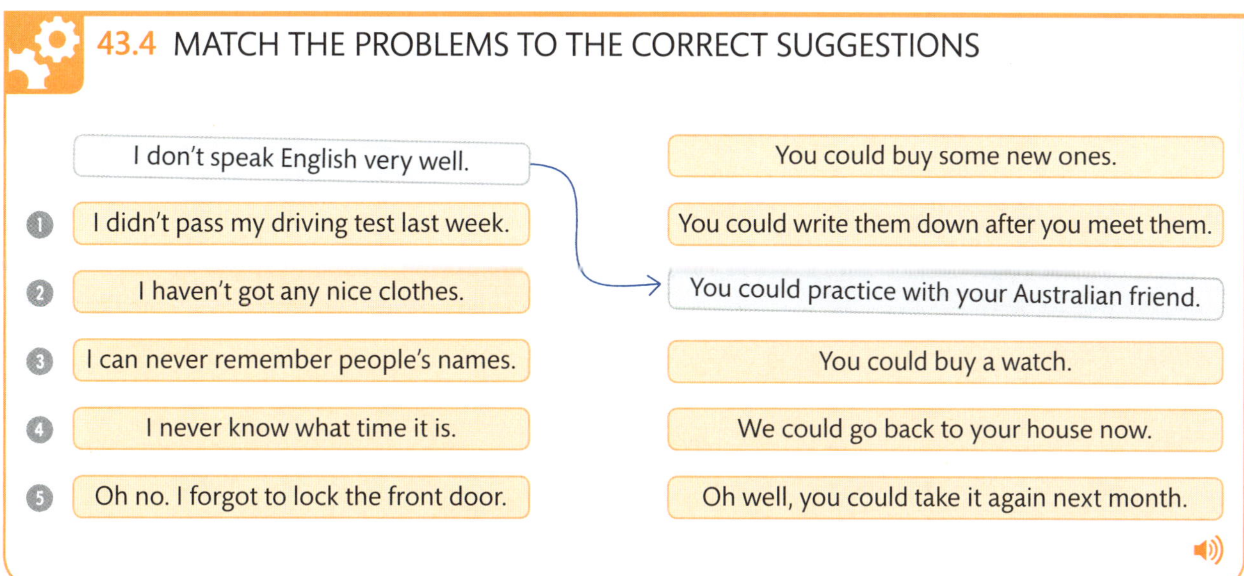

43.4 MATCH THE PROBLEMS TO THE CORRECT SUGGESTIONS

I don't speak English very well. → You could practice with your Australian friend.

1. I didn't pass my driving test last week.
2. I haven't got any nice clothes.
3. I can never remember people's names.
4. I never know what time it is.
5. Oh no. I forgot to lock the front door.

- You could buy some new ones.
- You could write them down after you meet them.
- You could practice with your Australian friend.
- You could buy a watch.
- We could go back to your house now.
- Oh well, you could take it again next month.

43.5 CHOOSE THE CORRECT SUGGESTIONS FROM THE PANEL, THEN SAY THE SENTENCES OUT LOUD

I play the piano, but I'm not very good.
You could *play every day*.

1. I haven't got enough money for a vacation.
   You could ______________.
2. I'm going out, but nobody can look after Fido.
   You could ______________.
3. I want to have a picnic, but it's raining.
   You could ______________.
4. I'd like to rent a house, but it's too expensive.
   You could ______________.
5. How can I write a book by December?
   You could ______________.

share with a friend | save $10 a week | ~~play every day~~

take him with you | eat it inside | write 500 words every day

43.6 KEY LANGUAGE USING "COULD" AND "OR" FOR SUGGESTIONS

When people give suggestions using "could," they often give more than one option to choose from.

Our friends are coming over for dinner, but the oven's broken.

We could make a salad or we could order a pizza.

Use "or" to give an alternative suggestion.

43.7 FURTHER EXAMPLES USING "COULD" AND "OR" FOR SUGGESTIONS

I can't drive, but I want to travel along the coast.

You could take a bus or travel in a friend's car.

You don't have to repeat the modal verb "could" after "or."

What should I wear to Jan's wedding?

You could wear your new dress or a skirt.

If the main verb is the same for both suggestions, you don't repeat it after "or."

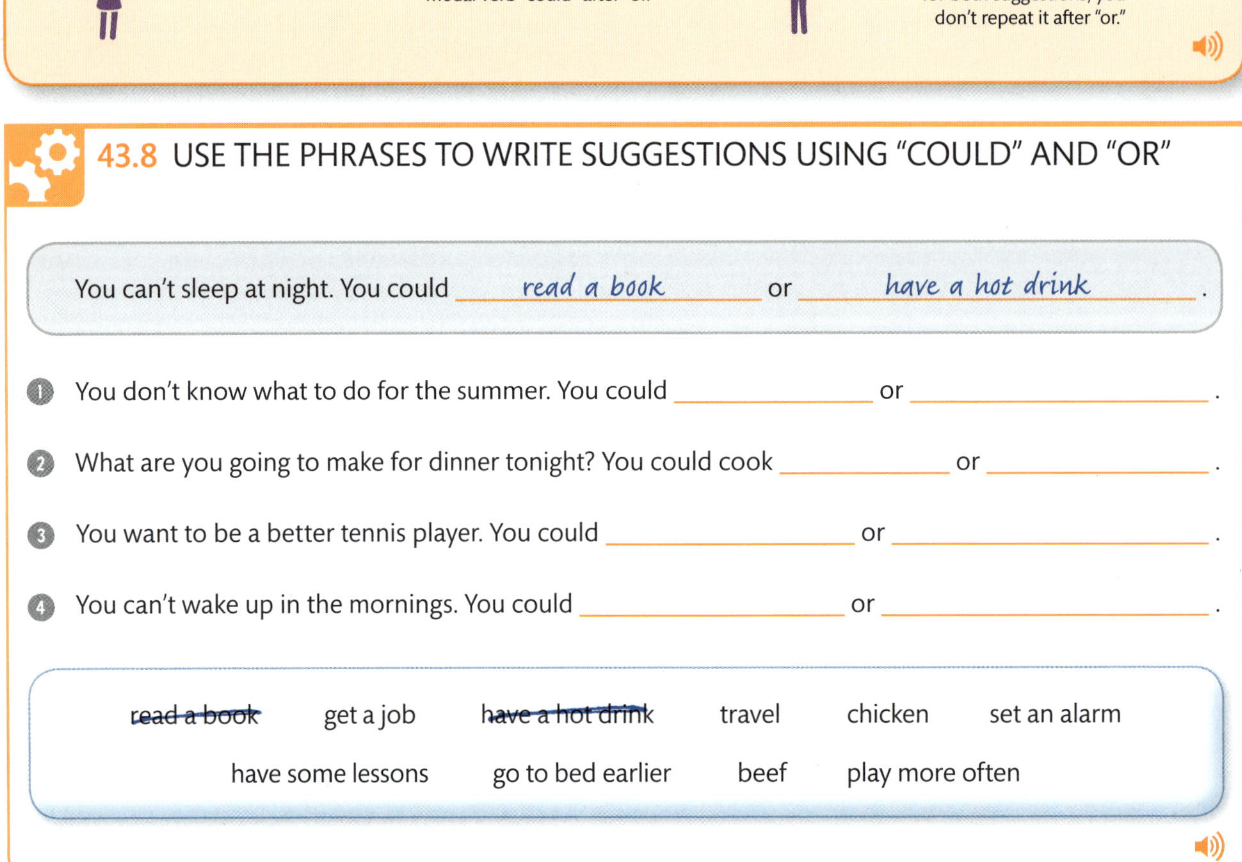

43.8 USE THE PHRASES TO WRITE SUGGESTIONS USING "COULD" AND "OR"

You can't sleep at night. You could *read a book* or *have a hot drink*.

1. You don't know what to do for the summer. You could ______ or ______.
2. What are you going to make for dinner tonight? You could cook ______ or ______.
3. You want to be a better tennis player. You could ______ or ______.
4. You can't wake up in the mornings. You could ______ or ______.

~~read a book~~ get a job ~~have a hot drink~~ travel chicken set an alarm have some lessons go to bed earlier beef play more often

43.9 LISTEN TO THE AUDIO AND MARK THE TWO SUGGESTIONS GIVEN TO SOLVE EACH PROBLEM

Anya can't understand her English teacher very well. She could...
ask him to speak slowly. ☐ **ask for notes on the lesson.** ☑ **record the lesson.** ☑

1. Jim hasn't got time to do the chores at home. He could...
   get his children to help. ☐ **get a cleaner.** ☐ **not worry about it.** ☐

2. Mandy needs to get a new job. She could...
   look in the newspaper. ☐ **ask friends.** ☐ **look at a website.** ☐

3. Some students aren't very good at writing in English. They could...
   read more English books. ☐ **write in English every day.** ☐ **email a new friend in English.** ☐

4. It's hard to find time to exercise. People could...
   take the stairs. ☐ **take the elevator.** ☐ **walk to the store.** ☐

43 CHECKLIST

"Could" for suggestions ☐ **Aa** Advice ☐ Making suggestions ☐

REVIEW THE ENGLISH YOU HAVE LEARNED IN UNITS 41–43

NEW LANGUAGE	SAMPLE SENTENCE	☑	UNIT
USING "MIGHT" WITH FUTURE POSSIBILITIES	I might have a vacation.	☐	41.1
USING "MIGHT" WITH UNCERTAINTY	I might go to town. I'm not sure. I don't know. I might have some pizza.	☐	41.7
USING "SHOULD" TO GIVE ADVICE	It's very sunny. You should wear a hat.	☐	42.1
USING "SHOULDN'T" TO GIVE ADVICE	You're sick. You shouldn't go to work today.	☐	42.2
USING "COULD" FOR SUGGESTIONS	You could get a new car.	☐	43.1
USING "OR" FOR SUGGESTIONS	We could make a salad or order a pizza.	☐	43.6

44 Vocabulary

44.1 HOUSEHOLD CHORES

clean the windows

sweep the floor

scrub the floor

mop the floor

vacuum the carpet

dust

take out the garbage (US)
take out the rubbish (UK)

tidy

go to the store (US)
go to the shops (UK)

buy groceries

chop vegetables

cook dinner

set the table

clear the table

do the dishes (US)
do the washing up (UK)

dry the dishes

load the dishwasher

do the laundry (US)
do the washing (UK)

hang clothes (US)
hang out the washing (UK)

do the ironing

fold clothes

make the bed

change the sheets

do the gardening

mow the lawn

water the plants

wash the car

paint a room

hang a picture

walk the dog

feed the pets

mend the fence

45 Around the house

You can use the present perfect form of a verb to talk about something that has happened in the past and has consequences in the present.

New language The present perfect
Vocabulary Household chores
New skill Talking about the recent past

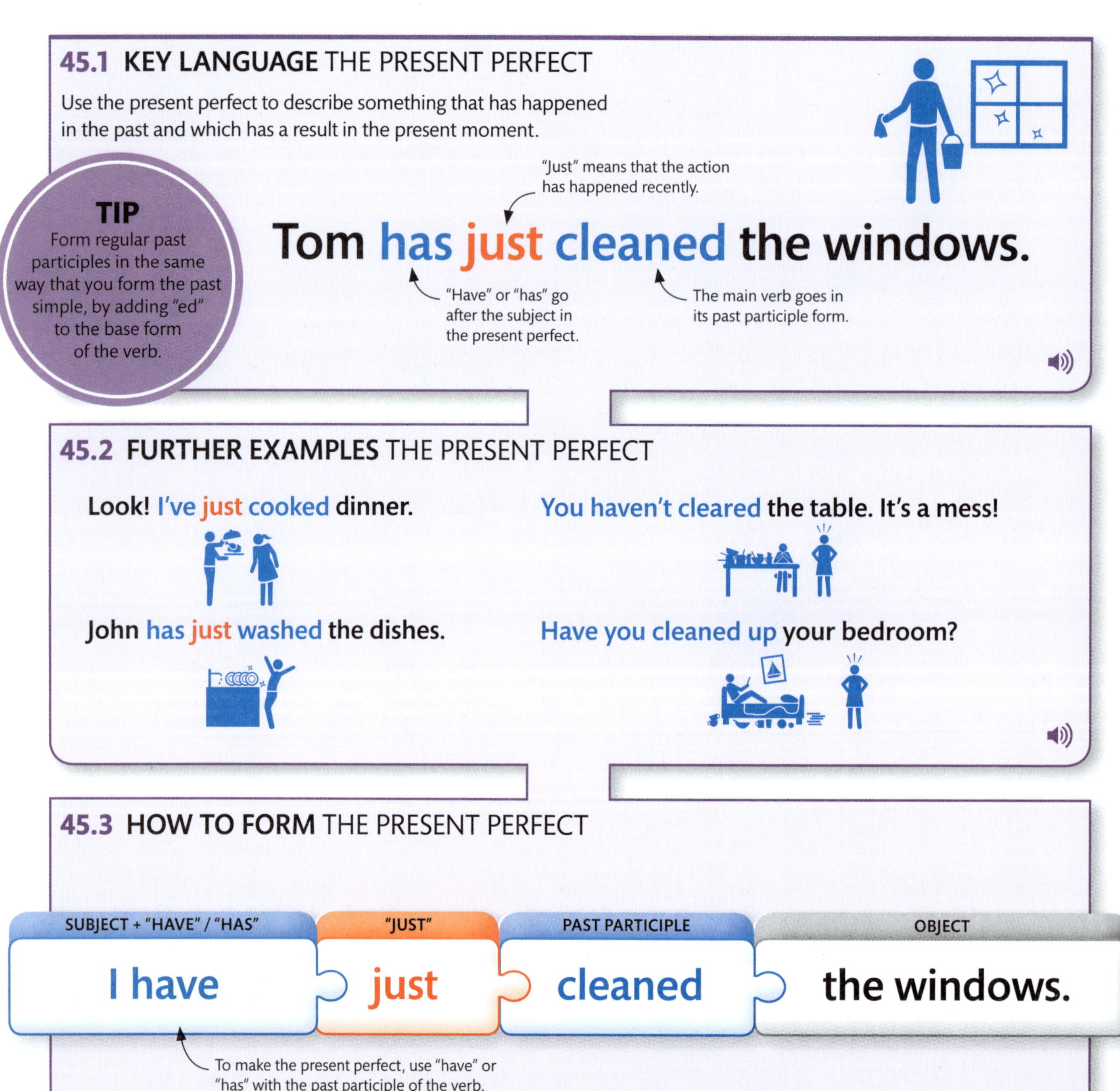

45.4 KEY LANGUAGE FORMING IRREGULAR PAST PARTICIPLES

There are no rules for forming irregular past participles, but some irregular past participles have similar endings.

I am → I've been

you eat → you've eaten

they see → they've seen

we do → we've done

I put → I've put

you leave → you've left

they keep → they've kept

we hear → we've heard

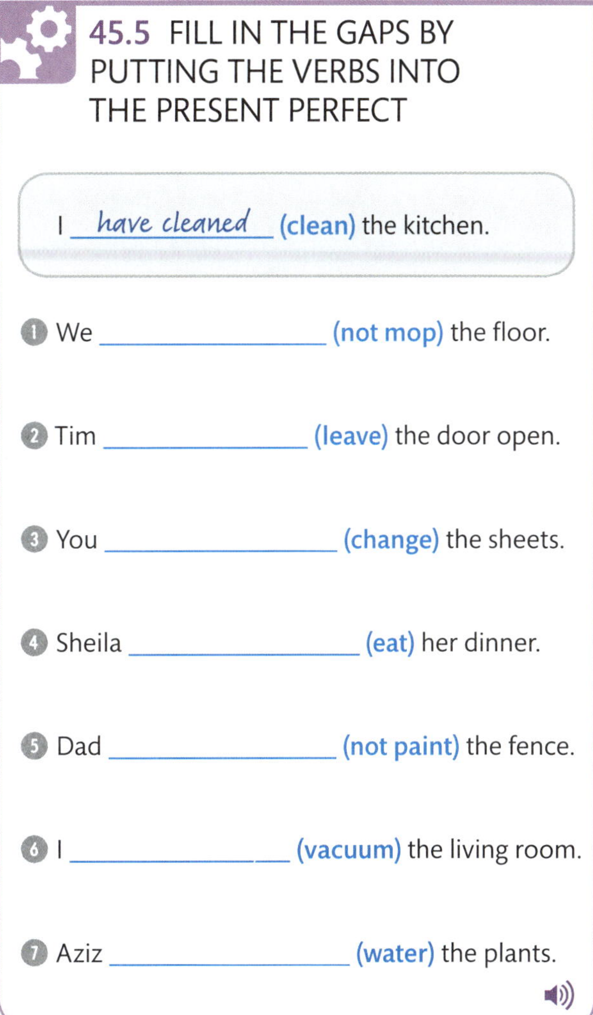

45.5 FILL IN THE GAPS BY PUTTING THE VERBS INTO THE PRESENT PERFECT

I *have cleaned* (clean) the kitchen.

1. We ______________ (not mop) the floor.
2. Tim ______________ (leave) the door open.
3. You ______________ (change) the sheets.
4. Sheila ______________ (eat) her dinner.
5. Dad ______________ (not paint) the fence.
6. I ______________ (vacuum) the living room.
7. Aziz ______________ (water) the plants.

45.6 FILL IN THE GAPS TO WRITE EACH SENTENCE THREE DIFFERENT WAYS

He has washed his clothes.	He hasn't washed his clothes.	*Has he washed his clothes?*
1. They have cleaned the car.	______________	______________
2. ______________	______________	Have you mopped the floor?
3. ______________	I haven't taken the garbage out.	______________
4. You have painted the house.	______________	______________
5. ______________	______________	Has John cooked dinner?

45.7 FIND EIGHT REGULAR AND IRREGULAR PAST PARTICIPLES AND WRITE THEM NEXT TO THE CORRECT VERBS

C	L	E	A	T	E	N	N	E	N	H	L
L	V	P	C	H	A	D	U	W	Z	S	N
O	Q	D	O	N	E	P	Y	T	I	E	S
S	B	Z	K	Y	A	X	G	O	N	E	F
E	H	Q	L	X	G	J	A	T	D	N	K
D	E	B	E	E	N	S	E	H	A	K	E
K	A	G	Y	H	T	F	L	Z	J	K	J
E	D	W	T	N	G	K	E	P	T	Z	L

1. go = *gone*
2. have = ________
3. close = ________
4. eat = ________
5. am = ________
6. keep = ________
7. see = ________
8. do = ________

45.8 REWRITE THE SENTENCES, CORRECTING THE ERRORS

Ellen **have** left her keys at home.
Ellen has left her keys at home.

1. We have **cook** dinner for you.
2. Ben and Ellen **has** gone to the supermarket.
3. The children have **see** the movie.
4. Sheila has **clean** the bathroom.
5. The dog **haven't** eaten all its food.
6. They've **be** to the mall to buy you a present.

45.9 LISTEN TO THE AUDIO AND ANSWER THE QUESTIONS

Adam and Becky are getting ready to have a party.

Has Adam cleaned the bathroom?
Yes, he has. ☑ **No, he hasn't.** ☐

1. Have they bought enough drinks?
   Yes, they have. ☐ **No, they haven't.** ☐
2. Has Becky put the chicken in the oven?
   Yes, she has. ☐ **No, she hasn't.** ☐
3. Has Adam talked to his sister?
   Yes, he has. ☐ **No, he hasn't.** ☐
4. Has Adam's sister sent him a present?
   Yes, she has. ☐ **No, she hasn't.** ☐
5. Has Adam moved his car?
   Yes, he has. ☐ **No, he hasn't.** ☐

45.10 REWRITE THESE VERBS AS PAST PARTICIPLES

tidy = *tidied*

1. clean = ______
2. wash = ______
3. cook = ______
4. change = ______
5. mop = ______
6. walk = ______
7. clear = ______
8. brush = ______

45.11 SAY THE SENTENCES OUT LOUD, FILLING IN THE GAPS BY PUTTING THE VERBS FROM THE PANEL IN THE PRESENT PERFECT

Mark has *washed* the dishes.

1. The children have ______ the car.
2. The cat has ______ all its food.
3. Jemma has ______ the window.
4. Jill has ______ her desk.
5. Paul has ______ his wallet on top of the car.

clean ~~wash~~ tidy break leave eat

45 CHECKLIST

The present perfect ☐ **Aa** Household chores ☐ Talking about the recent past ☐

46 Events in your life

Both the present perfect and the past simple can be used to talk about things that happened in the past, but you use them differently.

New language The present perfect
Aa Vocabulary Adventure sports
New skill Talking about past events

46.1 KEY LANGUAGE THE PRESENT PERFECT AND THE PAST SIMPLE

Use the past simple to talk about something that happened at a definite time. Use the present perfect when you don't specify a particular time.

Have you ever been to France?

Yes, I **visited** Paris in 2010.

You give a specific date, 2010, so use the past simple.

2010 NOW

You don't give a specific date, so use the present perfect.

Yes, I **have visited** Paris many times.

2003 2008 2010 2014 NOW

46.2 FURTHER EXAMPLES THE PRESENT PERFECT AND THE PAST SIMPLE

PAST SIMPLE	PRESENT PERFECT
I **saw** a great movie last week.	I **haven't seen** that movie.
Jo **didn't climb** Mount Fuji last year.	Saki **has climbed** Mount Fuji twice.
Madison **ate** too much last night.	Jack **hasn't eaten** curry before.

46.3 **VOCABULARY** ADVENTURE SPORTS

scuba diving | rock climbing | paragliding | windsurfing | bungee jumping | surfing

46.4 CROSS OUT THE INCORRECT WORDS IN EACH SENTENCE

Natalia visited / ~~has visited~~ China last year.

1. I love the movie *Casablanca*. I watched / have watched it more than nine times.
2. Our dog Rex ate / has eaten all Mary's birthday cake last night.
3. Jack didn't visit / hasn't visited the Colosseum when we were in Rome last year. He was too sick.
4. Did you go / Have you been to the swimming pool downtown yesterday?

46.5 SAY THE SENTENCES OUT LOUD, FILLING IN THE GAPS

Have you ever been surfing?
Yes, *I've been surfing* many times.

1. Has Chloe ever been bungee jumping?
Yes, ________ many times.

2. Has Liam ever visited Yosemite National Park?
Yes, ________ in 2014.

3. Have you ever seen *Gone with the Wind?*
Yes, ________ last night.

4. Have you ever been paragliding?
No, ________ .

5. Have any of your friends been scuba diving?
Yes, Mia ________ many times.

46.6 KEY LANGUAGE "BEEN / GONE"

You can use "be" and "go" in the present perfect to talk about your trips to places, but they have different meanings.

I haven't seen Joan recently. Where is she?

She's gone to Florida.

She is still in Florida.

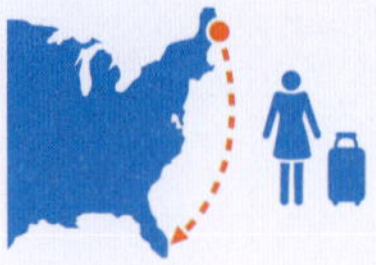

Hi, Joan. You're looking well.

Yes, I've been to Florida.

She went to Florida, but now she is back home.

46.7 FURTHER EXAMPLES "BEEN / GONE"

Where's Ben?

He's gone to the mall.

You look relaxed.

Yes, we've been in Bermuda. We had a great time.

Where's Ariana?

She's gone windsurfing.

What's Julie doing?

She's been swimming and now she's doing her homework.

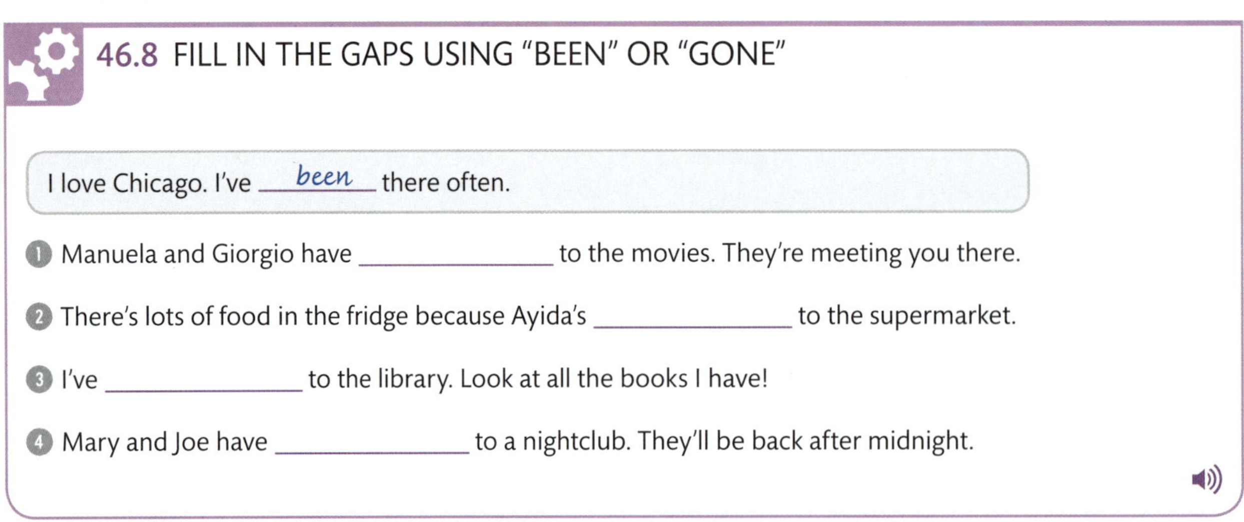

46.8 FILL IN THE GAPS USING "BEEN" OR "GONE"

I love Chicago. I've *been* there often.

1. Manuela and Giorgio have ____________ to the movies. They're meeting you there.
2. There's lots of food in the fridge because Ayida's ____________ to the supermarket.
3. I've ____________ to the library. Look at all the books I have!
4. Mary and Joe have ____________ to a nightclub. They'll be back after midnight.

46.9 READ THE POSTCARD AND WRITE THE VERBS UNDER THE CORRECT HEADINGS

PRESENT PERFECT

we've seen

1 ______

2 ______

PAST SIMPLE

we got

3 ______

4 ______

Hi Chris,
We're in Sydney! We got here five days ago and we've seen so much. On Monday, we visited the Sydney Opera House, and on Tuesday we went on a boat under Harbour Bridge. We haven't been to Bondi Beach yet, but I think we're going tomorrow. We've eaten some great food, too! Wish you were here.
Love,
Olivia x

46.10 LISTEN TO THE AUDIO AND ANSWER THE QUESTIONS

Martin has been bungee jumping three times.
True ☐ **False** ☑

1 Sammy went to China in 2011.
True ☐ **False** ☐

2 Nigel has never cooked a meal for visitors.
True ☐ **False** ☐

3 Debra has been rock climbing many times.
True ☐ **False** ☐

4 Andrew has never used a tablet before.
True ☐ **False** ☐

46.11 REWRITE THE SENTENCES, CORRECTING THE ERRORS

I've **gone** windsurfing many times.
I've been windsurfing many times.

1 She hasn't **be** to the circus.
______

2 I **meet** my best friend when I was six.
______

3 You **eat** all the chocolate last night.
______

4 He hasn't **try** paragliding.
______

46 CHECKLIST

The present perfect ☐ | **Aa** Adventure sports ☐ | Talking about past events ☐

47 Events in your year

One of the uses of the present perfect is to talk about events in a time period that hasn't finished. Use the past simple for a time period that is completed.

New language "Yet" and "already"
Vocabulary Routines and chores
New skill Talking about the recent past

47.1 KEY LANGUAGE PRESENT PERFECT AND PAST SIMPLE

If the time period referred to is ongoing, use the present perfect. Use the past simple to talk about a completed event.

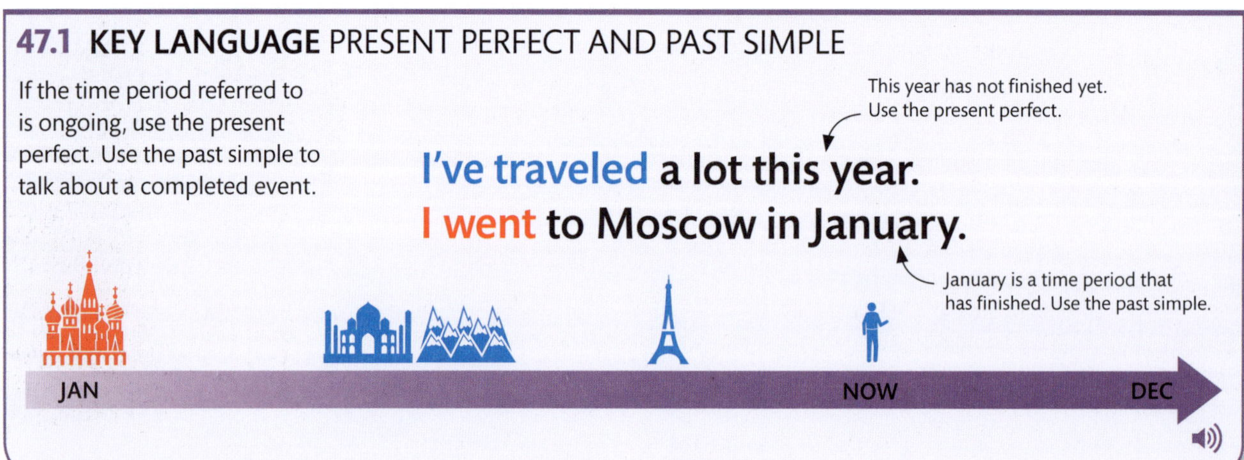

47.2 FURTHER EXAMPLES PRESENT PERFECT AND PAST SIMPLE

I haven't had any coffee this morning.

The photocopier broke yesterday.

I've had a lot of meetings today.

My manager called me last night.

47.3 FILL IN THE GAPS BY PUTTING THE VERBS IN THE PRESENT PERFECT OR PAST SIMPLE

I'm flying to New York again tomorrow. I *have been* (be) there five times this year.

1. Alvita is very happy. She ____________ (win) the prize for the best chocolate cake yesterday.
2. This is a great party. I ____________ (meet) lots of really fun and interesting people.
3. Martha looks happy. She ____________ (be) to the movies with Miles.
4. Mary can't drive. She ____________ (fall) and ____________ (break) her arm last week.

47.4 READ THE ARTICLE, THEN ANSWER THE QUESTIONS, SPEAKING OUT LOUD

41 SPORT TODAY

TENNIS STAR'S DIFFICULT YEAR

Sarah Jackson speaks to our sports reporter.

Sarah Jackson is a tennis player from the US. She has won five tennis championships, but she hasn't played in any competitions this year.

"I haven't had a good year. I broke my leg in January and I didn't play tennis for three months. It was really painful and it took me a long time to get well."

There are four big competitions for tennis players, known as the Grand Slams: the Australian Open, the French Open, Wimbledon, and the US Open. Sarah has already missed two of them.

"It's difficult for tennis players. You want to do well in the big competitions, but sometimes you can't."

The next grand slam is Wimbledon, but Sarah isn't going to play this year. "It's sad, but I'm just not ready for Wimbledon at the moment."

But the year hasn't been all bad: "I don't usually go on vacation," she told us, "but in March I went to the Caribbean. I had a really good time and relaxed. I also ate some great food and went swimming."

How many tennis championships has Sarah won?

She has won five tennis championships.

1. What hasn't Sarah done this year?

2. What did Sarah do in January?

3. How long didn't she play tennis for?

4. How many grand slams has Sarah missed this year?

5. What did Sarah do in March this year?

47.5 KEY LANGUAGE "YET"

"Yet" means "until now." It shows that you have an intention to do something.

Have you ordered the pizzas?

No, I haven't ordered them yet.

You haven't ordered the pizzas, but you will order them later.

47.6 KEY LANGUAGE "ALREADY"

Use "already" when something has happened, possibly sooner than expected.

I'll order the pizzas now.

It's OK. I've already ordered them.

You've ordered the pizzas before the other person expected.

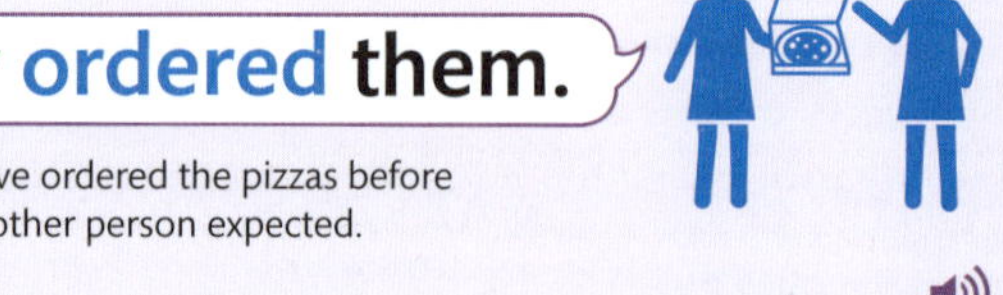

47.7 FURTHER EXAMPLES "ALREADY" AND "YET"

Has Rob cooked the dinner?

No, not yet.

You can use "yet" in short answers.

What time is Andrew going to get here?

He's already arrived.

47.8 MATCH THE QUESTIONS TO THE CORRECT ANSWERS

When is Phil going to get here? → He's already arrived.

1. Am I too late to play football?
2. Has Amy learned how to drive yet?
3. Can you send an email to Rachel?
4. Have you watched this movie?

- No, the game hasn't started yet.
- I've already done it.
- He's already arrived.
- No, not yet.
- Yes, I've already seen it.

47.9 LISTEN TO THE AUDIO AND ANSWER THE QUESTIONS

Sharon and Paul are getting ready to leave home and go on vacation.

Paul hasn't booked a taxi yet.
True ☐ False ☑

1. Paul hasn't made the sandwiches yet.
True ☐ False ☐

2. Sharon has already called her mother.
True ☐ False ☐

3. Sharon hasn't checked if the dog is OK yet.
True ☐ False ☐

4. The dog has already been for a walk.
True ☐ False ☐

5. Sharon has already mailed her letter.
True ☐ False ☐

47.10 LOOK AT SANTIAGO'S "TO DO" LIST AND WRITE ANSWERS TO THE QUESTIONS AS FULL SENTENCES USING "ALREADY" AND "YET"

Has Santiago fed the cat yet?
Yes, he's already fed the cat.

Has he put out the garbage yet?
No, he hasn't put out the garbage yet.

To do list

~~Feed the cat~~
Put out the garbage
~~Clean the kitchen~~
~~Buy milk and bread~~
~~Mail letter~~
Make birthday cake
Call Grandma
Take dog for walk

1. Has he cleaned the kitchen yet?

2. Has he bought milk and bread yet?

3. Has he taken the dog for a walk yet?

4. Has he made the birthday cake yet?

5. Has he mailed the letter yet?

6. Has he called his grandmother yet?

47 CHECKLIST

"Yet" and "already" ☐ **Aa** Routines and chores ☐ Talking about the recent past ☐

48 Eating out

"Eating out" means having a meal outside your home, usually in a restaurant. To do this, you need to know the language for making a reservation and ordering food.

New language Restaurant phrases
Aa Vocabulary Food preparation
New skill Ordering a meal in a restaurant

48.1 KEY LANGUAGE ORDERING A MEAL

A restaurant meal often has three courses.

TIP
In US English, you can use "entrée" or "main course" to describe the main dish in a meal.

48.2 VOCABULARY EATING OUT AND FOOD PREPARATION

appetizer (US) / starter (UK)

entrée (US) / main course (UK)

dessert

the check (US) / the bill (UK)

reservation / booking

roast

bake

broil (US) / grill (UK)

boil

fry

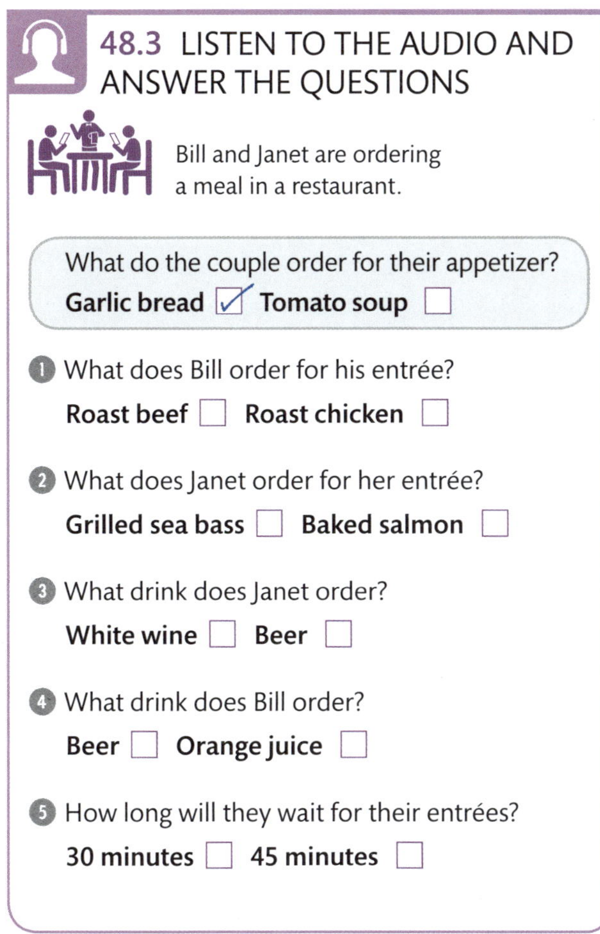

48.3 LISTEN TO THE AUDIO AND ANSWER THE QUESTIONS

Bill and Janet are ordering a meal in a restaurant.

What do the couple order for their appetizer?
Garlic bread ☑ **Tomato soup** ☐

1. What does Bill order for his entrée?
Roast beef ☐ **Roast chicken** ☐

2. What does Janet order for her entrée?
Grilled sea bass ☐ **Baked salmon** ☐

3. What drink does Janet order?
White wine ☐ **Beer** ☐

4. What drink does Bill order?
Beer ☐ **Orange juice** ☐

5. How long will they wait for their entrées?
30 minutes ☐ **45 minutes** ☐

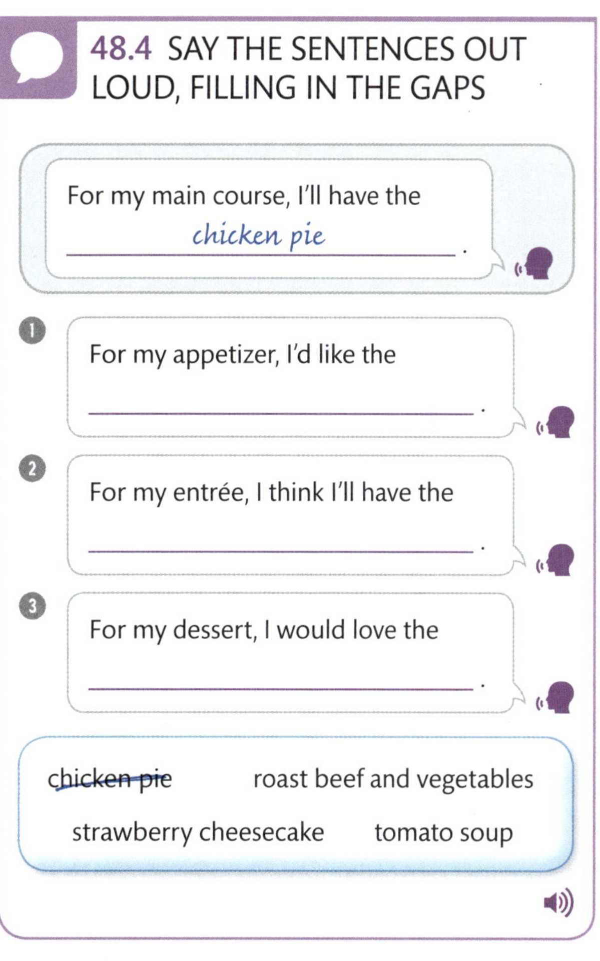

48.4 SAY THE SENTENCES OUT LOUD, FILLING IN THE GAPS

For my main course, I'll have the *chicken pie*.

1. For my appetizer, I'd like the ______.

2. For my entrée, I think I'll have the ______.

3. For my dessert, I would love the ______.

~~chicken pie~~ roast beef and vegetables strawberry cheesecake tomato soup

48 CHECKLIST

Restaurant phrases ☐ **Aa** Food preparation ☐ Ordering a meal in a restaurant ☐

49 Achievements and ambitions

English uses different phrases to talk about future wishes or desires, definite future plans, and past achievements. Use them in conversation to talk about your life.

New language Desires and plans
Vocabulary Travel and adventure sports
New skill Talking about your achievements

49.1 KEY LANGUAGE DESIRES AND PLANS

Use expressions such as "I'd like to" for desires. Use "I'm going to" for definite plans.

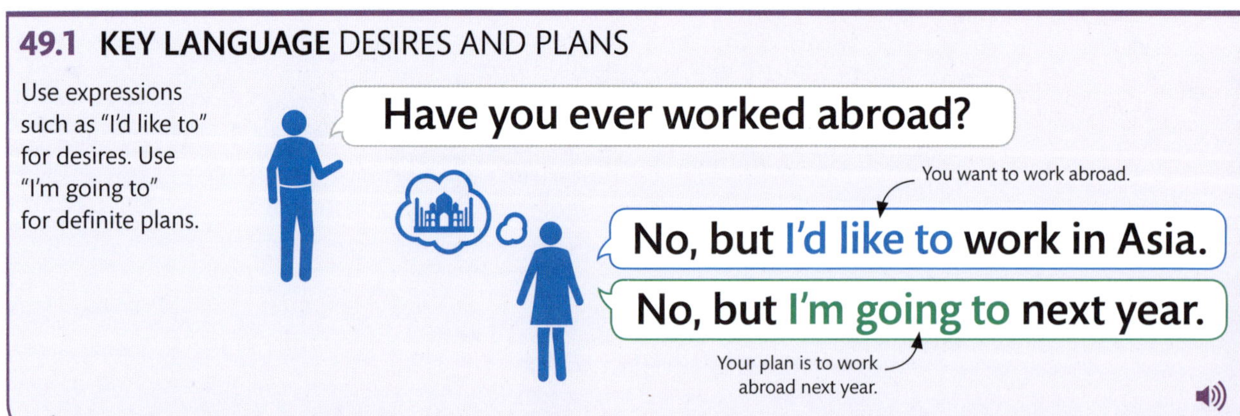

49.2 FURTHER EXAMPLES DESIRES AND PLANS

I'm very excited. We're going to hike the Inca Trail next year.

I haven't climbed Mount Fuji, but I'm going to do it this summer.

I've never been to South America, but I want to go.

I've never seen a whale. I'd like to go whale-watching later this year.

49.3 MATCH THE QUESTIONS TO THE CORRECT ANSWERS

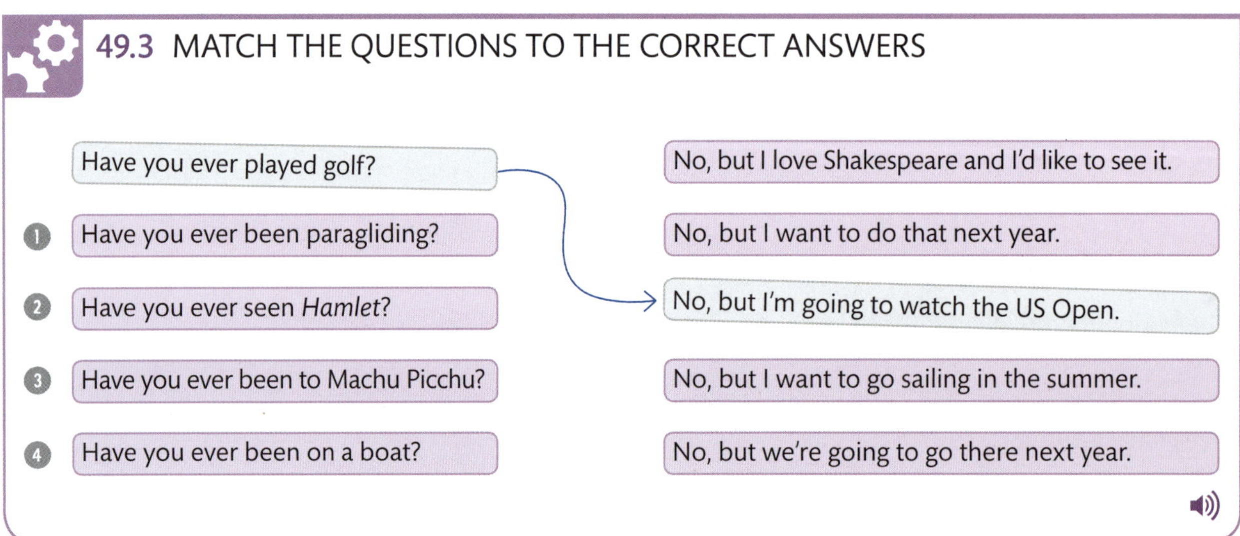

Have you ever played golf? → No, but I'm going to watch the US Open.

1. Have you ever been paragliding?
2. Have you ever seen *Hamlet*?
3. Have you ever been to Machu Picchu?
4. Have you ever been on a boat?

No, but I love Shakespeare and I'd like to see it.
No, but I want to do that next year.
No, but I'm going to watch the US Open.
No, but I want to go sailing in the summer.
No, but we're going to go there next year.

49.4 LISTEN TO THE AUDIO AND MARK WHAT BRETT HAS OR HASN'T DONE

Radio presenter Ken Wallace interviews stunt man Brett Ellis.

49.5 READ THE CLUES AND WRITE THE ANSWERS IN THE CORRECT PLACES ON THE GRID

1 D e s 2 e r t

3

4 5

6

7

8

9 10

~~Desert~~ sail dolphins Australia drive

football Chinese make mountain English

ACROSS

1. Davina is going to ride a camel across the Gobi ____Desert____ .
3. Harry wants to ________ along the Pacific Coast Highway.
6. Dan would like to go swimming with ________ in Mexico.
7. Flo would like to study ________ in Beijing.
9. Susie wants to see kangaroos in ________ .

DOWN

2. Javier wants to speak ________ every day.
4. Ben would like to climb a ________ .
5. José wants to play ________ with the Dallas Cowboys.
8. Gary is going to ________ a short movie with his friends.
10. Melinda wants to ________ her boat around the world.

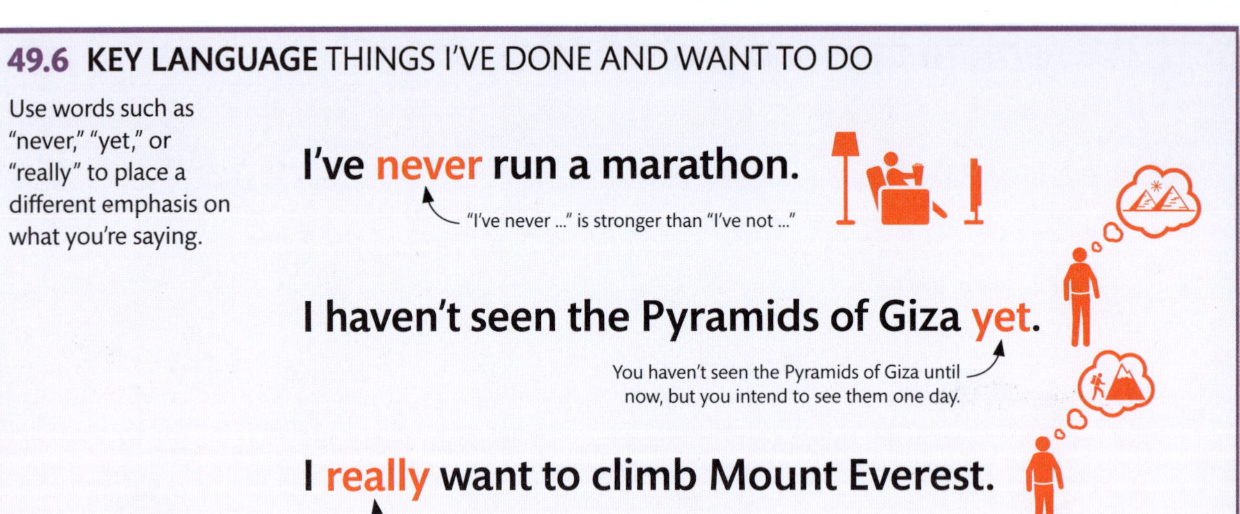

49.6 KEY LANGUAGE THINGS I'VE DONE AND WANT TO DO

Use words such as "never," "yet," or "really" to place a different emphasis on what you're saying.

I've never run a marathon.

"I've never ..." is stronger than "I've not ..."

I haven't seen the Pyramids of Giza yet.

You haven't seen the Pyramids of Giza until now, but you intend to see them one day.

I really want to climb Mount Everest.

Your desire to climb Mount Everest is strong.

Aa 49.7 MATCH THE PICTURES TO THE CORRECT SENTENCES

I haven't been up in a hot-air balloon, but I'm going to do that for my birthday in August.

I haven't traveled in a helicopter yet, but I'm going to fly over New York in one soon.

I haven't been to a music festival yet, but my friends really want to take me to one next summer.

I've never learned to ski, but my friend Sanjay is going to teach me next year.

I've never been on TV, but I'm going to be on a TV quiz show in a few weeks. I'm very excited.

1

2

3

4

49.8 READ THE EMAIL AND ANSWER THE QUESTIONS

John has been surfing in South Africa and Australia.
True ☐ False ☑

1. John has never seen a lion.
True ☐ False ☐

2. John and Jo have been on safari before.
True ☐ False ☐

3. John and Jo are going to China this year.
True ☐ False ☐

4. John wants to go to Japan this summer.
True ☐ False ☐

5. Jo has never been on an elephant.
True ☐ False ☐

To: Jo Abernathy

Subject: Things I want to do this year

Hi Jo,

I want to plan our year, so we can do more things. We've already been surfing in Australia and Hawaii, but we haven't surfed in South Africa yet. I've also never seen a lion, so I want to go on safari. We've never done that before. Also, I know we're going to China next year, but this summer I want to go to Thailand. I'd really like to ride an elephant, and I know you haven't done that yet. What do you think?

John

49 CHECKLIST

Desires and plans ☐ **Aa** Travel and adventure sports ☐ Talking about your achievements ☐

REVIEW THE ENGLISH YOU HAVE LEARNED IN UNITS 45-49

NEW LANGUAGE	SAMPLE SENTENCE	☑	UNIT
THE PRESENT PERFECT	Tom has just cleaned the windows.	☐	45.1, 45.3
THE PAST SIMPLE AND THE PRESENT PERFECT	I visited France in 2010. I have visited France many times.	☐	46.1
"YET" AND "ALREADY" WITH THE PRESENT PERFECT	I haven't ordered the pizza yet. I've already ordered the pizza.	☐	47.5, 47.6
ORDERING A MEAL	"Have you made a reservation?" "Yes, I have." "Excuse me! Can we have the check, please."	☐	48.1
DESIRES AND PLANS	I'd like to work in Asia. I'm going to work there next year.	☐	49.1, 49.2, 49.6

R Reference

R1 ADJECTIVES

An **adjective** is used to describe the qualities of a noun. It usually comes before the noun that it is describing. Some adjectives have irregular comparative and superlative forms.

A **comparative adjective** is used to describe the difference between two things. Use it before the word "than" to compare people, places, or things. If an adjective is three syllables or longer, use "more" or "less" before the adjective and "than" after it.

A **superlative adjective** is used to talk about extremes, or to describe a person or thing that possesses a certain quality more than anyone or anything else. For long adjectives, add "the most" or "the least" before the adjective to make the superlative.

ADJECTIVE	COMPARATIVE	SUPERLATIVE
angry	angr**ier**	angr**iest**
bad	**worse**	**worst**
beautiful	beautiful	beautiful
big	big**ger**	big**gest**
busy	bus**ier**	bus**iest**
cheap	cheap**er**	cheap**est**
clean	clean**er**	clean**est**
close	close**r**	close**st**
cold	cold**er**	cold**est**
dangerous	dangerous	dangerous
deep	deep**er**	deep**est**
difficult	difficult	difficult
early	earl**ier**	earl**iest**
easy	eas**ier**	eas**iest**
exciting	exciting	exciting
expensive	expensive	expensive
far	far**ther** (US)	far**thest** (US)
	further (UK)	**furthest** (UK)
fast	fast**er**	fast**est**
few	few**er**	few**est**
friendly	friendl**ier**	friendl**iest**
good	**better**	**best**
happy	happ**ier**	happ**iest**
hard	hard**er**	hard**est**

ADJECTIVE	COMPARATIVE	SUPERLATIVE
heavy	heav**ier**	heav**iest**
high	high**er**	high**est**
horrible	horrible	horrible
hot	hot**ter**	hot**test**
important	important	important
interesting	interesting	interesting
large	large**r**	large**st**
late	late**r**	late**st**
long	long**er**	long**est**
lucky	luck**ier**	luck**iest**
new	new**er**	new**est**
nice	nice**r**	nice**st**
noisy	nois**ier**	nos**iest**
old	old**er**	old**est**
pretty	prett**ier**	prett**iest**
quiet	quiet**er**	quiet**est**
sad	sad**der**	sad**dest**
safe	safe**r**	safe**st**
simple	simple**r**	simple**st**
short	short**er**	short**est**
small	small**er**	small**est**
tall	tall**er**	tall**est**
warm	warm**er**	warm**est**
young	young**er**	young**est**

R2 COMMON STATE VERBS

State verbs are usually used to express a state of being, i.e. to say how things are or how someone feels. They can be used to talk about emotions, possession, senses, or thoughts. They are not usually used in continuous tenses.

MEANING	STATE VERB	SAMPLE SENTENCE
feeling / wanting	**like / love**	I **like / love** Italian ice cream.
	need	We really **need** to spend more time together as a family.
	prefer	Some people **prefer** summer to winter.
	want	The band **wants** to become famous and make money.
thinking	**believe**	I **believe** your story, but it is rather unlikely.
	doubt	Lots of people **doubt** that he can do the job properly.
	know	Do you **know** where we parked the car?
	mean	What do you **mean** when you say you aren't ready?
	think	What do you **think** about the proposed policy?
	understand	Could you speak more slowly? I don't **understand** you.
being / existing	**appear / seem**	It **appears / seems** that the house has already been sold.
	exist	Strange creatures **exist** at the bottom of the sea.
possessing	**belong**	Excuse me, that book **belongs** to me.
	have / own	My cousin **has / owns** three classic cars.
	include	Did you **include** Lucy in the guest list?
sensing	**feel**	Does your leg **feel** better today?
	hear	I can **hear** you, but I'm not sure what you're saying.
	hurt	My arm really **hurts**. I think I should go to see the doctor.
	see	Can you **see** the blackbird in the bush over there?
having a quality	**feel**	This rug **feels** so soft. It would be lovely to walk on.
	smell	Something **smells** delicious. Is it the soup?
	sound	That **sounds** like thunder, or is it just fireworks?
	taste	This milk **tastes** a bit sour. I think it's gone bad.

R3 MODAL VERBS

Modal verbs modify the meaning of the main verb, expressing various notions such as possibility or obligation. They don't change form to match the subject, and they are always followed by a main verb in its base form.

CAN

"Can" can be used to describe what someone or something is able to do. It can also be used to ask permission or make a request.

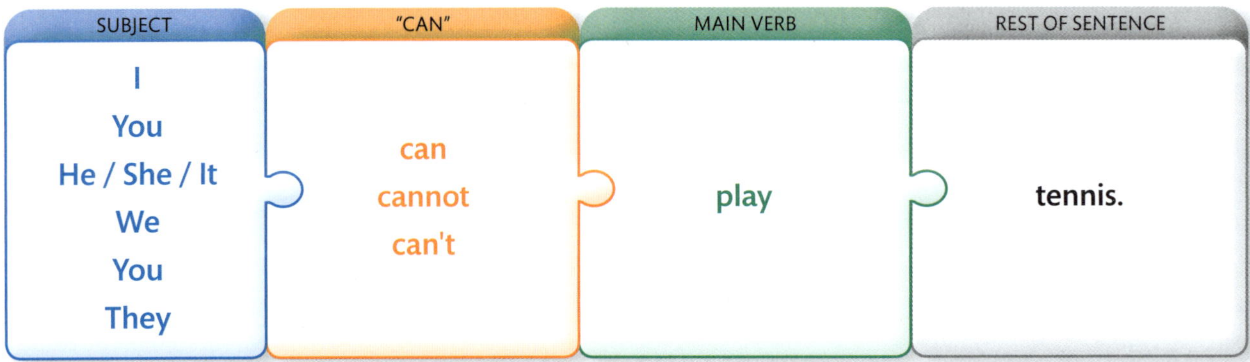

COULD

"Could" can be used in a variety of ways. It can be used to describe what something or someone was able to do in the past. It can also be used to make a polite request, offer a suggestion or solution, or ask for permission. It introduces possibilities but not preferences. It is not as strong as "should".

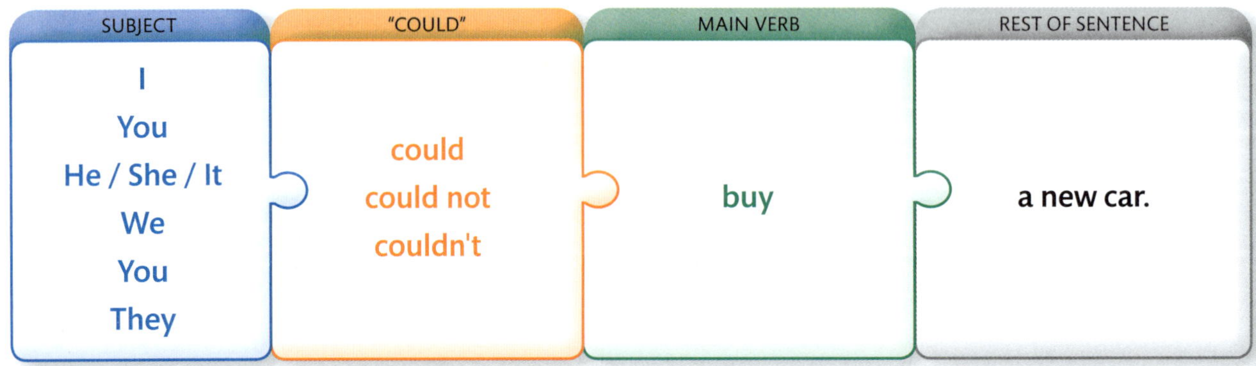

MIGHT

"Might" can be used to talk about something that a person may or not do in the future. It can also be used to express uncertainty. It is only a possibility and not an assertion.

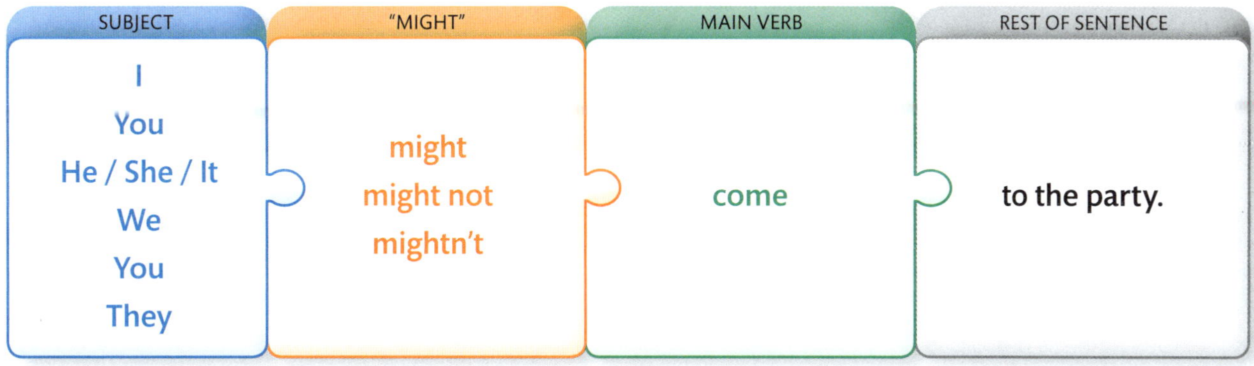

SHOULD

"Should" can be used to give advice. It can also be used to state what you expect will happen.

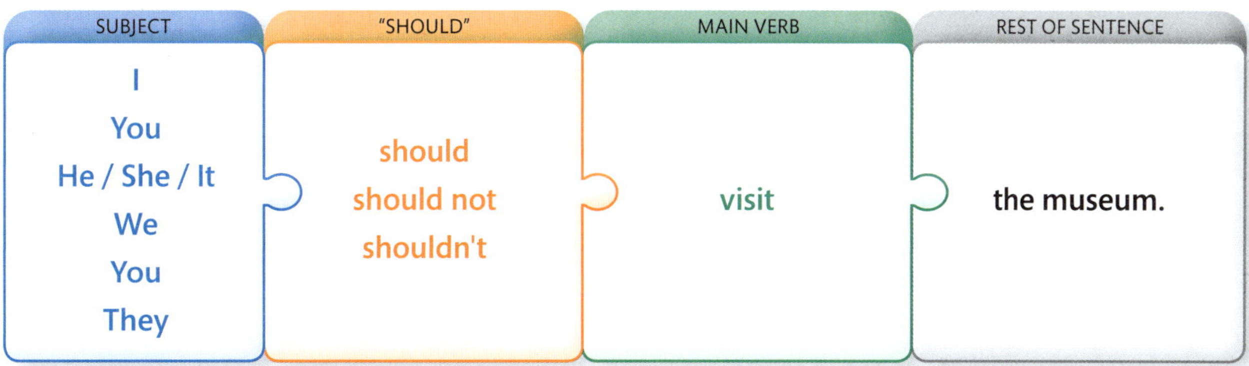

WOULD

"Would" can be used to express something that someone wants to do. It can also be used to describe what someone used to do in the past.

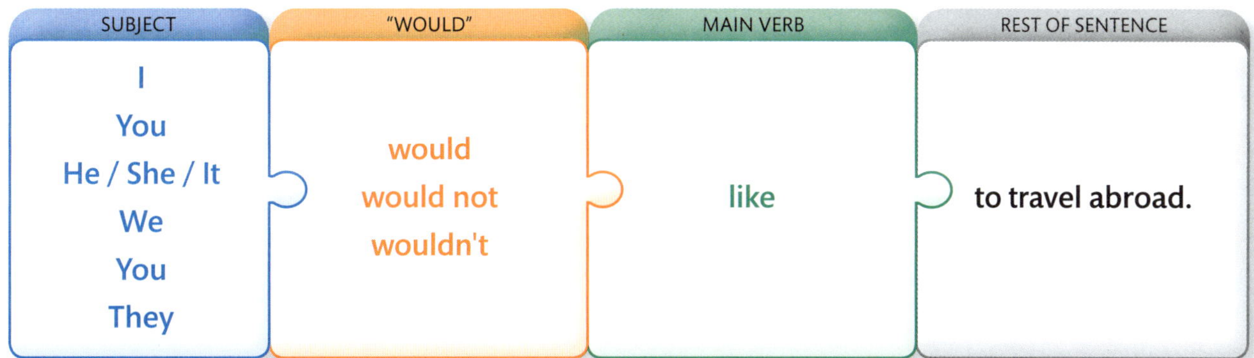

R4 THE PRESENT CONTINUOUS

The **present continuous** is used to talk about something that is happening now in the present moment. There are no irregular verb forms in the present continuous. Note that state verbs are not usually used in continuous tenses.

POSITIVE	NEGATIVE	QUESTION
I am / I'm talking	I'm not talking	Am I talking...?
You are / You're talking	You're not / You aren't talking	Are you talking...?
He is / He's talking	He's not / He isn't talking	Is he talking...?
She is / She's talking	She's not / She isn't talking	Is she talking...?
It is / It's talking	It's not / It isn't talking	Is it talking...?
We are / We're talking	We're not / We aren't talking	Are we talking...?
You are / You're talking	You're not / You aren't talking	Are you talking...?
They are / They're talking	They're not / They aren't talking	Are they talking...?

R5 THE PRESENT PERFECT: REGULAR VERBS

The **present perfect** is used to talk about events in the past that have an effect on the present moment. It is formed using the verb **"to have"** plus the past participle of the verb that describes the event. See R10 for a list of irregular past participles.

POSITIVE	NEGATIVE	QUESTION
I have / I've helped	I've not / I haven't helped	Have I helped...?
You have / You've helped	You've not / You haven't helped	Have you helped...?
He has / He's helped	He's not / He hasn't helped	Has he helped...?
She has / She's helped	She's not / She hasn't helped	Has she helped...?
It has / It's helped	It's not / It hasn't helped	Has it helped...?
We have / We've helped	We've not / We haven't helped	Have we helped...?
You have / You've helped	You've not / You haven't helped	Have you helped...?
They have / They've helped	They've not / They haven't helped	Have they helped...?

R6 THE FUTURE WITH "GOING TO"

When discussing the future, **"going to"** is used to talk about decisions that have already been made, or to make predictions when there is evidence in the present moment to support them.

POSITIVE	NEGATIVE	QUESTION
I am / I'm going to	I'm not going to	Am I going to...?
You are / You're going to	You're not / You aren't going to	Are you going to...?
He is / He's going to	He's not / He isn't going to	Is he going to...?
She is / She's going to	She's not / She isn't going to	Is she going to...?
It is / It's going to	It's not / It isn't going to	Is it going to...?
We are / We're going to	We're not / We aren't going to	Are we going to...?
You are / You're going to	You're not / You aren't going to	Are you going to...?
They are / They're going to	They're not / They aren't going to	Are they going to...?

R7 THE FUTURE WITH "WILL"

When discussing the future, **"will"** is used to talk about decisions made at the time of speaking, to make predictions about the future that are not supported by evidence, to offer to do something, or to make promises.

POSITIVE	NEGATIVE	QUESTION
I will / I'll	I will not / I won't	Will I...?
You will / You'll	You will not / You won't	Will you...?
He will / He'll	He will not / He won't	Will he...?
She will / She'll	She will not / She won't	Will she...?
It will / It'll	It will not / It won't	Will it..?
We will / We'll	We will not / We won't	Will we...?
You will / You'll	You will not / You won't	Will you...?
They will / They'll	They will not / They won't	Will they...?

R8 THE PAST SIMPLE: REGULAR VERBS

The **past simple** is used to describe events that happened at a definite time in the past, or to describe the state of things at a particular point in time. It is used to refer to completed actions in the past. The past simple forms of regular verbs usually end in "-ed".

POSITIVE	NEGATIVE	QUESTION
I worked	I did not / I didn't work	Did I work...?
You worked	You did not / You didn't work	Did you work...?
He worked	He did not / He didn't work	Did he work...?
She worked	She did not / She didn't work	Did she work...?
It worked	It did not / It didn't work	Did it work...?
We worked	We did not / We didn't work	Did we work...?
You worked	You did not / You didn't work	Did you work...?
They worked	They did not / They didn't work	Did they work...?

R9 THE PAST SIMPLE: "TO BE"

The **past simple** form of **"to be"** is completely irregular. It is the only verb in the past simple which changes depending on the subject.

POSITIVE	NEGATIVE	QUESTION
I was	I was not / I wasn't	Was I...?
You were	You were not / You weren't	Were you...?
He was	He was not / He wasn't	Was he...?
She was	She was not / She wasn't	Was she...?
It was	It was not / It wasn't	Was it...?
We were	We were not / We weren't	Were we...?
You were	You were not / You weren't	Were you...?
They were	They were not / They weren't	Were they...?

R10 THE PAST SIMPLE AND PAST PARTICIPLE: IRREGULAR VERBS

Some verbs have irregular forms for the **past simple** tense and the **past participle**. The tables below list some of the most common.

BASE FORM	PAST SIMPLE	PAST PARTICIPLE
be	was / were	been
begin	began	begun
break	broke	broken
bring	brought	brought
build	built	built
buy	bought	bought
catch	caught	caught
choose	chose	chosen
come	came	come
cost	cost	cost
cut	cut	cut
do	did	done
draw	drew	drawn
drink	drank	drunk
drive	drove	driven
eat	ate	eaten
fall	fell	fallen
fight	fought	fought
find	found	found
fly	flew	flown
forget	forgot	forgotten
freeze	froze	frozen
get	got	gotten (US) / got (UK)
give	gave	given
go	went	gone
grow	grew	grown
hear	heard	heard
have	had	had
hit	hit	hit
hold	held	held
hurt	hurt	hurt
keep	kept	kept
know	knew	known
lend	lent	lent

BASE FORM	PAST SIMPLE	PAST PARTICIPLE
leave	left	left
lose	lost	lost
make	made	made
mean	meant	meant
meet	met	met
put	put	put
read	read	read
ride	rode	rode
ring	rang	rung
run	ran	run
say	said	said
see	saw	seen
send	sent	sent
sit	sat	sat
sell	sold	sold
show	showed	shown
shut	shut	shut
sleep	slept	slept
speak	spoke	spoken
sing	sang	sung
spend	spent	spent
stand	stood	stood
steal	stole	stolen
swim	swam	swum
swing	swung	swung
take	took	taken
teach	taught	taught
tell	told	told
think	thought	thought
throw	threw	thrown
understand	understood	understood
wear	wore	worn
win	won	won
write	wrote	written

Transcripts of listening exercises

UNIT 1

1.6 ex: Hi. I'm Charlie and I am a doctor.
1.6.1 Hello, my name's Altan. I am American.
1.6.2 Hi, I'm Latifa. I'm an engineer.
1.6.3 My name's Ollie. I'm British and I'm 26 years old.
1.6.4 My name's Kathleen. I am a chef and I'm from Australia.
1.6.5 I'm Sammi. I'm 46 years old and I'm a vet.

UNIT 3

3.6
Friend: I like this photo of your family, Emma. You all look great!
Emma: Thanks. That's my dad beside me. He is wearing a wonderful gray suit and his favorite tie. I'm wearing my red dress and my favorite hat.
Friend: Is that your older brother?
Emma: Yes, that's Max. He loves that suit and that silly hat.
Friend: He looks funny. And that's Julie next to him, yeah?
Emma: Yes, she always wears jeans, but in this photo she's wearing her lovely blue skirt with a green jacket.
Friend: And she's beside your mother?
Emma: No, it's my cousin, Jada. She loves wearing strong colors.
Friend: I like her yellow jacket. It's very bright!
Emma: I know!

3.12
Friend: Hi Sam. It's very quiet in here. What are all your housemates doing?
Sam: Well, Ed's not watching TV. He's reading a book instead.
Friend: And what's Dan doing?
Sam: He's watching TV. There's a movie on now.
Friend: OK, and where's Manu? I can hear some music.
Sam: Actually, Manu's doing some exercise. The music is George playing his guitar. He's in a band.
Friend: Oh, that's great. And how about Jamal? Is he walking the dog?
Friend: He wanted to, but it's raining, so he's staying inside. I think he's playing a computer game.
Friend: Shall we join him?
Sam: Sure, let's ask him.

UNIT 4

4.5
Martha: Hi, Jack. It's Martha.
Jack: Oh, hi, Martha. How are you?
Martha: Great! How are you?
Jack: I'm fine. I'm relaxing in the yard at the moment. The sun is lovely today.
Martha: So nice that I'm gardening all day today! Is Rachel with you?
Jack: She's cooking in the kitchen.
Martha: Is Fleur helping her?
Jack: Not really. She's listening to music in her bedroom. She always does that on a Sunday afternoon. And Jacob's reading a book. He has a lot of work to do for university.
Martha: Well, say hi to everyone for me. And can you ask Rachel to call me later?
Jack: Sure.
Martha: We need to talk about...

4.9 ex: Friend: Hi, Jim! Is that your new tablet?
Jim: No, it's my smartphone.
Friend: Wow. It's big.
Jim: I know. I love it!
4.9.1
Friend: Hi, Lucas. What are you doing?
Lucas: Oh, it's silly. I'm cleaning my shirt. There's spaghetti on it!
4.9.2
Friend: Hi, Orla. Are you playing a game on your computer?
Orla: No, I'm doing some work on it.
4.9.3
Friend: Hi, Livia. Are you going out?
Livia: Yes.
Friend: You look nice. That's a lovely dress.
Livia: Oh, thanks. It's a skirt and top. It's my favorite outfit, actually.
4.9.4
Friend: Hi, David. What are you doing on your tablet?
David: I'm writing an email right now, but I do lots of things on it. I read books on it in the evening.
Friend: Oh, me too. I've got lots of books on mine.
4.9.5
Friend: Hi, Dewain. Have you got new headphones?
Dewain: Yep! Do you like them?
Friend: They're really nice ones. Are you listening to music?
Dewain: Not music, no. I'm listening to news on the radio.
4.9.6
Friend: Hi, Rochelle! Is that heavy? Can I help you carry it?
Rochelle: No, thanks. I'm fine. It's my new laptop. It's really light.
4.9.7
Friend: Hi, Julio. Is that a new tablet?
Julio: No, it's an e-reader. I'm reading a great book on it at the moment.

UNIT 7

7.6 ex: Jack: Oh, no. Where's my notes? My pen? I can't remember. Er... Ladies and gentlemen, welcome to... er... what's it called? Er... This building is... Help!
7.6.1
Jill: I'm great. Life's good at the moment. I've got a new job and a new boyfriend. And at the moment, I'm on holiday. Yay!
7.6.2
Sami: There's nothing on TV. No good movies to watch. No books to read. Nothing to do.
7.6.3
Ian: We're here on the Serengeti, waiting for the lions. They come here every day to drink at about midday, and here they come now.
7.6.4
Lindi: I can't believe it. Where are my keys? Where are they? I'm so late for work! Come on!
7.6.5
Jenny: It's our last exam. I'm so happy. I can't wait to finish my course.

7.6.6
Jimmi: Wow, this is a very upsetting film. I'm crying so much.
7.6.7
Minna: Oh, no, a spider! I hate spiders!
7.6.8
Aziz: That was a long day. Work was difficult. I had a lot of meetings. I'm tired. I'm going to bed early tonight.

UNIT 9
9.7 ex: A: So, what are you doing right now?
B: Well, I usually go fishing on Fridays, but at the moment, I'm sailing a boat.
A: That sounds great.
B: Yes, there are lots of surfers in the ocean and dolphins, too.
A: Wow, amazing! I'm so jealous!
9.7.1
Voicemail: Please leave a message after the tone.
Boyfriend: Hi, Michelle. It's me. I know we usually go to a restaurant on Friday evenings, but tonight I want to cook you a meal. Let me know what you want to eat. Anyway, see you later. Love you.
9.7.2
A: It's the intermission, but I'm going back on stage in a few minutes. I usually act in plays, but tonight I'm singing. I'm so nervous, but I think it's going well.
A: Good luck!
9.7.3
Husband: Hi, Daniella. What are the children doing? They usually watch TV after school.
Daniella: Oh, well right now, they're drawing pictures. They're having fun.
Husband: Great. Can you read them a story later on?
Daniella: Of course!

UNIT 13
13.7
Phil: This is Phil Watson on Talk 102, and now it's time for the weather with Ray Jupiter.
Ray: Hi, Phil.
Phil: So, Ray, tell us, what's the weather like?
Ray: Well, it's warm in some parts of the US today. It's 70 degrees Fahrenheit in Kansas, 72 degrees in Denver and 76 degrees in Boston. That's warm. But in Canada, it isn't. In Quebec it's 60 degrees, in Calgary it's 55 degrees, and in Vancouver it's 52 degrees.
Phil: Brrrr! That is cold, Ray.
Ray: Wait, there's more, Phil. There's some rain on the west coast of America, in San Francisco and Portland, and there's a storm right now in Seattle, so don't travel on the roads at the moment there.
Phil: Thanks for letting us know, Ray.
Ray: But it's not just storms – no. There's ice in Edmonton and Vancouver, and there's heavy snow in Anchorage, Alaska today. So wear a sweater, gloves, and a hat.
Phil: So, where is the sun today, Ray?
Ray: Well, it's sunny with some clouds in Phoenix and Dallas, but you want blue skies and no clouds, don't you, Phil?
Phil: That's right, Ray.
Ray: Well, you want to go to Houston, Texas. There are no clouds there today and the temperature is about 80 degrees Fahrenheit. It's a great place to go for some sun.
Phil: Well that's great, Ray. And now, let's go to the news...

UNIT 15
15.11
Selma: OK, Joe. Let's look at these vacation brochures for the Bahamas and Costa Rica. What do you think?
Joe: Well, Selma, the Bahamas is hot, but Costa Rica is hotter because it's nearer the equator.
Selma: Hmm. And it's easier for us to fly to Costa Rica than it is to fly to the Bahamas. The flight time is a lot shorter.
Joe: Yes, you're right. And the Bahamas is more expensive than Costa Rica, so we need more money to go to there.
Selma: Ah, yes. That's a good point. And Costa Rica has lots of beautiful beaches.
Joe: True, but the Bahamas has beautiful beaches, too.
Selma: Yes, but this is a picture of Tahiti Beach in the Bahamas, and here is Playa Hermosa in Costa Rica.
Joe: Ah, yes. Playa Hermosa is more beautiful than Tahiti Beach.
Selma: I agree.
Joe: Costa Rica is also more exciting than the Bahamas. It's a bigger place and there's more to see there. There are beaches and there's a volcano and a jungle.
Selma: That's it, then. Let's go to Costa Rica. It sounds really good!
Joe: OK, let's book it today.

UNIT 16
16.5
Ben: Hi, Joel. Hi, Sarah.
Joel: Oh, hi, Ben.
Sarah: Hi, Ben.
Joel: Oh, that's a nice car. Is it new?
Ben: Yeah, I bought it last week.
Sarah: It looks fast.
Ben: Well, it's faster than yours.
Sarah: Yeah, but mine's really old. Joel's got the fastest car. He loves fast cars.
Joel: I know. You're right. And I'm the tallest.
Sarah: No, you're not. Ben's the tallest.
Ben: You know I'm taller than you, Joel.
Joel: Yes, OK. Hey, is that your new phone, Sarah?
Sarah: Yes. Do you like it?
Joel: It's nice, and it's really small.
Ben: Yeah, mine's a lot bigger and heavier than that.
Joel: Mine, too.
Sarah: Yeah, I like small phones. They're easier to carry around. I've got a new laptop, too.
Joel: Wow, that's nice. I really need a new laptop.
Ben: Me, too. Mine is really heavy. Was it expensive?
Sarah: Yes, it was 1,000 dollars.
Ben: Wow. Mine only cost 500.
Joel: Ha! Mine was 250 dollars.
Sarah: Yes, Joel, but your apartment is a lot more expensive than mine.
Joel: True. Ben's apartment is the most expensive, though.
Ben: Yes, but it's a great place. I love the views.
Sarah: It is nice. Anyway, I got my laptop for my birthday.
Joel: When was that?
Sarah: Last week.
Joel: So, how old are you?
Sarah: 21.
Joel: Oh, I'm older than you, then. I'm 22 next month.
Ben: And I'm 23 already, so I'm the oldest.
Joel: Oh, Ben. You're so old.

UNIT 18

18.10

TV host: Hello and welcome to *Big, Bigger, Biggest*, the quiz show where size is important! And today on the show we have Rita Adams. Hi, Rita. So, are you ready to play?

Rita: Yes. I think so.

TV host: So, here's the first question. Which is the largest state in the US? Is it Texas, Virginia, or Alaska?

Rita: Oooh, I don't know. Virginia is big, but I think Texas is bigger.... or is it Alaska? Yes... Alaska.

TV host: Correct. Well done! So, next question. Which city is the farthest from the equator? Is it Taipei, Manila, or Bangkok?

Rita: Oh. I'm not very good at geography. It's not Manila... is it Taipei? Yes, I think that's it.

TV host: Amazing! That's the right answer. OK, now a question about countries. Which is the smallest South American country, Brazil, Peru, or Suriname?

Rita: Oh! That's easy. I've been there. It's Suriname. It's the smallest country in South America.

TV host: Correct. Three out of three. You're doing great. The next question is about deserts.

Rita: Oh, no.

TV host: Which is the biggest desert: the Mojave, the Sahara, or the Kalahari?

Rita: I've no idea. I can only guess. The Kalahari?

TV host: Oh dear. Wrong. It's the Sahara. It's over 3.6 million square miles. OK. Next question. Which is the tallest building: Big Ben, the Eiffel Tower, or Pisa Tower (also known as "the leaning tower of Pisa")?

Rita: Hmm. I've been to all three. The Eiffel Tower is definitely taller than the other two.

TV host: So your answer is...?

Rita: The Eiffel Tower.

TV host: Correct. Well done. OK, last question. Which is the highest mountain – is it K2, Kilimanjaro, or Mont Blanc?

Rita: I know this one. Everest is the highest mountain in the world, and I'm sure that K2 is the second highest. So it must be K2.

TV host: That's the correct answer. So now we move on to the second round...

UNIT 19

19.3 ex: Five hundred and thirty

19.3.1 Four thousand, five hundred

19.3.2 Four hundred and sixty-seven thousand

19.3.3 Nine hundred and eighty-nine

19.3.4 Seventy-two thousand, four hundred and twenty-seven

19.3.5 Four million, one hundred and twenty-five thousand and twenty-five

UNIT 21

21.3

Addie: Hi, Mel.

Mel: Hi, Addie. How are you?

Addie: I'm fine, thanks. Hey, I have a new phone and I can't see my old calendar on it. Can I check some dates with you?

Mel: Sure!

Addie: Thanks! We've got a concert on the 22nd of March; I remember that.

Mel: OK, good. And it's Alice's party on April 5th. Have you got that in there?

Addie: No, I haven't, so that's good to know. When's our theater trip?

Mel: It's not until November 17th.

Addie: Oh, OK. That's in my diary now. And I plan to visit my parents on the 5th of June.

Mel: That's in three months, Addie! You should really go see them sooner than that.

Addie: Yeah, you're right. Then there's that music festival. When's that?

Mel: It's August 31st.

Addie: Good, got it! What else is there? Ah, our trip to Toronto!

Mel: That's on September 13th.

Addie: Hmm... I think that's all. Unless you can think of anything else?

Mel: What about Naneen's birthday? Do you know when that is?

Addie: Is it the 19th of May?

Mel: You remembered!

Addie: I'm such a good friend!

21.6

Dahlia: My name's Dahlia and I was born in 1971 in Los Angeles, but my family moved to San Francisco when I was five years old. I started school in San Francisco. That was in 1976.

Then I stayed in San Francisco until I went to college. I went to college in New York because it's such a cool city. I finished my degree in 1993. After that, I lived in different cities around the world for a few years. I got my first job in 1996. I worked for a bank in New York. I didn't like that job very much, but I met my husband at the bank. We got married in 2004. Now we live in New Jersey and we're very happy. We had our first child, our daughter, in 2008. She's called Bethany and she's very beautiful.

UNIT 22

22.6

Quiz master: OK, everyone; here are the answers to our quiz about important dates in history.

The 24th of June, 1497, was the day that Giovanni Cabotto arrived in North America. The 11th of November, 1918, was the day that the First World War ended.

The 9th of February, 1964, was the day that The Beatles appeared on TV in the US for the first time. About 73 million Americans watched them play.

The 16th of July, 1969, was a very important day. Humans landed on the Moon for the first time.

The 10th of May, 1994, was a great day. Nelson Mandela was elected President of South Africa.

So, how many questions did you get right? Add up your scores...

22.12 ex: You can see that this is a supermarket now, but in the 1950s, this was a train station. But now there are no trains.

22.12.1 This is a lovely building. It was a museum in the 1960s, but now it's a theater. Many people come here to see different shows.

22.12.2 The next building is very big. It was a factory in the 1940s. You can see that now it is a school. There are about 800 students here, so it is very noisy.

22.12.3 This is a beautiful building. It's lots of large apartments now, but in the 1950s, it was a hospital. There is also a movie theater next to it, so it's a great place to live.

22.12.4 This is the last place on our tour. You can see it's a lovely garden now, but in the 1950s, it was an outdoor swimming pool. There is a new café over there next to the garden so if you want a drink, go and get one...

UNIT 23

23.8

Arno: Hi there! My name's Arno and I'm recording a short life story for the new podcast *Years, Fears, Joys, and Tears.*

So, let's start at the beginning. I was born in the small town of Monville in Canada, in 1971. My family moved to the US when I was three years old. That was in 1974.

I started school in 1975. It was a great school. I loved English and drama. I started college in 1989, and I studied drama. I acted in my first film in 1991. It was a thriller.

In 1993, I visited lots of different countries. I backpacked to lots of amazing places. I moved to the UK in 1995 to teach drama. I really enjoy teaching my students and running our small theater.

I guess that's it. You're right up to date with my life story!

UNIT 24

24.5 ex:

Interviewer: So, Diana. You're an excellent musician and you started very young.

Diana: Thanks! Well, I could play the piano when I was five years old. I could read music then, too.

Interviewer: When could you write music?

Diana: That was more difficult. I could do that when I was eight.

Interviewer: Very young.

24.5.1

Interviewer: Hi, Louis! You started studying when you were very young.

Louis: Yes, well. My mom and dad were teachers. They taught me when I was really little.

Interviewer: So what could you do first?

Louis: I loved mathematics. I could do that when I was four. But I couldn't read when I was four.

Interviewer: And when could you write?

Louis: I think I was five or six.

24.5.2

Interviewer: How old are you, Imelda?

Imelda: I'm 16 years old.

Interviewe: And you can already drive a car and fly a plane!

Imelda: That's right. I could drive when I was nine. Dad taught me on our farm. I could fly a plane when I was ten. I fly with my father, of course. He's a pilot.

Interviewer: Amazing! And you can ride a horse!

Imelda: Yeah. I could do that when I was seven. All these things are really easy.

Interviewer: They are for you, anyway.

24.5.3

Interviewer: So Irina, how many languages can you speak?

Irina: I can speak three: French, Spanish, and English.

Interviewer: Wow! And how did you learn?

Irina: Well, I was born in England, but my mother's French and my father's Spanish. They wanted me to learn all three languages, so she spoke to me in French, he spoke to me in Spanish, and my teachers spoke to me in English.

Interviewer: Great.

Irina: Yes. But most children start to speak when they are two or three. I couldn't speak until I was four, but then I could speak all three languages.

UNIT 26

26.15

Marcus: Hi, Daniella. Did you go to Sara's birthday party yesterday?

Daniella: Yes, and I had a great time!

Marcus: Cool! What time did you get there?

Daniella: Well, the party started at 7pm, but I got there at 8. Lots of other people arrived later than me, at about 9.

Marcus: And did you wear your green skirt?

Daniella: It wasn't clean, so I wore my red dress. I didn't want to wear jeans because the party was in an expensive bar.

Marcus: And what did you give Sara? Did you buy her that new novel?

Daniella: Actually, I bought her a watch because she has so many books. She likes flowers, too, but I didn't have time to get any.

Marcus: Did you meet anyone interesting there?

Daniella: I met Lana's brother, Sam. Do you know him?

Marcus: I don't think so.

Daniella: He's friends with Will.

Marcus: Oh yes, I know him. And was the food good?

Daniella: Yes, but I didn't eat much. I just had some pizza. It was really nice.

Marcus: Did people dance?

Daniella: Oh yes, the music was great. There was some rock and pop music, but I loved the jazz band. I danced to their songs. It was a great party!

Marcus: Glad you had a great time.

UNIT 28

28.3

Radio presenter: I'm Gareth Cook and this is Chat FM... and now it's *Movie Time!* Let's talk about the movies you can see this weekend at a movie theater near you.

So first, there's a new action movie out this weekend. It's a crime story called *Get Me Out of Here*. There are lots of car chases in this one, so it's very exciting.

Next is a romantic comedy called *Falling for You*. In this, Bella, the main character, meets Juan in a funny way. Bella is skating and she has a nasty fall. Juan helps her. He becomes her hero and they fall in love. I can't tell you what happens next.

Do you enjoy horror movies? Then go and see *Dark Woods*. It's about a man camping in the woods one dark night. Then, terrible things start to happen. It's really scary.

And for the children this weekend, there's a very funny movie called *Space Pigs*. I don't need to explain the story, but the kids will love it!

Finally, *Andromeda 25* is a great science fiction movie. It's the story of Captain Samuel L. Dawson. He wants to find a faraway planet, so he goes on a long and difficult journey through space to find it.

So, those are the best movies to see this weekend. I hope you enjoy them...

28.5

Jack: So, Chrissy. What did you think of the play?

Chrissy: *The Midnight Walk*... an interesting title. Yes, I enjoyed it. What did you think?

Jack: Yeah, I really liked it, too. I wasn't sure about the title, but the story was good. It was an exciting adventure.

Chrissy: Yes, it wasn't boring. And the actors were great!

Jack: Yes. I didn't know any of them, but they were all really good.

Chrissy: The villain was the best, I thought.

Jack: I was scared of him. He was a really evil character.

Chrissy: I know. The hero had a hard job fighting against him. He was very brave.

Jack: But the one thing I didn't like was the music.

Chrissy: Yeah, it wasn't very good and I don't think the play needed it.

Jack: No, I know what you mean!

Chrissy: Great night out, though. Thanks for coming along with me!

UNIT 29

29.4

Friend: Hi, Bea. Did you have a good time in India?

Bea: Yes, I did. It was great, thanks.

Friend: What did you do? Did you visit the Taj Mahal?

Bea: Yes, I did. Mom and I went there in our first week. It was beautiful.

Friend: Did you ride on an elephant?

Bea: I did, but my mom didn't. It was really good fun.

Friend: What else did you do?

Bea: We went to the Himalayas. They're beautiful mountains. We went walking there.

Friend: Great. Did you go to the beach too?

Bea: Yes, we did. We went to Kerala. It was beautiful.

Friend: And did you eat lots of Indian food?

Bea: I did. Mom didn't like it, so she ate fruit and salad most of the time.

Friend: Your poor mom.

Bea: But we both had a great vacation.

UNIT 30

30.5

Interviewer: OK, Tom. So you want a job as a manager at our department store?

Tom: That's right, yes.

Interviewer: Good. So the first thing I want to ask you about is your qualifications. Why did you study English at college?

Tom: I like English, and I'm good at it. It's a useful degree for lots of different jobs.

Interviewer: Uh huh... Yes... And you worked at a music store until 2011. What did you do at the store?

Tom: I talked to the customers about music and did lots of things in the shop... taking the money and things like that.

Interviewer: And why did you leave the music store?

Tom: Ah... I worked there until I finished my degree.

Interviewer: OK, thanks. So, are you good at working with people?

Tom: I'm very good, yes. I'm also good at working in a team. I get along well with most people, so that's not a problem.

Interviewer: So why do you want this job?

Tom: Well, I want to work for a bigger company. I like your store, and you sell some excellent products.

Interviewer: OK. When can you start work?

Tom: I can start in one month.

Interviewer: Excellent, well thank you very much. Have you got any questions...

UNIT 31

31.5

Arjun: Hi, Gemma.

Gemma: Hey, Arjun.

Arjun: How are you? How's work?

Gemma: Oh, it's OK. I like the job, but my manager isn't very good. He doesn't give people enough time to do things.

Arjun: Oh, no. Where do you work now?

Gemma: I'm in an office in town. I work for a construction company.

Arjun: That's good. I work for the supermarket on Vine Street. I like my job, but I want a job that pays more money.

Gemma: So do most people. Do you work from nine-to-five?

Arjun: Yes.

Gemma: Mine's a nine-to-five job, too. Some people don't like that, but I do.

Arjun: Me, too. I don't want to work in the evenings or early in the mornings.

Gemma: Neither do I. Oh, but I really want a holiday.

Arjun: Are you going on holiday soon?

Gemma: Not until December. That's six months! I want to get away from the customers now.

Arjun: Oh, I like talking to the customers. That's the best part of my job!

UNIT 32

32.5 ex: A: Martin wants a meeting. We need to talk about some things.

B: Yes, we all want one, too. Can we do it this afternoon?

A: OK. Let's have one at 3pm, then.

32.5.1

A: I think Sharon in Room 212 needs a new computer before the weekend. Is that right?

B: It is.

A: And does anybody else need one?

F: No. Just Sharon.

32.5.2

Theodore: Hello, Jill, I've got some great news about the business. Is anyone around?

Jill: No, Theodore, it's just you and me here today.

Theodore: OK. I'll just tell you, then. We're going to buy the store on March 23rd...

32.5.3

A: Where is everybody going?

B: We're going to lunch.

A: What, all of you?

B: Yes. It's Daniella's birthday, so we're going to the restaurant on Hope Street.

A: Great. I'll come, too.

32.5.4

A: Oh, no! Look, everything's wet. All my papers are ruined.

B: Nobody closed the window last night.

A: I know. It's very annoying!

32.5.5

Colleague: Hey, Joseph. Do you know what's happening in the new year?

Joseph: Sure, aren't we moving offices?

Colleague: Yeah. How do you know about that?

Joseph: It was in an email that was sent to everyone last week. Didn't you read it? We all know about the move.

Colleague: I need to read my emails more often.

UNIT 35

35.5

Friend: Hi, Sarah. How are you? Are you very busy at the moment?

Sarah: I'm really busy. I'm training for a marathon, so I'm going running on Monday.

Friend: Oh, great. And then we're going sailing on Tuesday.

Sarah: I know. I'm really excited about that.

Friend: Me, too. I love sailing. And when are you doing that parachute jump you told me about?

Sarah: Friday. I'm getting really nervous about it.

Friend: It's fine. Don't worry. I think you'll enjoy it! Are you going on vacation this year?

Sarah: Yes, I am. I'm going to Mexico for two weeks, but I'll be back in time for my birthday.

Friend: That sounds great! When is your birthday, then?

Sarah: It's on September the 13th. I'm having a party. Can you come?

Friend: Of course. And are you doing anything this weekend?
Sarah: I'm going to London on Saturday. I'm meeting Gemma there and we're going on the London Eye.
Friend: Sounds good. I'm going there in December with the drama club to see a show.
Sarah: Oh yes, I'm going on that trip, too. I'll see you there.

UNIT 36

36.10 ex: Friend: Hi, Tom. So what are you going to do this year?
Tom: Well, I want to learn French, but I'm not going to do that this year. Instead, I'm saving my money. I'm going to buy a new car by December.
36.10.1
Friend: So, Jack. Do you have any resolutions for this year?
Jack: I want to do lots of things... go to Europe, buy a new car. But I'm not going to do those this year. Instead, I'm going to join a gym. I want to get fit before the summer.
36.10.2
Friend: Have you got any new year's resolutions, Samantha?
Samantha: At the moment, I'm playing the piano a lot, but I really want to write my own music.
Friend: That sounds good. When are you going to do that?
Samantha: At weekends!
36.10.3
Friend: Hi, Debbie. Got any new year's resolutions?
Debbie: Yes, now that I've got a car I'm going to travel more.
Friend: In the summer?
Debbie: I travel a lot in the summer already, so I'm going to start traveling more in the winter because my life is usually really boring at that time of the year.
36.10.4
Friend: Hi, Joseph. Got any plans for the year?
Joseph: I'm going to college in October, so I want to learn how to cook.
Friend: When are you going to do that?
Joseph: I want to learn by this time next month, so I can cook my girlfriend a meal for her birthday.
Friend: Great!

UNIT 39

39.6
Pete: Hi, Jenny. Are you excited about the birthday party?
Jenny: Not really. There's so much to do.
Pete: Well, your friends and family can help. What do you need to do?
Jenny: First, I need to clean the house.
Pete: Oh well, your sister will do that in the morning.
Jenny: Well, yes. You're right... she's really tidy. I also need to find some good music.
Pete: Marsha will do that. She always takes her CDs to people's parties.
Jenny: You're right, but I also need to get some party games.
Pete: Oh. Sam will do that. She has a huge collection of party games.
Jenny: OK. I'll ask her about that. Then I need a birthday cake.
Pete: Your mom will bake one. She won't let you have a party without a cake.
Jenny: Yes, OK. And the last thing... I need someone to do the food.
Pete: Your brother will do that. He loves cooking burgers and sausages on the barbecue.
Jenny: Yeah, OK.
Pete: Anything else?
Jenny: No, I don't think so.
Pete: Well, let me know. I can help, too.
Jenny: Thanks, Pete. That's great.

UNIT 40

40.5.1
Daughter: Dad! Did you get the novel *Wuthering Heights* from the library for me? I have to read it for my studies.
Dad: Oh, sorry. I didn't have enough time to go to the library today.
Daughter: Well, in that case I'll have to watch the film on TV instead.
Dad: Good idea!
40.5.2 Martin: Hi, Sam. It's Martin.
Sam: Oh, hi, Martin. Are you still coming tonight?
Martin: Yes, but it's really windy right now, so I won't cycle into town.
Sam: Oh, OK. Do you want me to pick you up in the car?
Martin: No, I'll walk. It's not very far.
Sam: OK, great. See you later.
40.5.3
Wife: I'm hungry, André. What are we going to have for dinner?
André: Burger and fries, I think. Oh, but there's no burgers.
Wife: Sorry. I ate them for lunch.
André: Well, there's pizza. That's all we've got.
Wife: Sounds great. We'll have that, then.
40.5.4
Boyfriend: So, Jen. Are we going to the theater tonight?
Jen: We can't. There aren't any shows on.
Boyfriend: Oh, in that case, let's go to the movies instead. I want to see that new spy thriller.
Jen: That's a good idea!
40.5.5
A: What are you going to wear to the party? This red dress is lovely.
B: Or this green one? It's my favorite.
A: Oh, yes. I like that.
B: But I always wear it, so I'll wear the red one tonight.
A: Great!

UNIT 41

41.9 ex: Wife: Morning! Are you OK, John? You don't look very well. Are you going to work today?
John: I'm not sure. I don't think so, but I'll have a cup of coffee and see how I feel.
Wife: Oh, good idea. You might feel better after that.
41.9.1
Friend: Hey, Mel. Are you going to Sam's party this evening?
Mel: I need to finish some work first, so I don't know.
Friend: OK. Well, I'm going at 9pm, so you can come with me later.
Mel: All right, I might. I'll give you a call.
41.9.2
Friend: Hi, Donna. Are you and Elise going swimming today?
Donna: We can't. We've got a late meeting, but we might go tomorrow.
Friend: OK. Well, let me know!
41.9.3
Elliot: Hi, it's me, Elliot. I'm on the bus. I think it arrives in town at 8pm, but I'm not sure. Anyway, in case I'm late, go inside and I'll meet you there. See you in the concert. I'm very excited!

41.9.4
Friend: What are you going to study in college next year, Elsa?
Elsa: I'm not sure. Mathematics or geography, I think.
Friend: Not English?
Elsa: I'm not very good at that, so I'm going to study something else.
41.9.5
Friend: Morning, Delilah. Just calling to check – are you driving to work today?
Delilah: I don't think so. The traffic was really bad yesterday so I'm going to walk.
Friend: Oh, me, too. Should I meet you at the bus stop on the way?
Delilah: Sure. We can walk together from there.

UNIT 42
42.7 ex: Friend: How are you going to get to work tomorrow, James? There are no buses on Sundays.
James: Oh... I'm not sure.
Friend: You should walk. It's good exercise.
James: Good idea!
42.7.1
Organizer: OK, everyone! Our theater trip is next Friday and I know many of you want to go. You don't need to pay any money now, but on the day of the trip, you should bring $10 for your ticket.
42.7.2
Maya: Matt, I'm annoyed with this mess and I can't find anything. You need to clean up.
Matt: I know, but I've got to finish some work first. It's really important.
Maya: OK. Well, you should do that first. But then can you please clean up?
Matt: I promise.
42.7.3
Sheila: Hi, Martin.
Martin: Hi, Sheila. How are you?
Sheila: I'm really tired. I've got so much work at the moment. I work every night and go to bed late.
Martin: You should try getting up earlier. That might be better for you.
Sheila: I'll try that!
42.7.4
Atif: My computer, it's broken!
Atif's sister: Oh, Atif! You should borrow one from your friend Barney. I think he's got an old one.
Atif: Yeah, maybe. Or I'll buy a new one when I have enough money.
42.7.5
Teacher: All right, everyone. The exam starts in five minutes. Remember, this is a speaking exam, so you should speak clearly. Good luck!

UNIT 43
43.9 ex: Friend: Hi, Anya. Are you enjoying your new English course?
Anya: Not really. The teacher speaks very fast and I can't understand him.
Friend: Ah... that's too bad! Well, you could record lessons on your phone and listen again later.
Anya: That's a good idea.
Friend: And you could ask the teacher for notes.
Anya: Great. I'll do that, too.
43.9.1
Friend: Hi, Jim. How are you?
Jim: Yeah, I'm all right, but my house is really messy. I never have time to do chores. I usually don't worry about it, but it's really bad at the moment.
Friend: You could get a cleaner or you could get your children to help you.
Jim: Two good ideas!
43.9.2
Friend: Hi, Mandy. Are you looking for a new job?
Mandy: I am, yes, and I asked my friends, but I can't find anything.
Friend: Oh, you could try the newspaper. It has job ads on Fridays.
Mandy: That's true.
Friend: Or you could look online. There's a new job website.
Mandy: Good idea! I'll do that. Thanks!
43.9.3
Teacher: Right, class. Well, I know some of you can't write in English very well and you want some ideas on how to improve. You could make friends with someone from an English-speaking country. Then you can email them in English. You could also read some English books as this can help your writing, too.
43.9.4
Doctor: I'm a doctor and I meet lots of patients. They all want to stay fit. It's difficult to find time to exercise in a busy week. But they could make small changes to their routines. They could take the stairs instead of the elevator. And walk to the store instead of driving.

UNIT 45
45.9
Becky: Right, Adam. It's five o'clock and the party starts at seven, so we haven't got much time.
Adam: I know, Becky.
Becky: So, have you cleaned the bathroom?
Adam: I did that this morning. Don't worry.
Becky: OK. Good. And how about the drinks?
Adam: Well, I've bought some beer and wine.
Becky: And I got some juice from the supermarket, but have we bought any milk?
Adam: No.
Becky: Oh, we'll need to buy some because people will want tea and coffee.
Adam: OK. I'll get some in a minute. Hey, the oven's on. Have you put the chicken in the oven?
Becky: Ooooh, no, I forgot. I'll do that in a few minutes. Have you phoned your sister?
Adam: Why?
Becky: She needs to talk to you about something.
Adam: Oh I know. I talked to her this afternoon. She can't come tonight.
Becky: Oh, that's a shame!
Adam: I know, but at least she sent me a birthday present in the mail.
Becky: Great. One last thing... have you moved the car?
Adam: Why do I need to do that?
Becky: It's easier for people to park.
Adam: That's a good idea. I will. Right, I think we're almost ready.

UNIT 46
46.10 ex: Friend: Hi, Martin. Are you OK?
Martin: Yeah. I've just been bungee jumping.
Friend: Wow! Was that your first time?
Martin: Yes, but I want to go again.
Friend: I've been three times or more. I love it!
46.10.1
Friend: Hi, Sammy. I'm going to China for my summer vacation.
Sammy: Really?
Friend: Did you go last year?
Sammy: Actually, no. I've never been to China, but Ben went in 2011. He had a great time.
Friend: Great. I'll talk to him about it. Thanks.

46.10.2
Friend: So, Nigel. When are you going to cook dinner for us?
Nigel: Erm...
Friend: What's the problem?
Nigel: I'm not a good cook. I don't often cook for myself, and I have never cooked for visitors.
Friend: Never mind. You just need some practice. We'll be round for dinner on Tuesday.
46.10.3
Friend: So, Debra. Are you ready to go rock climbing?
Debra: Yeah, sure.
Friend: Have you been before?
Debra: Loads of times. Remember, I'm from Canada. We have some amazing mountains back home.
Friend: Great! Let's go, then.
46.10.4
Friend: Here's the tablet, Andrew. Can you write your name here?
Andrew: Where?
Friend: Here. Haven't you used a tablet before?
Andrew: I'm sorry, but I haven't.
Friend: OK. So, press here and then touch the letters.
Andrew: Mmm... thanks.

UNIT 47

47.9
Sharon: Right, Paul. We've only got a few hours before we go on vacation.
Paul: I know, Sharon. I'm so excited!
Sharon: I'll order a taxi. We need to be at the airport before 5pm.
Paul: Oh, I've already done that. It's coming at 4pm.
Sharon: Oh, well done, that's great. Thanks for doing that.
Paul: That's OK, but I haven't made the sandwiches yet.
Sharon: No. Do we need any?
Paul: Food's expensive on the flight. I think it's a good idea... don't you?
Sharon: OK, sure. Well, you do that. I need to call my mother.
Paul: Oh, haven't you called her yet?
Sharon: No, I haven't. And it's her birthday, so I need to call her before we leave.
Paul: OK. And we also need to check the dog is OK at Helen's house.
Sharon: No, we don't. I've done that. Helen called me earlier. Rex is fine, and he's already been for a walk.
Paul: Well, that's good. So, is that everything now?
Sharon: Well, I need to mail a letter, but I can do that on the way.
Paul: Great. We should make it on time.

UNIT 48

48.3
Bill: I like this restaurant, Janet.
Janet: Me, too, Bill... and I'm really hungry.
Waiter: Are you ready to order?
Bill: I am. Are you?
Janet: Erm... Could we have a few more minutes?
Waiter: Of course. No problem.
Janet: What are you going to have?
Bill: Hmm, either the roast beef or the roast chicken.
Janet: I think I'll have the fish, but I'm not sure. Are you going to have an appetizer?
Bill: Maybe garlic bread.
Janet: Good idea.
Bill: Excuse me... waiter?
Waiter: Hi.
Bill: We're ready to order.
Waiter: OK, great. Would you like any appetizers?
Bill: We'll have the garlic bread for two.
Waiter: And for the entrées?
Bill: I'll have the roast beef.
Water: Good choice, sir. And for you, madam?
Janet: What can you recommend?
Waiter: The grilled sea bass is excellent, and so is the baked salmon.
Janet: Hmm.... salmon would be nice. I think I'll have that.
Waiter: An excellent choice. Would you like vegetables with that?
Janet: Yes, please.
Waiter: And what would you like to drink?
Janet: Can I have a glass of white wine, please?
Waiter: OK. And for you, sir?
Bill: I'd like a beer, but I'm driving, so I'll have an orange juice.
Waiter: Great. I'll get your drinks, and there will be a 30-minute wait for your entrées.
Bill: That's OK.
Waiter: Great. Can I take your menus?

UNIT 49

49.4
Ken: This is Ken Wallace on Radio 99.1 FM, and today in the studio we have Brett Ellis. Hi, Brett.
Brett: Hi.
Ken: So, Brett is a stuntman. He's been in lots of movies doing dangerous things.
Brett: Yeah, and I love it. It's fun.
Ken: Recently, you jumped over some cars on your motorbike – is that right?
Brett: Yeah, I've done that a few times. I jumped over five cars last time.
Ken: And that was for an action movie?
Brett: That's right. And in my next movie, I'm going to jump out of a helicopter and ski down a mountain.
Ken: Wow, great! Haven't you done that before?
Brett: I've jumped out of a helicopter, but not wearing skis.
Ken: Aha! And in your last film, did you climb up a waterfall?
Brett: That's right. It was Angel Falls in Venezuela, but I've climbed a few waterfalls. It looks really good in an action movie! I like doing it.
Ken: Yes... really dangerous... scary! Is there anything you'd really like to do?
Brett: Hmm. I've done a lot of things, but I haven't ever lived on a desert island. I'd like to live on my own and cook my dinner over a fire on the beach. I've never done that.
Ken: Well, maybe in your next movie.
Brett: Or maybe for my next vacation.
Ken: Maybe. Well, thanks, Brett, for talking to us today...

Answers

01

1.4

1. You **are** 40 years old.
2. I **am** from New Zealand.
3. He **is** my cousin.
4. We **are** British.
5. They **are** mechanics.
6. She **is** my sister.
7. We **are** scientists.
8. She **is** 21 years old.

1.5

1. You **are** British.
2. He **is** a farmer.
3. They **are** 13 years old.
4. We **are** French.
5. I **am** an engineer.

1.6

1. True
2. False
3. False
4. True
5. True

1.7

1. I am Jack.
2. I am 40 years old.
3. I am Canadian.
4. I am an engineer.
5. He is Jack.
6. He is 40 years old.
7. He is Canadian.
8. He is an engineer.
9. They are 40 years old.
10. They are Canadian.

1.10

Note: All answers can also be written without contractions.

1. He **isn't** playing tennis.
2. She **isn't** a waitress.
3. He **isn't** 30 years old.
4. We **aren't** teachers.
5. **I'm not** at work.
6. Lyla **isn't** a cat.

1.11

Note: All answers can be written with or without contractions.

1. Kaleh isn't their mother.
2. There isn't a bank on this street.
3. That isn't his laptop.
4. They are not her grandparents.
5. Alyssa and Logan aren't your friends.

1.14

1. Is Alvera a nurse?
2. Are those my keys?
3. Are Ruby and Farid artists?
4. Are they best friends?

1.15

1. **Is** Holly your mother?
2. **Are** they from Argentina?
3. **Are** these your dogs?
4. **Is** this Main Street?

02

2.4

1. He **wakes up** at 7 o'clock.
2. I **start** work at 10am.
3. They **leave** home at 8:45am.
4. We **finish** work at 4pm.
5. My friend **has** dinner at 6:30pm.
6. I **cook** dinner every night.
7. My parents **eat** lunch at 2pm.
8. Mia **gets up** at 5 o'clock.
9. My cousin **works** with animals.

2.5

1. We **leave** work at 5:30pm.
2. Pam **eats** lunch at 1:30pm.
3. We **walk** in the park.
4. His son **goes to** work at 9am.
5. My brother **leaves** work at 4:45pm.
6. They **eat** dinner at 8pm.

2.6

1. My son **watches** TV all night.
2. He **goes** shopping on Fridays.
3. We **eat** breakfast at 7am.
4. My cousin **works** inside.
5. Georgia **starts** work at 9am.
6. They **do** their chores.

2.10

1. I go to work every day.
   I do not go to work every day.
2. He watches TV in the evening.
   He doesn't watch TV in the evening.
3. They do not work in an office.
   They don't work in an office.

2.13

1. Do you like basketball?
2. Do you like running?
3. Do you like pizza?
4. Does he like basketball?
5. Does he like running?
6. Does he like pizza?
7. I don't work on the weekend.
8. I don't work on Mondays.
9. My sister doesn't work on the weekend.
10. My sister doesn't work on Mondays.
11. They don't work on the weekend.
12. They don't work on Mondays.

03

3.4

1. Sharon **is** reading a book.
2. I **am** carrying my laptop.
3. My cat **is** climbing a tree.
4. We **are** working at the moment.
5. They **are** having their dinner.
6. He **is** talking to his dad.
7. I **am** driving to work right now.
8. They **are** watching the movie.

3.5

1. They **are coming** home now.
2. We **are playing** a board game.
3. Jane **is cooking** dinner.
4. He **is drinking** some water.
5. We **are listening** to music.
6. I **am washing** my hair.
7. You **are winning** the game.
8. We **are visiting** New Zealand.

3.6

1. Emma
2. Max
3. Julie
4. Emma's cousin

3.10

1. We **aren't** playing with them.
2. The baby **isn't** sleeping.
3. He **isn't** watching the game.
4. You **aren't** wearing boots.
5. She **isn't** cooking lunch.
6. We **aren't** meeting right now.
7. I **am not** eating with them.

3.11

1. They **aren't going** to the park.
2. I**'m not eating** this meal.
3. You **aren't wearing** this coat again.
4. Frank's dog **isn't sitting** by the fire.
5. My dad **isn't carrying** the heavy box.

3.12

1. Dan's watching a movie.
2. Manu's exercising.
3. George's playing his guitar.
4. Jamal is playing a computer game.

3.13

1. They are climbing a tree. They aren't climbing a tree.
2. They are surfing. They aren't surfing.
3. They are washing the car. They aren't washing the car.

04

4.5

1. Martha 2. Rachel 3. Fleur 4. Jacob

4.6

1. What are John and Mike watching? **They are watching a movie.**
2. What is Sida singing? **She is singing "Happy Birthday."**
3. Where are you going? **We are going to the store.**
4. What are Anna and Sue eating? **They are eating chocolate.**
5. What are Ali and Sam doing? **They are cooking dinner.**

4.8

1. Sam is **wearing** red pants.
2. Jack is **reading** on an e-reader.
3. You are **listening** to headphones.
4. Sam is **cleaning** her bike.
5. I am **using** my smartphone.

4.9

1. his shirt
2. a computer
3. a skirt
4. writing
5. the radio
6. her laptop
7. his e-reader

4.10

1. What is Kimi cleaning?
2. What is Jill doing?
3. What is Jack using?
4. What is Max holding?
5. What is Marge carrying?

4.11

1. Emir is going to New York.
2. They are holding books.
3. She is carrying a laptop.

05

5.3

ACTION VERBS: **go, learn, read, eat**
STATE VERBS: **want, love, hate, remember**

5.5

1. I **have** a big house by the ocean.
2. My sister **hates** this new TV show.
3. Thomas **knows** your dad.
4. Finn **wants** a new bike.
5. I **see** the cat and dog.

5.6

1. She **is going** to the store now.
2. Fred **doesn't like** pizza.
3. I always **sing** in the bath.
4. He **is reading** a book at the moment.
5. Jo **remembers** my birthday.
6. Li **is playing** tennis at the moment.
7. We **don't want** to leave.

07

7.4

1. bored
2. calm
3. confident
4. stressed
5. miserable

7.5

1. Ben **is feeling** bored.
2. Luis **is feeling** irritated.
3. I **am feeling** sad.
4. You **are feeling** calm.
5. Kate and I **are feeling** happy.
6. Gina **is feeling** confident.
7. We **are feeling** excited.
8. I **am feeling** tired.

7.6

1. True
2. False
3. False
4. True
5. True
6. False
7. True
8. True

7.10

1. Joe's **very** unhappy.
2. Bella and Edith are **really** sad.
3. Lin is **very** nervous.
4. She is **very** confident.
5. They're **so** tired.

7.11

1. I'm at the airport. I'm waiting for the flight. I don't have a book. There's nothing to do. I'm really **bored**.
2. I'm watching a movie on TV. It's a love story. The man and his wife are in different countries. They're very **sad**.
3. We're at the concert. We're waiting for my favorite band in the world to come on stage. We're at the front. I'm so **excited**.
4. I'm at the supermarket. There's no milk, no butter, no flour, and no sugar. All the things that I need for the cake. I'm so **angry**.
5. I'm waiting to meet my new boss. She's talking to everyone in the office. I don't know what to say to her. I'm very **nervous**.

09

9.4

1. Sarah and I normally **play** tennis on Wednesdays, but today we **are swimming**.
2. Today, I **am having** soup for lunch, but I usually **have** a sandwich.
3. We often **watch** TV in the evenings, but tonight we **are having** a party.
4. Ben and Tom usually **work** until 6pm, but tonight they **are working** until 9pm.
5. Melanie **is skiing** in France this winter, but she normally **goes** to Italy.
6. Today, you **are drinking** water, but you often **have** coffee after lunch.

9.6

1. Denzel **is seeing a show.**
2. Selma **is doing her project**.
3. Marlow **is playing hockey.**
4. Roxy **is making dinner.**
5. Rainey **is eating with friends.**
6. Malala is **having coffee**.
7. Altan is **taking a break**.

9.7

1 A 2 B 3 C

9.8

1. Sally usually **swims**, but right now **she's playing** soccer.
2. Abe normally **reads**, but tonight **he's listening** to music.
3. They often **play** golf, but today **they're playing** hockey.
4. I usually **take** a shower, but today **I'm taking** a bath.

11

11.2

1. My brother isn't **feeling** very well this morning.
2. George **is** sick, so he's staying in bed today.
3. I **am** sick, so I'm not going to work.
4. Ayshah **isn't** feeling well, so she's going home.
5. Luca and Ben **aren't** feeling well today.

11.5

1. Mary's back **hurts**.
2. John has a **broken** leg.
3. I've got a **pain** in my finger.
4. She has a terrible **toothache**.

11.6

1. I have a pain in my arm.
2. John has got an earache.
3. His head hurts.
4. Aziz has got a pain in his back.

13

13.3

1. The weather is beautiful here. It's hot and sunny, and I'm having a great time.
2. There's a lot of snow, so the children are having a great time. They want to learn how to ski.
3. This is a beautiful place, but I really want it to be sunny. It's dark and cloudy all the time.

13.4

1. Oh no! I hate this weather. It's **raining** again.
2. I can't ride my bike in these conditions. It's too **foggy**.
3. Be careful! There's **ice** on the road.
4. Wow! It's really **stormy** outside today.

13.6

1. freezing
2. cold
3. hot
4. boiling
5. warm

13.7

1. 55ºF
2. Seattle
3. Anchorage
4. Houston

13.8

1. There's a lot of ice.
2. It's very windy.
3. It's very rainy.
4. It's sunny.
5. There are a lot of clouds.

15

15.4

1. An **elephant** is larger than a **lion**.
2. **Three** o'clock is earlier than **seven** o'clock.
3. **Ice cream** is colder than **coffee**.
4. A **mouse** is smaller than a **cat**.

15.5

1. lower 2. higher 3. larger
4. later 5. easier 6. earlier
7. hotter 8. closer

15.9

1. The Hotel Supreme is very expensive. It's **more expensive than** the Motel Excelsior.
2. The physics exam is really difficult. It's **more difficult than** the biology exam.
3. Your dress is very beautiful. It's **more beautiful than** my dress.
4. This TV program is really interesting. It's **more interesting than** the other ones.

15.10

1. This laptop is **more expensive than** this phone.
2. Seven o'clock is **later than** three o'clock.
3. A game of chess is **more difficult than** a game of cards.
4. A horse is **bigger than** a rabbit.

15.11

1. False 2. True 3. False 4. False

15.12

1. Paris is **more beautiful** than Dallas.
2. Noon is **earlier** than 5pm.
3. A cheetah is **faster** than a bear.
4. Gold is **more expensive** than silver.
5. Rock is **harder** than paper.
6. Water is **warmer** than ice.
7. Skiing is **more exciting** than walking.

16

16.5

1. Ben
2. Sarah
3. Joel
4. Ben
5. Sarah

16.6

1. The African elephant is the **heaviest** animal on land.
2. The **fastest** animal in the world is the peregrine falcon.
3. The **longest** word in the English dictionary has 45 letters.
4. The Sahara is the **biggest** desert in the world.
5. The giraffe is the **tallest** animal on Earth.

16.10

1. Antarctica is **the coldest place on Earth.**
2. Mumbai is **the biggest city in India.**
3. Alaska is **the largest state in the US.**
4. The inland taipan is **the most dangerous snake in the world.**

16.11

1. The Grand
2. The Plaza
3. The Plaza
4. The Grand
5. The Rialto

16.12

1. Moscow is a very large city. It is **the largest** city in Europe.
2. The Missouri River is 2,540 miles long. It is **the longest** river in North America.
3. The cheetah is a very fast animal. It is **the fastest** land animal on Earth.
4. The Kali Gandaki Gorge is 3.46 miles deep. It is **the deepest** gorge in the world.

18

18.3

1. Do you want to visit New York **and** Chicago?
2. Would you like to study chemistry **or** physics?
3. Would you like a burger **and** a soda?
4. Do you want to go home **or** go to a restaurant?

18.6

1. **What** is the biggest country in Africa?
2. **What** would you like to eat for your dinner?
3. **Which** jacket do you want to wear, the blue one or the red one?
4. **Which** is your favorite color, red, green, yellow, or blue?

18.9

1. John's Bar has the best music.
2. The Big Cahuna is the farthest from the beach.
3. The Seaview Café has the best ice cream.
4. The Big Cahuna has the worst food.
5. The Little Olive has the best seafood.

18.10

1. Taipei
2. Suriname
3. Sahara
4. Eiffel Tower
5. K2

19

19.3

1 4,500
2 467,000
3 989
4 72,427
5 4,125,025

19.4

1 Three thousand, one hundred and seven.
2 Twenty-three thousand, four hundred and seventeen.
3 Three hundred and forty-five thousand, nine hundred and seventy-two.
4 Twenty-three million, four hundred and fifty-six thousand, nine hundred and eighty-seven.

21

21.3

1 B
2 F
3 A
4 G
5 E
6 C
7 D

21.6

1 1976
2 1993
3 1996
4 2004
5 2008

21.7

1. My birthday is on December 5.
2. My birthday is on the 11th of March.
3. My meeting is on December 5.
4. My meeting is on the 11th of March.
5. Nami's birthday is on December 5.
6. Nami's birthday is on the 11th of March.
7. Nami's meeting is on December 5.
8. Nami's meeting is on the 11th of March.
9. I was born 20 years ago.
10. I was born 41 years ago.
11. He was born 20 years ago.
12. He was born 41 years ago.

22

22.4

1 You **were** at the museum last week.
2 There **were** five people here yesterday.
3 The students **were** there on Monday morning.
4 My mom **was** an artist in the 1990s.
5 I **was** in college in 1989.
6 Sal and I **were** at the theater last night.
7 My dad **was** a builder until 1995.

22.5

1 True
2 False
3 False
4 False

22.6

1 1918
2 1964
3 1969
4 1994

22.10

1 They **weren't** very good at science.
2 I **wasn't** in Canada in 2002.
3 You **weren't** at the party last night.
4 We **weren't** in our house last year.
5 There **wasn't** a restaurant near the river.

22.11

1 Was he a good builder?
2 Were they late this morning?
3 Was she at a meeting yesterday?
4 Were you happy in college?
5 Were we in New Zealand for two weeks?
6 Were you in the swimming pool?

22.12

1 B
2 B
3 A
4 A

22.13

1. I was a student last year.
2. I was a student in 2008.
3. I was a student for four years.
4. They were students last year.
5. They were students in 2008.
6. They were students for four years.
7. I was in Australia last year.
8. I was in Australia in 2008.
9. I was in Australia for four years.
10. They were in Australia last year.
11. They were in Australia in 2008.
12. They were in Australia for four years.
13. They were good friends last year.
14. They were good friends in 2008.
15. They were good friends for four years.

23

23.4

1 The music was good, but I **didn't dance** very much.
2 My friend **didn't listen** to the band on Saturday night.
3 Last week, I **cleaned** my brother's new car for him.
4 Did you **watch** a fun movie last night?
5 Ben and Franklin **played** tennis for five hours yesterday.

23.7

1. On Tuesday morning, she **played** squash.
2. On Tuesday afternoon, she **phoned** her boss.
3. On Wednesday, she **tried** sushi at a Japanese restaurant.
4. On Thursday morning, she **cleaned** the bathroom.
5. On Thursday night, she **visited** Aziz in hospital.
6. On Friday, she **invited** friends to her birthday party.
7. On Saturday, she **walked** in the park.
8. On Sunday, she **cooked** dinner for her parents.

23.8

1. 1974
2. 1989
3. 1991
4. 1975
5. 1993
6. 1995

23.10

1. She moved to the US when she was 19 years old.
2. They started swimming when they were 25 years old.
3. We visited Japan when we were 27 years old.
4. I received this gift when I was 31 years old.

23.11

1. She moved to New York in 1996.
2. She visited Asia in 2008.
3. She started her first job in 2010.

24

24.4

1. I could cook Italian food.
2. We couldn't play the piano.
3. She could paint a picture.
4. They couldn't make a cake.

24.5

1. do mathematics
2. ride a horse
3. three languages

24.6

1. When I was five, I couldn't play chess.
2. When I was five, I couldn't ride a bike.
3. When I was five, I couldn't swim.
4. When I was five, I couldn't skate.
5. When I was seven, I couldn't play chess.
6. When I was seven, I couldn't ride a bike.
7. When I was seven, I couldn't swim.
8. When I was seven, I couldn't skate.
9. When you were five, you could play chess.
10. When you were five, you could ride a bike.
11. When you were five, you could swim.
12. When you were five, you could skate.
13. When you were seven, you could play chess.
14. When you were seven, you could ride a bike.
15. When you were seven, you could swim.
16. When you were seven, you could skate.

26

26.4

1. begin
2. break
3. take
4. sell
5. buy
6. get
7. write
8. make
9. sit

26.5

1. C
2. G
3. B
4. A
5. F
6. E
7. D

26.6

Wow! This morning a bear **ate** my breakfast. We are in the Redwood Park and last night we camped in the forest. We **made** a fire and it was very quiet, so my friend and I **slept** well. The next morning, we **went** to the river to get water. When we got back to the tent, we **saw** the bear. I **felt** really scared. We **ran** back to the campsite and we are safe now!

26.9

1. **First** Sheila put her best clothes on.
2. **First** do your homework. **Then** go out and play.
3. Ben passed his test. **Next** he bought a car.
4. Eat dinner. **After that** you can have some dessert.
5. **First** he ate a large breakfast.

26.10

1. **After that** they got lost. Then they decided to camp and put the tent up.
2. They were scared of the sounds in the forest. But **finally** they went to sleep.
3. **In the morning** they washed in the river. They went back to their tent for food.
4. **After that** they saw a bear eating their food. After that it walked into the forest.
5. **Finally** Harold and Jack arrived safely back at the campsite.

26.13

1. What did she eat? **She ate a burger and fries.**

2 How much did he spend? **He spent about $500.**
3 What time did you leave the bar? **I left around 11pm.**
4 Did they go by bus? **Yes, because there were no trains.**
5 Did I get any mail? **You got three letters.**
6 Did we win the competition? **No, we lost.**

26.14

1 When **did the movie begin?**
2 Which **shirt did he choose?**
3 What **did she eat last night?**
4 What **did she read this morning?**
5 How many **fish did Aia catch at the lake?**
6 Who **did you see at the party last night?**
7 What **did he give his brother?**

26.15

1 a red dress
2 a watch
3 Sam
4 pizza
5 jazz

28

28.3

A 5
B 2
C 1
D 3
E 4

28.5

1 False
2 True
3 True
4 True
5 True
6 False

28.6

1. The movie is about three characters.
2. The movie is about a court case.
3. The movie is about a love story.
4. The play is about three characters.
5. The play is about a court case.
6. The play is about a love story.
7. It's a movie about three characters.
8. It's a movie about a court case.
9. It's a movie about a love story.
10. It's a play about three characters.
11. It's a play about a court case.
12. It's a play about a love story.

28.7

1 Millie enjoys singing.
2 Millie learns to sing in her bedroom.
3 The name of her music teacher is Miss Cafferty.
4 The villain is Miss Cafferty.
5 No. Millie is played by a child.

28.8

1 Millie **hates** singing.
2 Millie has **ugly** costumes.
3 Many of the actors were **terrible**.
4 The songs are very **bad**.
5 I really **hated** the music.

28.9

1 villain
2 documentary
3 comedy
4 play
5 author
6 adventure

29

29.4

1 B
2 A
3 D
4 C
5 E

29.5

1 Did I have lunch today? **No, you didn't.**
2 Did the dog eat its dinner? **Yes, it did.**
3 Did they go to Venezuela? **No, they didn't.**
4 Did we win the competition? **Yes, we did.**

29.6

1 Did they give Ellie a present?
2 Did you stay in an expensive hotel?
3 Did his mother buy a lot of postcards?
4 Did your brother climb a mountain?
5 Did their parents take lots of photos?

29.9

1 How did you get to the station? **By taxi.**
2 Where did you stay? **In the Hotel Bella Vista.**
3 Why did you stay there? **Because it was cheap.**
4 Who did you go on vacation with? **Daniella and Toni.**

29.10

1 By boat
2 On Saturday
3 Macy's
4 Some clothes
5 Oysters

29.11

1 Who **did you go on vacation with**?
2 Where **did you stay in London**?
3 What **did you eat in Chinatown**?
4 How **long did you go abroad** for?
5 When **did you leave the US**?

30

30.2

1 True
2 False

3 True
4 False
5 False

30.4

1 My **qualifications** include degrees in biology and chemistry.
2 The interview at the bank went really well. I've **got the job**.
3 The manager read my **résumé** and said it was really good.
4 I can **start** the job in January.
5 You need to **have an interview** before you can get the job.

30.5

A 5
B 2
C 1
D 6
E 3
F 4

31

31.5

1 False
2 True
3 True
4 False
5 True

31.6

1 What **did Sharon get yesterday?**
2 What **did your boss have this morning?**
3 What **do you want?**
4 Who **did the staff phone last month?**
5 Who **did you see on TV last night?**

31.10

1 What did the manager say?
2 Which customer did you speak to?
3 Who gave Emma that book?
4 What started at 7am?

31.11

1 What did the dog break?
2 Who ate the last piece of cake?
3 Which TV program starts at 9pm?
4 What did they eat?
5 Who has a better job now?
6 Who did you see yesterday?

31.12

1 What **did Arjun start last month?**
2 What **does the office have?**
3 Who **is waiting outside?**
4 What **does Mark want to be?**
5 What **does the boss want this year?**

32

32.3

1 Please ask **someone** to phone Mr. Richards immediately.
2 Mrs. Turner didn't give **anyone** any work to do this week.
3 Can I give **anyone** a lift to the station tomorrow morning?
4 Mr. Phillips needs **someone** to go with him to the hospital.
5 I'm sorry, but there isn't **anyone** in the office at the moment.

32.5

1 **Somebody** in room 212 needs a new computer.
2 Theodore tells **someone** the good news about the business.
3 **Everyone** is going for lunch at the restaurant to celebrate Daniella's birthday.
4 **Nobody** closed the window last night before they left the office.
5 **Everyone** knows that we have a new office.

32.6

1. Everybody went to the meeting.
2. Everybody went to the party.
3. Everybody wrote to the customer.
4. Everybody finished their work today.
5. Someone went to the meeting.
6. Someone went to the party.
7. Someone wrote to the customer.
8. Someone finished their work today.
9. Nobody went to the meeting.
10. Nobody went to the party.
11. Nobody wrote to the customer.
12. Nobody finished their work today.

33

33.4

1 I was very tired last night. **Were you?**
2 We didn't go to the party. **Didn't you?**
3 Frank wasn't feeling well. **He wasn't?**
4 The cat likes its new food. **Does it?**

33.5

1 **Was** it?
2 There **is**?
3 **Did** you?

35

35.4

1 John's cousins **are coming** to the party tomorrow.
2 I **am going** to the dentist tomorrow morning.
3 My family and I **are visiting** my grandma on Saturday.
4 The managers in my office **are having** a meeting this afternoon.
5 A famous band **is playing** in Central Park this weekend.
6 He **is studying** for his test tomorrow.

35.5

Ⓐ 3
Ⓑ 6
Ⓒ 1
Ⓓ 4
Ⓔ 7
Ⓕ 2
Ⓖ 5

35.8

1. Sorry, I can't. I'm visiting my parents this evening.
2. I'd like to, but I'm going to France this weekend.
3. That sounds nice, but I'm going swimming on Tuesday.
4. I'd love to, but I'm looking after my nephew tomorrow.

35.9

1. I'd like to, but **I'm going to dinner with Marco and Olivia**.
2. Sorry, I can't. **I'm going to lunch with Aziz**.
3. That would be fun, but **I'm going to the theater to see a musical**.
4. That sounds nice, but **I'm looking after Sandy's baby**.
5. I'd like to, but **I'm going to a yoga class**.

36

36.4

1. I **am not going** to eat sushi for dinner.
2. Debra **is going to get** a new job soon.
3. My friends **are going to cook** a meal for me next week.
4. Manuel **is going to learn** how to scuba dive this summer.
5. We **are going to travel** to Dubai in December.

36.5

1. False
2. True
3. True
4. False
5. False

36.8

1. He is going to paint his bedroom by the end of this month.
2. He is going to join a gym by this time next month.
3. He is going to book a vacation by the end of March.
4. He is going to get fit by the summer.
5. He is going to buy a new car by December.

36.9

1. Tim is going to buy a new boat by October.
2. Sally and Jane are going to go on vacation on the weekend.
3. I am going to write a book by this time next year.
4. We are going to run a marathon tomorrow.

36.10

1. Jack is going to join a gym before the summer.
2. Samantha is going to write music at weekends.
3. Debbie is going to travel more in the winter.
4. Joseph is going to learn how to cook by this time next month.

37

37.3

1. Watch out! You **are going to step into** that puddle.
2. The dog **isn't going to eat** its food. I think it's sick.
3. Oh no! She **is going to fall off** the ladder.
4. John is terrible at golf! He **isn't going to win** the tournament.
5. It's very windy! His umbrella **is going to blow away**.
6. You're carrying too much. You **are going to drop** everything.

37.4

1. John and Jill are putting their coats on. They **are** going to leave now.
2. I saw the weather forecast. It **is** going to snow this afternoon.
3. It's my birthday, so I **am** going to get a present from my husband.
4. Larry and John have gone home to get their tennis rackets. They **are** going to play tennis.

37.5

1. He is **not going to** be in the next Olympics.
2. Marco is **going to** study art at university.
3. He is **not going to** be the main character in a musical.
4. Marco is **going to** fail his English exam.
5. He is **going to** play soccer next weekend.

37.6

1. fall over
2. crash into
3. fail
4. pass
5. break

37.7

1. The man is going to **fall into** the pond.
2. The snowman is going to **fall over**.
3. It is going to **rain** later today.
4. The boy in the blue shirt is going to **win**.
5. The store is going to **close** now.

37.8

1. I am going to be late for work.
2. I am going to make a fruit cake.
3. I am going to play soccer.
4. Sheila is going to be late for work.
5. Sheila is going to make a fruit cake.
6. Sheila is going to play soccer.
7. We are going to be late for work.
8. We are going to make a fruit cake.
9. We are going to play soccer.
10. They are going to be late for work.
11. They are going to make a fruit cake.
12. They are going to play soccer.

39

39.4

1. John **will not eat** pizza.
2. Maria **will enjoy** the new dance class.
3. Susie and Bella **will be** early for work this week.
4. The children **will not understand** this information.

39.5

1. He'll bring chocolates.
2. She'll make a salad.
3. He'll not bring anything.
4. I'll bring drinks.
5. They'll buy cheese.

39.6

1. Who will find the party music? **Marsha will do it.**
2. Who will bring the party games? **Sam will do it.**
3. Who will bake a birthday cake? **Jenny's mother will do it.**
4. Who will cook the food? **Jenny's brother will do it.**

39.10

1. Diane works very hard. **I think she'll pass her exams.**
2. Chiara loves traveling. **I think she'll enjoy visiting Rome.**
3. Carl failed his driver's test again. **I don't think he'll ever pass it.**
4. Georgia can't sing very well. **I don't think she'll be in the musical.**

39.12

1. Bob is going to **eat** all his dinner.
2. It is going to **snow** this afternoon.
3. The dog will **eat** these leftovers.
4. The car is going to **turn** left.
5. John thinks he will **go out** tonight.

40

40.4

1. It's my birthday, **so I'll cut the cake.**
2. I forgot my swimming trunks, **so I won't go in the water.**
3. I don't have any money, **so I won't go shopping.**
4. I can't find my train ticket, **so I'll get the bus.**

40.5

1. C 2. E 3. D 4. A 5. B

40.6

1. In that case we'll **go** by bus.
2. In that case I'll **have** tea.
3. In that case we'll **eat** at home.
4. In that case I'll **listen to** music.

40.9

1. False
2. True
3. False
4. True
5. True
6. True

40.10

1. I think I'll **have milk**.
2. I think I'll **leave at 6:30pm**.
3. I think I'll **play with Cassie**.
4. I think I'll **watch the news**.
5. I think I'll **go home**.

41

41.4

1. My dad might give me some money.
2. Helen might pass her driving test.
3. I might not eat a chocolate bar.
4. They might not have a party.

41.5

1. we will go
2. I'll bring
3. I won't bring
4. We might want

41.6

1. They won't make dinner.
   They might make dinner.
2. He won't be late again.
   He will be late again.
3. You might remember that.
   You will remember that.
4. She won't become a teacher.
   She will become a teacher.
5. We won't win the game.
   We might win the game.
6. The dog might eat this food.
   The dog will eat this food.

41.8

1. Where will you live next year? **I don't know. I might live in Boston.**
2. What will you do before you start college? **I might get a summer job. I'm not sure.**
3. How much money are you taking on vacation? **I'm not sure. I might take about $300.**

41.9

1. She might.
2. No, they're not.
3. He might.
4. No, she won't.
5. No, she won't.

41.10

1. Aban might learn French.
2. Aban won't run a marathon.
3. Nadiya will become a doctor.
4. Nadiya might write a book.
5. Nadiya won't do a bungee jump.
6. Jack will get a dog.
7. Jack might buy a motorcycle.
8. Jack won't move house.

42

42.4

1. You shouldn't open this door.
2. She should play the guitar every day.
3. He shouldn't wear that tie with that shirt.
4. You should take a tablet twice a day.
5. They shouldn't ride their bikes here.

42.5

1. We **shouldn't** swim at this beach.
2. People **should** be quiet in the library.
3. Shoppers **should** email.
4. They **should not** walk on the ice.
5. You **shouldn't** drive too fast.

42.6

1. I've got too many clothes. **You should sell some of them.**
2. I eat too much junk food. **You should eat more fruit.**
3. I don't know my neighbors. **You should have a block party.**
4. I feel tired all the time. **You should get more sleep.**
5. I need more exercise. **You should join a gym.**
6. I'm so lonely. **You should get a dog.**
7. I've nothing to wear tonight. **You should go shopping.**

42.7

1. bring $10
2. finish his work
3. get up earlier
4. use a friend's computer
5. speak clearly

42.8

1. People **should** visit the library more often.
2. People **should** have a shower before swimming.
3. You **shouldn't** eat anything in a laboratory.
4. You **shouldn't** go through that blue door.
5. Students **shouldn't** speak during their exams.

43

43.4

1. I didn't pass my driving test last week. **Oh well, you could take it again next month.**
2. I haven't got any nice clothes. **You could buy some new ones.**
3. I can never remember people's names. **You could write them down after you meet them.**
4. I never know what time it is. **You could buy a watch.**
5. Oh no. I forgot to lock the front door. **We could go back to your house now.**

43.5

1. You could **save $10 a week.**
2. You could **take him with you.**
3. You could **eat it inside.**
4. You could **share with a friend.**
5. You could **write 500 words every day.**

43.8

1. You don't know what to do for the summer. You could **get a job** or **travel.**
2. What are you going to make for dinner tonight? You could cook **chicken** or **beef.**
3. You want to be a better tennis player. You could **have some lessons** or **play more often.**
4. You can't wake up in the mornings. You could **set an alarm** or **go to bed earlier.**

43.9

1. get his children to help; get a cleaner
2. look in the newspaper; look at a website
3. read more English books; email a new friend in English
4. take the stairs; walk to the store

45

45.5

1. We **have not mopped** the floor.
2. Tim **has left** the door open.
3. You **have changed** the sheets.
4. Sheila **has eaten** her dinner.
5. Dad **has not painted** the fence.
6. I **have vacuumed** the living room.
7. Aziz **has watered** the plants.

45.6

1. They haven't cleaned the car.
   Have they cleaned the car?
2. You have mopped the floor.
   You haven't mopped the floor.
3. I have taken the garbage out.
   Have you taken the garbage out?
4. You haven't painted the house.
   Have you painted the house?
5. John has cooked the dinner.
   John hasn't cooked the dinner.

45.7

1. gone
2. had
3. closed
4. eaten
5. been
6. kept
7. seen
8. done

45.8

1. We have **cooked** dinner for you.
2. Ben and Ellen **have** gone to the supermarket.
3. The children have **seen** the movie.
4. Sheila has **cleaned** the bathroom.
5. The dog **hasn't** eaten all its food.
6. They've **been** to the mall to buy you a present.

45.9

1. No, they haven't.
2. No, she hasn't.
3. Yes, he has.
4. Yes, she has.
5. No, he hasn't.

45.10

1. cleaned
2. washed
3. cooked
4. changed
5. mopped
6. walked
7. cleared
8. brushed

45.11

1. The children have **cleaned** the car.
2. The cat has **eaten** all its food.
3. Jemma has **broken** the window.
4. Jill has **tidied** her desk.
5. Paul has **left** his wallet on top of the car.

46

46.4

1. I love the movie *Casablanca*. I **have watched** it more than nine times.
2. Our dog Rex **ate** all Mary's birthday cake last night.
3. Jack **didn't visit** the Colosseum when we were in Rome last year. He was too sick.
4. **Did you go** to the swimming pool downtown yesterday?

46.5

1. Yes, **she has been bungee jumping** many times.
2. Yes, **he visited Yosemite National Park** in 2014.
3. Yes, **I saw *Gone with the Wind*** last night.
4. No, **I have not been paragliding**.
5. Yes, Mia **has been scuba diving** many times.

46.8

1. Manuela and Giorgio have **gone** to the movies. They're meeting you there.
2. There's lots of food in the fridge because Ayida's **been** to the supermarket.
3. I've **been** to the library. Look at all the books I have!
4. Mary and Joe have **gone** to a nightclub. They'll be back after midnight.

46.9

1. We haven't been
2. We've eaten
3. We visited
4. We went

46.10

1. False
2. True
3. True
4. True

46.11

1. She hasn't **been** to the circus.
2. I **met** my best friend when I was six.
3. You **ate** all the chocolate last night.
4. He hasn't **tried** paragliding.

47

47.3

1. Alvita is very happy. She **won** the prize for the best chocolate cake yesterday.
2. This is a great party. I **have met** lots of really fun and interesting people.
3. Martha looks happy. She **has been** to the movies with Miles.
4. Mary can't drive. She **fell** and **broke** her arm last week.

47.4

1. She hasn't played in any competitions.
2. She broke her leg.
3. She didn't play tennis for three months.
4. She has missed two grand slams.
5. She went to the Caribbean.

47.8

1. Am I too late to play football? **No, the game hasn't started yet.**
2. Has Amy learned how to drive yet? **No, not yet.**
3. Can you send an email to Rachel? **I've already done it.**
4. Have you watched this movie? **Yes, I've already seen it.**

47.9

1. True
2. False
3. False
4. True
5. False

47.10

1 He has already cleaned the kitchen.
2 He has already bought milk and bread.
3 He hasn't taken the dog for a walk yet.
4 He hasn't made the birthday cake yet.
5 He has already mailed the letter.
6 He hasn't phoned his grandma yet.

48

48.3

1 Roast beef
2 Baked salmon
3 White wine
4 Orange juice
5 30 minutes

48.4

1 For my appetizer, I'd like the **tomato soup**.
2 For my entrée, I think I'll have the **roast beef and vegetables**.
3 For my dessert, I would love the **strawberry cheesecake**.

49.3

1 Have you ever been paragliding? **No, but I want to do that next year.**
2 Have you ever seen *Hamlet*? **No, but I love Shakespeare and I'd like to see it.**
3 Have you ever been to Machu Picchu? **No, but we're going to go there next year.**
4 Have you ever been on a boat? **No, but I want to go sailing in the summer.**

49.4

1 Hasn't done
2 Has done
3 Hasn't done

49.5

1 Desert
2 English
3 drive
4 mountain
5 football
6 dolphins
7 Chinese
8 make
9 Australia
10 sail

49.7

1 I've never learned to ski, but my friend Sanjay is going to teach me next year.
2 I haven't been up in a hot-air balloon, but I'm going to do that for my birthday in August.
3 I've never been on TV, but I'm going to be on a TV quiz show in a few weeks. I'm very excited.
4 I haven't been to a music festival yet, but my friends really want to take me to one next summer.

49.8

1 True
2 False
3 False
4 False
5 True

Index

All entries are indexed by unit number. Unit numbers for main entries are in **bold**. Unit numbers with the prefix R, for example R1, refer to information in the reference section.

A

B

C

D

E

P

QR

S

T

Acknowledgments

The publisher would like to thank:
Jo Kent, Trish Burrow, and Emma Watkins for additional text; Thomas Booth, Helen Fanthorpe, Helen Leech, Carrie Lewis, and Vicky Richards for editorial assistance; Stephen Bere, Sarah Hilder, Amy Child, Fiona Macdonald, and Simon Murrell for additional design work; Simon Mumford for maps and national flags; Peter Chrisp for fact checking; Penny Hands, Amanda Learmonth, and Carrie Lewis for proofreading; Elizabeth Wise for indexing; Tatiana Boyko, Rory Farrell, Clare Joyce, and Viola Wang for additional illustrations; Liz Hammond for editing audio scripts and managing audio recordings; Hannah Bowen and Scarlett O'Hara for compiling audio scripts; George Flamouridis for mixing and mastering audio recordings; Heather Hughes, Tommy Callan, Tom Morse, Gillian Reid, and Sonia Charbonnier for creative technical support; Shipra Jain, Roohi Rais, Anita Yadav, Manish Upreti, Nehal Verma, Jaileen Kaur, Tushar Kansal, Vishal Bhatia, Nisha Shaw, and Ankita Yada for technical assistance.

DK would like to thank the following for their kind permission to use their photographs:
61 **Dorling Kindersley**: Peter Cook (center); Nigel Hicks (top center). 157 **Rough Guides, Courtesy of Sydney Opera House Trust**: Andrew Goldie (center).

All other images are copyright DK.
For more information, please visit **www.dk.com/uk/information/contact-us**.